MARKET RESEARCH

MARKET RESEARCH

a guide to planning, methodology & evaluation

3rd edition

paul hague

KOGAN
PAGE

First published by Kogan Page Limited in 1996
Reprinted 1997
Second edition 1999
Third edition 2002
Reprinted 2003

120 Pentonville Road
London N1 9JN
United Kingdom

22883 Quicksilver Drive
Sterling VA 20166–2012
USA

www.kogan-page.co.uk

British Library Cataloguing in Publication Data

A CIP record for this book is available from the British Library.

ISBN 0 7494 3730 8

Typeset by Jean Cussons Typesetting, Diss, Norfolk
Printed and bound in Great Britain by Bell & Bain Ltd, Glasgow

Contents

Preface to the third edition

As I sit down to write this third edition of *Market Research* I am struck, on the one hand, by how much some things have changed since the publication of the second edition in 1998 and, on the other, by how some things have stayed the same.

Since so much of market research is common sense anyway, it seems reasonable that the principles will not change. At the heart of market research is the need to ask the right question of the right person – even if we do tend to dress it up by studious approaches to interviewing and questionnaire design.

The changes surround the detail. The many examples used in the book have needed some freshening up, although not as much as I thought would be necessary. However, almost every telephone number and many of the addresses quoted in the earlier edition have changed, and I am struck by the shifting sands of businesses at a micro level.

A major change has taken place in what was described as 'desk research' in the earlier edition. Thirty years ago I spent weeks every year in libraries in Manchester and London. I am a great advocate of desk research as I know that there is so much for the market researcher to glean for next to nothing from the oceans of statistics and literature on the shelves. Knowing my way around the libraries used to give me something of an advantage since here were sources that you simply had to get to know by soaking yourself in them. Today I sit at my desk and type my search request into Google like everyone else. Searching has become so much easier and I do not feel that I have that special advantage anymore. Or have I? As I watch my colleagues searching the Net I see search strategies fail. I see good information passed over because they are not sure how to interpret its meaning. I have been prompted to re-write the chapter and to re-name it 'How to get information for next to nothing'. In this day and age, and admitting to a Yorkshire birthright, the new title seems more fitting than boring old 'Desk research'.

Today there is a great interest in customer satisfaction studies. They account for a significant spend on market research, especially in business to business markets where I specialize. I thought that the subject merited its own chapter in this new edition.

Market researchers do a great job collecting data but we do tend to fall at the final fence. Sometimes we fail to deliver the findings in a practical, useable and actionable form. We are sometimes too pure for our own good. The purpose of market research is to minimize business risk and every research project that gathers dust is an indictment to our profession. I have beefed up the chapter on 'Report writing' with sections on writing briefs and writing conclusions.

The greatest change of all for me, however, has been writing the book on my own. The previous two editions were written with Peter Jackson, my business partner for 25 years. In 1996 we sold our shares in the business we had built up and run for a quarter of a century and Peter took early retirement. This included retirement from writing books. When I read through the script, looking for revisions, I always felt more inclined to change the words that I penned rather than those that came from Peter. He wrote with clarity and perspicacity. He deserves to be walking the Cornish hills, but I do miss him.

Being slightly younger than Peter, and with market research blood in my veins, I couldn't make that same move. Instead I have joined forces with Ann Kemp, my field manager for more years than she would care to be reminded, and we formed B2B International Ltd. The market research industry has always kept me interested but starting a new company from scratch has rejuvenated me. I have surrounded myself with bright, young people who for the most part knew little about market research, and it has been my pleasure to work with them, train them and watch them fast overtake me.

In marketing, positioning is all. Products must be developed to meet the needs of particular sectors. Where then is this product – this book – aimed? The principal target is students of market research needing a first introduction and with little prior knowledge of the subject. Such students may be starting a university course with marketing and market research as their core subjects or taking market research as a subsidiary in a wider first or postgraduate degree or professional course. However, it is an introductory text and no more. Anyone with any level of serious interest is urged to broaden his or her knowledge by reading widely. The references at the end of the book point to where particular topics can be explored in more detail, although these are by no means exhaustive.

A second target is the market research practitioner. Perhaps the greatest contribution I can bring to this book is experience, gained through commercial market research for hundreds of clients and in thousands of projects, as well as principles and theory. It covers some of the things that a working craftsman should pass on to apprentices; some of the things that, looking back, I wished had been given to me when I started out in market research.

Something the market researcher quickly learns is that there are lots of ways of solving the same problem and someone, somewhere will have been there first. A good way of learning is to use and, if necessary, modify that previous experience, and with this in mind the third edition includes a CD ROM. The CD ROM contains examples of briefs, questionnaires, reporting templates and favourite sources of information. Readers are encouraged to use them where they will, recognising that there will almost certainly be some changes and improvements that can be made.

I have three aims or hopes for you the reader. Firstly I hope that I will be successful in sharing with you tips, theories and structures that you will find useful. Secondly I hope that the book will inspire you to use market research whenever you have a business decision to make that involves a serious element of risk. And last, but not least, I hope that the book will encourage you to forever keep asking why? – the most important question of all.

Paul Hague

What is market research?

Market research can be understood in terms of how the activity is carried out – designing questionnaires, planning respondent samples, methods of data collection and analysis etc – in other words the techniques of the discipline. Much of this book is concerned with this aspect of market research. A student of the subject needs to become familiar with the tools of the trade and how to use them. However, equally important is to understand what market research is for – why it is carried out. In some introductory books this is neglected or taken for granted but we believe an understanding of the 'why' of market research is essential and particularly for a student with little or no business background. Market research may be taught legitimately as an academic subject but it is first and foremost a practical discipline with a vital contribution to the whole business process. This first introductory chapter, therefore, deals with the contribution market research makes to wider activities as well as laying down a framework for later discussions of methods and techniques. The next chapter extends this theme by describing and illustrating, with case studies, some applications of market research.

RESEARCH FOR MARKETING DECISIONS

The purpose of market research is to assist and improve marketing decisions; selecting the optimum alternative or even setting the decision-making agenda –

what are the real marketing issues facing us? In any field, the basis of good decision making is having effective information available and using it. This applies throughout business including in finance, production, personnel as well as marketing and is also equally true for non-commercial organizations. Almost any information required in or contributing to marketing decision making and the methods used to acquire that information, can be considered to be market research but, as a distinct and specialized activity, it is the provision of information about the market that is usually the central concern.

If marketing is about the profitable satisfaction of market needs (a well-established definition but see Morello (1993) for an interesting view of this), we clearly have to understand our markets and the needs of consumers – individuals or organizations – that make up these markets. This understanding can be intuitive and based on 'common' sense and many successful decisions have been and continue to be based on no more than hunches. However, in competitive markets where implementing a decision may require major financial resources and where the costs of failure are high, there is a need for decision making based on more rigorous and reliable data. Additionally, many features of modern markets and marketing such as consumer diversity, internationalization and the ever accelerating pace of change, increase uncertainty and make the informal and intuitive approaches to understanding less secure. The more formal techniques of market research, which have been developed and matured over the last few decades, generally offer a basis for increased confidence in decision making and so reduce some of the risks that always will be present in markets. The size of the market research 'industry' – see Chapter 14 – attests to the recognition given by modern business to the importance of market research. What is surprising, however, is that major investments and strategic decisions are still made without adequate information. The reasons for this may include some professional failures on the part of market research practitioners such as an inability or unwillingness to be involved in decision making, as well as differences in the corporate cultures between research using and non-using organizations (see Elliott and Jobber, 1995).

What sort of decisions are involved in marketing and which can market research assist? They are as diverse as the businesses that make them. We shall come to some of the more common decision and information areas shortly as well as illustrating them in the next chapter, but for the moment the scope of market research can be introduced by thinking about just one sort of marketing decision – what to do about a product which is producing below average or unsatisfactory profits. Regardless of the product, there are in fact only three possible options, in isolation or combination; sell more, charge more or cut costs. Table 1.1 illustrates some (but not an exhaustive list) of the information, potentially available through market research, that might be required before deciding on how to improve these profits. In each case the information concerns an understanding of the market and the consumers making up the market. For example, if the profits are to be increased through selling more (raising extra revenue) there must be an opportunity to achieve this and some questions that may need answering before setting new volume targets include:

● Is the market in total or in specific segments big enough to provide the extra sales?
● What share of the market is held already? The larger this is the harder it may be to gain extra volume.
● Are there some barriers to achieving extra sales that will have to be addressed: poor distribution, low consumer awareness or possibly the product does not match many consumers' needs?

For the other strategies to increase profitability, relevant questions also need answering before a decision can be made confidently. Table 1.1 illustrates this.

Table 1.1 *Marketing strategies and relevant information to increase the profitability of a product*

Strategy	Marketing information
Sell more	Size of the total market for the product Breakdown of the market by segment Existing share held Availability of the product – eg retail penetration Consumer awareness of the product Consumer acceptance of the product
Charge more	Competitive pricing levels Price sensitivity of the market Consumer perceptions of the value of the product The importance of non-price issues Likely effect on consumer demand of price increases
Cut costs	Whether any resulting product reformulation would influence consumer perceptions of the product

While in this book the emphasis is on market research for marketing decisions, the techniques of market research are also widely applicable for assisting decision making in other areas. Examples include opinion polls (used for political marketing), social issues and policy making and personnel management (eg employee attitude surveys). In fact, writing of applying market research to such as social policy making may give the wrong impression; market research as a discipline has certainly developed some techniques of its own but the building bricks were brought in from other academic disciplines including sociology and psychology and often developed in applications such as social policy and investigating social 'problems'. Market research may have only become common business practice in the last three or four decades but its lineage stretches back well into the nineteenth century.

MARKETS AND MARKET RESEARCH

Market research can be applied in any type of market where buyers and sellers come together to exchange and increase value (ie of the supplier's profits and buyer's satisfaction). However, depending on the nature of the market there are differences in the approach and techniques required on the part of the market researcher. Anyone using market research will be primarily interested in the approach needed for his or her own type of market and even full-time professional researchers tend to specialize in markets as well as research techniques. The most fundamental division of markets is between those where the consumers are individuals or households buying for their own needs and satisfaction – these are usually referred to as consumer markets – and those where the consuming unit is an organization, a business, a public authority or other body. In such cases individuals may make the decision and act for the organization but it is not (or should not be) individual and personal needs that are being satisfied.

In consumer markets, the number of potential buyers of a product is often a significant proportion of a total population and therefore running into millions. Techniques used to research these markets include quantitative methods based on rigorous sampling as well as qualitative techniques which probe the complex consumer perceptions and motivations which provide the dynamics to these markets. Consumer markets can be further sub-divided and particularly between fast moving consumer goods (FMCGs) – food and similar frequent purchases and other markets – media, travel and leisure, financial, consumer durables etc. Modern marketing concepts and market research largely grew up in FMCG markets and this sector remains the area where most commercial market research is carried out. Consumer markets – FMCGs in particular – are also retail markets and anyone marketing through retail distribution needs to know as much about what is happening in the shops as among final consumers. What is happening at the store level is, therefore, a major concern and is the information output of some of the largest continuous market research programmes (eg by organizations such as Nielsen).

Any market where the consuming unit is an organization requires different market research techniques or at least a change of emphasis. For one thing the decision making process is often complex with different groups in the organization involved, each with distinct concerns (eg the production, technical, purchasing and financial departments may all influence decisions for engineering products). Also the structure of the markets is very different with often a few companies accounting for the majority of the demand for the product or service. At one time, all markets made up of organizations were referred to as 'industrial' but now it is common to speak of a separate business-to-business sector. These are markets where although the consumers are organizations, they are typically large in number. Often the products are for the 'office' rather than the factory floor and examples include equipment such as computers, copiers and franking machines but also services such as telecommunications and financial. In research terms, the main point about these business-to-business markets is that the methods developed for consumer markets, including large-scale and structured interviewing of statistically valid samples, can be and are adapted and applied.

The category 'industrial market' now tends to be used in a more restrictive sense for products and services required in manufacturing production. Often, these are also technical products requiring, on the part of anyone carrying out market research, at least an appreciation of the underlying technologies. The differences in the market research methods used in these areas reflect, as much as anything, structural differences in the markets being researched. The number of 'players' in the market – both suppliers and buyers – may be numbered in only tens and a very small interview programme may cover organizations accounting for 75 per cent of the market. Also, the Pareto principle applies to most business markets; the top slice of a few very large players accounts for the large majority of the market and a small 'judgement' sample, which includes such key respondents, will provide reliable data, whilst a random sample, which takes no account of industry sector, will produce only nonsense. This small scale has implications for how the research is organized. Much consumer market research needs considerable resources in order to collect valid data but in industrial markets one researcher with no or very limited assistance may be at no disadvantage. Also the necessary technique of understanding of products and technology is more likely to be found in a small specialized team or even one person.

Markets, whether consumer or industrial or business to business, are not confined to single countries. Increasingly marketing is international with global brands and marketing programmes. Various economic and political considerations are bringing about these changes including the General Agreement on Tariffs and Trade (GATT) and, for the UK, membership of the single market of the European Union (EU). In some markets it is increasingly the case that the scope of any research needs to be at least the whole of Europe; confining the research to the UK alone may be in future as parochial as restricting it to Lancashire. In both consumer and industrial/business-to-business markets the techniques are basically the same whether the UK or, say, the whole EU is covered in a market research project. However, there are some obvious differences of detail, not least of which is language. International research programmes are also logistically more complex and commonly require access to more extensive resources than may be required for domestic-only research (see Goodyear, 1996). However, as we discuss in Chapter 4, desk research is a cost effective tool requiring only limited resources and is capable of yielding important data on international markets.

THE SCOPE OF MARKET RESEARCH INFORMATION

Regardless of the market, the types of decisions that need to be taken tend to be similar. Whether the product is a confectionery bar or engineering component, the marketing plan needs to cover areas such as the product specification and its relation to consumer needs and requirements, branding, pricing, distribution methods, advertising support, marketing definition and segmentation, forecast sales levels etc. Each of these decisions requires information from the market to increase the chance of getting it right. Common information requirements met through market research are listed below (see Table 1.2) although this is by no means exhaustive and can of course be classified in different ways (eg as in the next chapter). Also no single research commission would cover all or even most areas; as argued later, research that is focused and restricted to what is really crucial to the decision is more likely to be effective.

Although each information area is potentially a requirement in all markets, the characteristics of specific markets means that there is considerable variation in the detailed coverage sought in each case. Market segmentation, for example, means something rather different for FMCGs than for engineering components. Similarly, in industrial markets there is often a greater need for understanding the structure of suppliers and their organization, while in consumer markets branding issues are often a far greater concern. The next chapter discusses applications of market research and, through case study examples, shows how market research can contribute to marketing decisions.

Table 1.2 *Common information areas met through market research*

The market	Market structure

The market

Total market size
Consumer profiles and requirements
Market segmentation
Trends – growing, declining

Consumer perceptions

Underlying needs
Perceptions of brands
Perceptions of suppliers and brands
Perceptions of suppliers and retailers

New product development
Unsatisfied product needs (gap analysis)
Acceptance of new products
Communication of new products
New product branding

Distribution/retailing

Distribution levels achieved
Sales at retail level and by type of
outlet
Retail requirements

Market structure

Major players – shares held
Branding – shares held
Distribution structure
Trends in positions held

Products

Analysis of available products
Product usage and consumption
patterns
Product differentiation
Product linkage to market and market
segmentation
Production innovation and life cycle
Consumer satisfaction with products
and service support

Pricing
Current pricing structures
Past trends
Price sensitivity
Predicted effects of price changes

Advertising and promotion

Campaign planning
Creative development
Promotion evaluation
Sales activity planning
Media data

QUANTITATIVE AND QUALITATIVE RESEARCH

One important classification of market research information, regardless of the type of market, is between *quantitative* and *qualitative*. Quantitative research is concerned with measurement of a market and includes areas such as market size, the size of market segments, brand shares, purchase frequencies, awareness measures of brands, distribution levels etc. Such quantitative data is required to some level of accuracy (though not in all cases to very high levels) and the methods used must be capable of achieving this. In consumer markets at least, quantitative information is almost always based on extrapolating from a sample to the general population or market and the research design and particularly the sampling methods (see Chapters 6 and 7) must be sufficiently rigorous to allow this.

Qualitative information is rather harder to define but the emphasis is on 'understanding' rather than simple measurement – advert A is recalled better than advert B (quantitative information), but *how* does A work as an advert and why is it more effective than B? Much qualitative research is concerned with empathizing with the consumer and establishing the meanings that he or she attaches to products, brands and other marketing objects. Another focus is motivation – eg why does one product rather than another meet consumer needs and what are these needs that are being met? As with quantitative information, qualitative research is conducted among a sample but in this case usually a small one since there is no attempt (or there should not be) to extrapolate in any rigorous way to the total population. In the case of attitudes to brands, for example, it will be considered adequate to be confident that a particular attitude syndrome exists to some extent among the population rather than seeking to say whether 10 per cent or 20 per cent of the population has these attitudes. Chapter 5 describes in more detail the aims of qualitative research and describes the techniques used.

Many marketing research practitioners see quantitative and qualitative research and information as complementary – often a particular marketing decision may call for both approaches (the information areas in Table 1.2 include quantitative and qualitative). However, there is also rivalry between the two with 'quants' seeing a lack of rigour or misplaced aims in much qualitative research (see Achenbaum, 1993) while 'quals' believe that by itself, quantitative research is often unable truly to explain, illuminate or point to solutions. To a large extent this reflects personnel and organization differences between these two branches of market research; researchers usually develop their careers in one area or the other and may work for organizations specializing in either quantitative or qualitative research. Except for a few who take extremist positions, most research practitioners recognize some role for both types of research; even the most hardened 'quants' see value in 'exploratory' qualitative research to help define concepts and to determine what needs measuring, and 'quals' nearly always agree that some things sometimes need expressing numerically as 'hard' data.

THE MARKET RESEARCH PROCESS

The collection of any facts relevant to a marketing decision can be considered as market research. However, we are concerned in this book with something rather more than an occasional and haphazard use of snippets. A formal definition of the market research process can be as follows:

> Market research – the systematic collection, analysis and interpretation of information relevant to marketing decisions.

For some, market research, as opposed to less rigorous use of information, is distinguished by the application of scientific methods to the provision of marketing information (eg see Achenbaum, 1993) and this same basic outlook is found in other social sciences such as sociology – we regard market research as falling into at least a broad definition of social science. However, there are other views on the 'science' issue and some do not regard the methodologies of sciences such as physics to be always or often useful in 'softer' areas such as human motivations and behaviour – the stuff of most market research.

Market research can be carried out as a one-off project to meet a specific requirement – eg whether or not to enter a new market – and this is called _ad hoc_ research, or it can involve continuous or regular tracking – eg to monitor the market share held by a product or brand. The purposes for which _ad hoc_ or for that matter continuous research are carried out are enormously diverse but the process followed in virtually any _ad hoc_ (and in principle most continuous) project is as illustrated in Figure 1.1.

The starting-point of any market research project is to define objectives – what is the work meant to achieve? If this is not done adequately – too often it is not – the effort put into the work will be wasted. Objectives are a statement of why the research is being carried out and link to what information is being sought. This subject is developed further in Chapter 3.

A plan of how this objective is to be met and how the information is to be obtained is then required. This is the research design and includes the aspects discussed in Chapters 6 and 7 in the case of quantitative research and in Chapter 5 in the case of qualitative research. The resources needed (including money) and the timescale involved are also important at the planning stage.

Data collection is the visible part of market research – the interviewer in the shopping mall pestering time-pressed shoppers to answer 'just a few questions'. Data collection is a vital part of the whole process but it is a mistake to think of it as the same as market research – all the other parts of the process are also vital. Unless planned to meet the objectives of the research, the questions asked will not yield meaningful data and without adequate analysis and interpretation 'raw' data can make no contribution to decision making. There are various types and techniques of data collection and the most fundamental division is between desk (secondary)

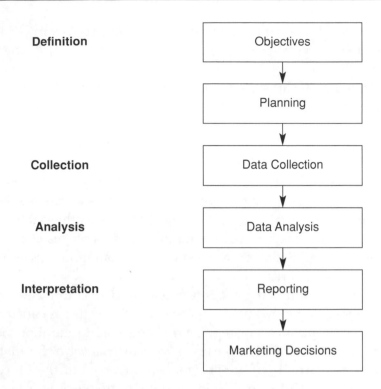

Figure 1.1 *The market research process*

research and fieldwork (primary) research. The practicalities of these approaches are covered in several later chapters – desk research in Chapter 4 and fieldwork methods in Chapter 9 and elsewhere.

Fieldwork normally involves interviewing and completing a questionnaire for each individual or organization in the sample (at least in quantitative research). This may be numbered in tens, hundreds or even thousands. The individual questionnaires and responses are usually of little or no interest; what is required is an aggregation of the whole sample or perhaps groupings within that sample. Data processing produces this and is discussed in Chapter 12.

Having produced an analysis and aggregation of the data (and this includes what is found through desk research) it needs interpreting and presenting in a meaningful way so that the decision maker can act on the results. This is the reporting stage of the process and may involve the researcher making recommendations on policy. Chapter 13 covers this subject.

The final step in the process is taking a decision, based on the research outcome, and acting on it. Occasionally the researcher and the decision maker are one and the same but more commonly the work is carried out for internal or external clients and there is an organization split between the research doer/provider and research user/decision maker. Poor integration of the two functions may be at the root of why, surprisingly, quite a lot of research is not acted on and the time and money involved is wasted. This may reflect that the research results are not appropriate (or thought to be not appropriate) to the decisions being made; a result of poor research design or planning. However, in other cases, the results are ignored because they do not match preconceptions; the new product is 'obviously' a winner even though the research pointed to a mismatch with market need, the company's service support is excellent and the dissatisfaction identified 'must be a sample fluke' or the new advertising is so creative that research 'just cannot capture its subtleties'. Occasionally such hunches and guesses are better than hard facts but this is rare. If a decision has been made before research is carried out and is in practice not going to be changed, why bother with the research? There is no point carrying out market research and then ignoring the findings.

THE ORGANIZATION OF MARKET RESEARCH

Market research projects can be carried out on a one-man or a one-woman basis with all stages in the process a single responsibility. However, except where data collection is confined to desk research or small-scale fieldwork (as in some types of qualitative research or in industrial market projects), logistics, budgets and the need to meet timetables require some division of labour and a team approach.

The tasks covered in the outline of the market research process can be divided rather crudely between 'thinking' and 'doing'. Thinking type tasks include planning the research, selecting an appropriate research design, developing questionnaires and similar tools, deciding how the data needs analysing and interpreting and communicating the results. These tasks require professional* level skills and a background in the body of theory underpinning market research. However, unlike the doing parts of the process, a large team is not usually required for these parts of the process; in many projects the work can be well handled by one person.

The two main doing parts of research are data collection and data analysis. Some types of data collection (eg desk research, qualitative fieldwork) are best carried out by professional level staff but in most cases this would be impractical or ruinously

---

* Market research is now more or less recognized as a distinct profession. It is based on evolving theory and is carried out to recognized codes of practice. However, it is an unregulated profession with no restrictions on entry.

expensive since quite sizeable teams are required for the data collection element of even average sized projects. Consider, for example, a quantitative study of a consumer market in which it is decided that 1,000 face-to-face interviews are required with a nationally representative sample. It may well be decided to plan this as a programme of 50 interviews around 20 sampling points spread around the country. The costs and time of travel point immediately to the need for a team of 20 interviewers (one per point) and to keep the fieldwork within an acceptable timetable and to avoid interviewer 'fatigue' it will be more common to use two to four interviewers per sampling point – 40 to 80 interviewers in total for an 'average' job. These interviewers need to be trained in gaining and carrying out interviews but there is no reason why they should be proficient also in other parts of the process. In practice this is how most market research fieldwork is carried out successfully – by teams of trained but not professional level staff.

Data processing is the area of market research where information technology (IT) has had the longest standing impact (IT is now spreading to other parts of the process, including data collection). On this basis, therefore, you might expect that, unlike data collection, data analysis is not labour intensive but this is not (yet) generally the case since much research requires a significant input of relatively simple clerical skills in 'coding' and 'data entry' (see Chapter 12). Again, therefore, the professional researcher needs the assistance of a sizeable team in order to carry out the work effectively. Also, the IT aspect of data processing has had the effect of bringing in new sorts of specialists ('spec writers') and, therefore, extending the team required for many types of project.

The teams put together to carry out market research projects may be organized 'in-house' or by commercial research companies or 'agencies'. Much of the pioneering work in market research was carried out by departments of large organizations carrying out research for their own internal clients. However, the economics of market research now strongly favour outsourcing to agencies. This is almost universally true of the doing parts of the process but also to an increasing extent the thinking elements as well. Where in-house research staff or departments exist their focus tends to be buying-in market research (and assuring its quality) at the front end or at the other end, ensuring the results obtained are effectively implemented and brought into the decision-making process. The very large majority of market research work is, therefore, now the responsibility of commercial research agencies which together form the 'industry' described in Chapter 14.

Possibly one consequence of the organizational split of market research between suppliers (agencies) and clients (the companies making the marketing decisions) is that market research does not realize its full potential in contributing to decision making. The researcher, however experienced and skilled, is often remote and a stranger to those making decisions. He or she is also insulated from other factors that may need to be taken account of in decision making – production capabilities, finance, wider corporate goals etc. In addition, rightly or wrongly, market researchers are often see as backroom boys; valuable in a narrow field but not capable of taking the broader view or contributing to long term strategy. Alongside perennial debates on methodological issues such as the merits of quantitative versus qualitative research, the need for researchers to be at the heart of decision making is a constant theme of the professional bodies and their publications – eg see Cowan (1994) and Freeling (1994).

2

Applications

Nearly all market research is carried out for a practical reason; a business opportunity has to be checked out, the cause of a problem needs identifying, some commercial risk must be reduced. Market research is an applied science and its output should result in action.

With this in mind we introduce the reader to the applications for market research at this early stage in the book. Applications provide a context which shows where market research fits in. This is important since because market research is the subject of our considerations, it could lead to the misapprehension that it sits at the centre of the business universe. Certainly market research plays an important role in business decision making, but ultimate success in markets is determined by many other factors, not least the commitment of the team, the size and mix of the marketing budget, and the ability to react to unforeseen problems. It is not always easy to review a business success and say that it was entirely due to the market research. At the most, a market researcher will only be able to say 'I played my part'.

In this chapter we classify the applications of market research into four main areas. We show how market research can:

1. help to establish the need for a product or service;
2. help get a new or a flagging product off the ground;
3. improve the performance of an established product;
4. show the way forward in strategic moves such as moving into new territories or making acquisitions.

A FRAMEWORK FOR MARKET RESEARCH APPLICATIONS

The demand for products (and services) waxes and wanes as fashions and technology change. It is argued that products, like humans, have a life with recognizable stages of youth, maturity and old age. When demand is plotted over time, a curve similar in shape to a sand dune is created with the early stages representing youth, at which time sales are small but beginning to take off rapidly. Maturity is a time of growth, eventually slowing down as demand peaks. Finally, in old age, the demand for the product falls away as it is replaced by something else.

This is a great oversimplification and recognising life cycles in industrial and consumer products can be difficult. It may be very evident in the hula hoop or carbon paper but where are Mars Bars in the cycle? Products can be supported and rejuvenated by promotions and improvements so that the smooth curve of the dune is not obvious. Bearing in mind this limitation, the life cycle paradigm offers a model into which we can slot many of the applications of market research.

Pre-birth: establishing needs

Market research can play an important role before the product (or service) has been launched. At this early time it is crucial to determine whether or not there is a need for the product, or more hopefully a need which is not being met. Research can be used to test the concept or idea.

Youth: getting the product off the ground

In the first and youthful stage of the life cycle, market research has many applications. It has an important input into the marketing plan. The price of the product must be set at an optimum level for winning sales and yielding a profit and market research can play its part here. So too marketing research can help in getting the packaging right, devising an advertising campaign and segmenting the market so that the right people can be targeted.

Maturity: improving product performance

As sales of the product build up and push towards the maximum that can be achieved, market research has an application in sharpening the act. It can be used to ensure that customers, once won, stay satisfied and loyal. It can determine what the brand means to people and suggest how it could be more attuned to the market so that maximum returns are achieved. During this period, the applications that were so vital in the youthful phase of the cycle will still have a relevance so that we would expect to see market research feeding into marketing planning, pricing, advertisement testing and the like.

Old age: working out the next move

In the autumn of the life cycle, market research has an application in finding new users for the product; modifications which will revitalize its sales, new segments which could be targeted. Market research can be used to explore export opportunities for the product or seek acquisitions to counterbalance the falling sales. At this stage market research also may be used to test new concepts which could replace the failing product.

Applications for market research within the life cycle framework are shown in Figure 2.1.

Using case histories and examples, we now look in more detail at the applications for market research.

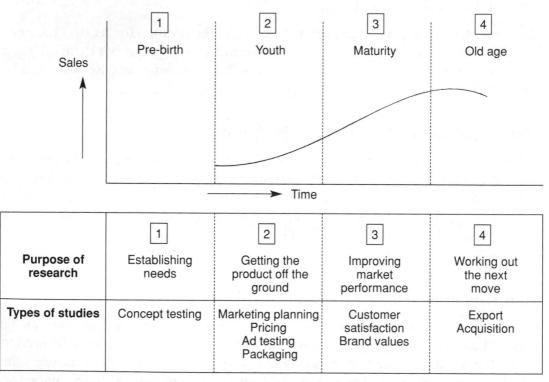

Purpose of research	1 Establishing needs	2 Getting the product off the ground	3 Improving market performance	4 Working out the next move
Types of studies	Concept testing	Marketing planning Pricing Ad testing Packaging	Customer satisfaction Brand values	Export Acquisition

Figure 2.1 *Applications for market research*

PRE-BIRTH: ESTABLISHING NEEDS

The success of market research in determining unmet needs for new products is mixed. Let us begin with some of the triumphs. Market research is credited with playing an important part in the launch of the Yorkie bar. During focus groups carried out on behalf of Rowntree Mackintosh, respondents lamented that the days when chocolate bars were thick and chunky, and when one piece was sufficient as a reward or to gratify were gone. This sparked an idea which was translated into a new product concept and the Yorkie bar was born. The brand name, the advertising and the associations with hunky truckers no doubt all played their part in the fortunes of the launch but market research can claim much credit for being in there at the beginning.

Market research has also been important in converting Manchester Airport from a regional player to a major European hub. The Airport recognized that to grow, it would have to persuade airlines to develop new routes – the equivalent of launching new products. It commissioned surveys with holiday makers and business travellers across the country to demonstrate to airlines that there was a massive pool of people in the North and Midlands who would use new routes. The objectivity of market research, backed by imaginative marketing campaigns to support airlines with their new routes, became a formula which Manchester Airport was able to repeat many times as it raised its status and joined the ranks of the largest international airports in Europe.

The launch of the Yorkie bar and the building of routes from Manchester Airport are more akin to _new product developments_ than those of _conceptually new products_. When a product is a true innovation, market research faces a tougher challenge and inventors may regard it with some scepticism. If the product is conceptually new, buyers need educating and conditioning and their imaginations need firing. It is hard to artificially concertina this conditioning process and so, in the testing of conceptually brand new products, much has to be left to the interpretation of the researchers.

Harry Drnec is chief executive officer of Maison Caurette the beer distributor based in the United States. He recounts the story of when he joined Gallo, the largest producer of wine in the world, and Ernst Gallo had decided that at a time when people were drinking an awful lot more beer, they weren't drinking enough wine.

Harry Drnec recognized that men drink more of everything than women and he set out to redress the balance. His idea was to market a wine-based drink, mixed with something to keep the alcohol down to five per cent of the drink. At the time of this conception, he kept the idea deliberately vague, suggesting fruit juice, sparkling water or tonic.

Drnec took the concept to his in-house market research department, which set up focus groups in nine cities over 14 days at a cost of more than $100,000. He sat in on every single one and listened to people regale the researchers with claims of how much they hated the product. The consumers assumed that the worst wine had been used in the product. They couldn't see why they should be told what proportions to mix it in or what to mix it with. To say there were negative impressions is a gross understatement.

Any sensible person listening to the research had to conclude that it was a complete failure and the product should not be launched. At the same time, about 100 miles away from Gallo's offices, there were two young men making a product in their garage called California Cooler. Four years later they sold out to Brown Foreman, a big US distiller, for £105 million and the 'wine cooler' became a phenomenon.

Not surprisingly, Harry Drnec hates market research. He can hardly be blamed. However, the problem may not be with the research but his expectations of it. He wanted consumers to see the potential as he did. And yet he had been living with the idea for months at least. Researchers know that consumers need time to get used to a new concept. Very often good concepts receive negative vibes at the early stage but they may still be winners if ultimately backed by promotions that turn people on.

Harry Drnec should have researched the background to the concept and relied as much on this as he did the taste tests. This would have told him that people are looking for lighter drinks, they are becoming more adventurous, they like the idea of healthier drinks etc etc. His mistake was not that he carried out market research but that he trusted it to come up with all the answers.

Drnec, H, 'My Biggest Mistake', *The Independent on Sunday*, 2 August 1992

Perhaps it is hardly surprising in the light of the above comments that three consultants were commissioned independently to research the future of an early Xerox copier. Two advised against the launch and the third forecast sales of 8,000 units over six years. Xerox ignored the advice, launched the copier and within three years installed 80,000 machines. The research failed because respondents could not know how they would react with a product they had never experienced.

Certainly there is a role for market research in determining the need for a new product but too much should not be expected. Market research can provide an understanding of the environment into which the new product will be sold – but not a lot more. It can do this by means of formal surveys or focus groups or it can be more unassuming. Toyota recognized that the ultimate fortunes of its new Lexus range were dependent on how it would be received in the United States. Consequently, before it developed the new car, it sent one of its senior managers to live with a family on the West Coast to get the feel of the importance and role of the car in American society. Toyota knew that it needed an understanding of the market into which the new car would be sold and it chose to obtain it by market research of an informal kind.

Clive Sinclair is an electronics expert and, like most inventors, has an instinct for unmet needs. He was right about the launch of the 'Black Watch' and computer games but not about the C5 (Marks, 1990). The C5 was a one-seater electronically driven vehicle which he developed for urban use but which flopped because the market was poorly defined and there was a lack of both quantitative and qualitative research. If market research had been used, it may have pointed to more suitable applications in closed environments such as amusement parks or golf courses.

YOUTH: GETTING THE PRODUCT OFF THE GROUND

In the early stages of a product's life cycle, market research comes into its own. All products (and businesses) need a marketing plan. It does not have to be a formal document; many successful entrepreneurs have their plan only in their head. However, if a business is to grow, it will almost certainly need to stand up to financial justification. Also, the members of the product or business team will need clear goals backed by an action plan showing how they will be met.

In marketing planning there are three crucial questions that must be answered:

1. Where does the product/company stand at this point in time?
2. Where does it wish to go?
3. How can it achieve its goals?

In answering the first question (where does the product/company stand?), market research provides an assessment of the size of the market, its growth prospects, the distribution routes, the market segments and the way they buy, and the suppliers and their strengths and weaknesses.

Market research also will help to establish goals for the product or company. Knowledge of the market size, structure and competition will show what can be achieved. Occasionally new products take off at an unexpected speed and surprise everyone. More often, the targets are too ambitious and the timescales too short because there has been no market research to indicate the ferocity of the competitive environment and the inertia of the would-be buyers.

The final component of the marketing plan is showing how the goals can be achieved. Here market research can be used to guide pricing decisions, packaging design, promotions, product design, service – all the elements of the marketing mix.

In the late 1980s Philips Lighting used market research to help launch a new range of lamps which had a soft hint of colour achieved through the development of pigments which could be electrostatically coated onto the inside of the bulb (Hague and Jackson, 1992). The lamp was called 'Softone'.

Prior to the launch, Philips commissioned market research to establish whether the new lamp had significant customer appeal as the shape of the bulb was novel at the time (squarish) and the light output was in pastel shades. The research was also required to establish the willingess of consumers to pay a price premium for a new lamp of this kind. In this prelaunch phase, it was thought necessary to show the product to consumers but also to have enough respondents to have confidence in their replies. This was especially important in the pricing questions where a guideline from a focus group or a few in-depth interviews would not have been sufficiently robust. Two hundred face-to-face interviews were carried out across the country with householders who were asked to examine the new products in a hall test (see Chapter 9 for a fuller explanation of this technique). A sample of 200 randomly selected lamp buyers could be expected to yield an accuracy of ±7 per cent and this was considered sufficiently acceptable for the decisions which had to be taken.

The findings of this early research showed that the square lamps were liked because they were different, distinctive and unconventional. Nearly 80 per cent of the sample said that they would be quite or very likely to buy a coloured lamp of this kind even though sales of conventional coloured lamps were quite low. No one believed that this percentage would be achieved in the eventual launch, but it was encouraging nevertheless. It was the pastel concept that excited people. Furthermore, a small price premium was acceptable to the majority.

The next step was to work out a suitable pack. For this the company used focus groups with women since they constituted the principal lamp buyers. Four groups were all that was necessary to judge the acceptability of the mocked-up packs. Each of the groups came back with the same story – what was required was a pack which showed the unique shape of the lamp, which clearly indicated the wattage and which majored on the colour co-ordination possibilities in the home by using the words 'a hint of …'. These words married well with a Dulux campaign running at the time which was also promoting subtle shades of off-white.

The promotional messages, the prices and the pack were all finalized. The researchers turned now to testing the advertising campaign. Once more hall tests were used, this time just two but in different locations. At each of the halls, 40 target respondents were asked to evaluate the effectiveness of a TV commercial which was in the form of animatics (a sort of moving storyboard) and three treatments of a press campaign. This was not a large sample but it just about exceeded the threshold of 30 interviews which is often used to separate qualitative from quantitative surveys. Having seen the advertisements, the great majority of respondents were enthusiastic about 'Softone' and were eager to buy the lamps for their innovative appeal. However, none of the advertisements had a particularly strong impact and it was considered that a more down-to-earth approach was needed for what was at the time a novel product.

The campaign was suitably modified and finalized with the help of this tactical research. The last step was to test the effectiveness of the advertising campaign in a period which spanned just over three years. Each wave of the tracking study required a sample of 2,400 lamp buyers, a number that was deemed sufficiently large to provide the necessary level of accuracy for the subcells of respondents in each of the 12 regions of the UK. Philips bought into the MAS Omnibus (see Chapter 14 for a discussion on omnibus surveys) as this offered the most economical means of obtaining such a large sample for the relatively simple requirement of checking the awareness and recall of the 'Softone' brand name.

The graph in Figure 2.2 summarizes the two key sets of results from the tracking exercise, showing how, over the period after the launch, awareness of both the product and brand name more than doubled, with increases which appeared

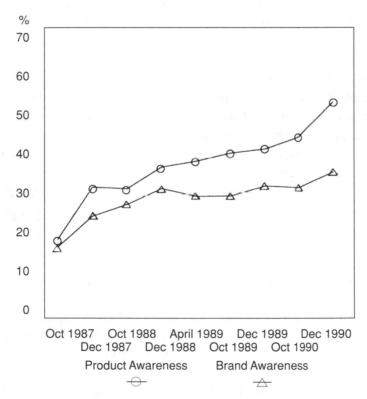

Figure 2.2   *'Softone' product and brand awareness*

specifically related to the advertising activity. (A small cautionary note here. The link between the advertising and recall seems pretty conclusive but it could have been due to some other simultaneous effect such as increased distribution and availability in the stores.)

MATURITY: IMPROVING PRODUCT PERFORMANCE

All the market research applications that we have discussed so far are also applicable in a mature market. As a product reaches saturation in its market and as the competition is reduced to just a handful of players by rationalization and take-overs, market research finds applications for fine tuning. Thus, market research is used to test new advertising concepts, track the effectiveness of the advertising, keep a check on optimum pricing, and provide facts and figures on the market size and trends for planning purposes and goal setting. It is especially important at this stage to ensure long-term customer satisfaction. Gone are the days when a company could rely on winning and keeping customers with very little effort. Most marketplaces are battlefields in which a neglected customer is soon picked off by a company which is prepared to try harder. There is a high cost in winning a customer in the first place and so, once on board, it pays to keep them. Customer satisfaction studies help this process.

Some very basic levels of customer satisfaction cannot be ignored, just because they are not market research measurements. The volume of sales and number of complaints are sure indicators of some level of satisfaction. However, the griping may be from a small number of seasoned complainers and the falling or rising sales may be as much the result of a boom or a recession as customer satisfaction. Most companies need an independent measure of the level of satisfaction which they can compare against other suppliers and track over time to see if things are improving or getting worse. For this they turn to market research. (For a more detailed explanation of customer satisfaction research see Chapter 11.)

OLD AGE: WORKING OUT THE NEXT MOVE

Eventually the sales of products begin to wane. Everything that can be done to bolster sales has been done but new products are taking over and demand is falling. Before this stage has been reached, it is likely that market research will have been used to explore the opportunities for product modifications and improvements. This could result in a rejuvenation of the life cycle as illustrated in Figure 2.3.

There may be other ways to buttress the sales. New markets could be found for

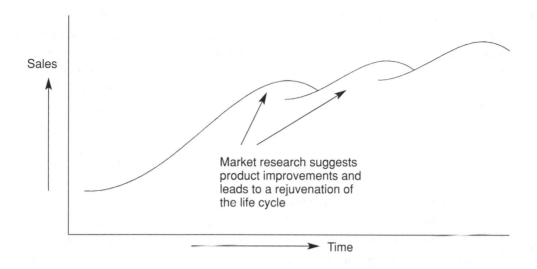

Figure 2.3 *Rejuvenation of the product life cycle*

the products. European car manufacturers have found new markets for their ageing but still serviceable engine and body plants in the Eastern bloc and China. A high market share enjoyed by the Japanese in their domestic markets has been the driving force which for many years has forced them to look outward for economies of scale. Cornflakes, cola and cars offer ready examples of ageing but still successful products which have had to move into export markets to find new growth opportunities.

Finding opportunities for an established product in an export market is an ideal application for market research. If there are problems in winning market share close to home, imagine the difficulties of building a business hundreds or thousands of miles away when there is no firm base of knowledge on the size of the market, its trends, the competition, the prices, the buyers and differences of culture.

Like good research of any kind, the best export market research is highly focused. Sometimes it is necessary to research the world market but more often this is a worthless exercise. The really successful exporters pick off just one or two countries at a time. They know that research across a number of countries can lead to effort being spread too thinly.

Market research is not just a tool for use by manufacturers of commercial products and services. The army is a mature if not ageing institution which has seen recruitment plummet due to a demographic trough in which there are smaller numbers of potential recruits in the 16 to 19 year old age groups. The army needed a campaign that would work harder than ever in its efforts to draw recruits from this smaller population. To help it in its task it commissioned research (Byrne and Langmaid, 1990). The study showed the most effective means of communicating the excitement of the army to young people and so enabled the army's advertising agency to devise three television campaigns. Market research also tracked the performance of the commercials. It measured recall before and after the campaign and this provided a deeper understanding of how the campaigns were working. However, of greater practical importance, the research resulted in a highly effective campaign, attracting a large number of potential soldiers to army recruitment offices.

Back in the world of commerce, Whessoe plc grew in the 1960s and 1970s to become a very sizeable manufacturer of heavy fabrications for offshore markets. As the offshore oil market matured and dried up in late 1990s, the company was left high and dry. No amount of product modification would boost a demand which did not exist; the company had to change direction. A decision was made that Whessoe would grow its small instrumentation division by acquisition. In the search for suitable targets, it found Elcon, an Italian manufacturer of instrumentation and controls. Elcon claimed that it had achieved a dominant position in its domestic market and was making successful inroads into the United States. It also assured Whessoe that its intrinsically safe products, designed for hazardous areas, stood comparison with any competition and met an important and growing need. These assertions needed testing independently and had to be grounded firmly on facts, not opinion.

Market research was carried out in Europe and the United States to test Elcon's claims. The results showed that Elcon did have a large share of the Italian market, so much so it had little chance of achieving any further growth in that territory. In the rest of Europe there were opportunities but they were limited by the narrow niche in which the company was positioned and this had to be taken into consideration in the purchase negotiations. In the United States, Elcon had not achieved the position it had thought. For sure there were great opportunities in that market but, at the time of the acquisition, Elcon had not organized itself in the best way to exploit them.

Whessoe was soon armed with a greater knowledge of the market than Elcon itself. Firstly, it knew what the up and down-sides were of the acquisition and it was able to work out a strategy for building sales of the company even before the take-over was executed. Also, it was able to impress Elcon at the time of the negotiation with its knowledge and so be sure that there could be no misunderstandings during the discussions. The acquisition went ahead and Elcon was integrated successfully into the growing Whessoe instrumentation division. During the next few years, Whessoe repeated this formula, sometimes using market research to track down targets, at other times using it to check them out. The result has been the formation of a substantial and healthy company with a completely different profile to the ageing dinosaur of the previous decade.

3

Planning market research

Where market research fails to live up to expectations the cause is nearly always poor initial planning – the issues which the research needed to address were not thought through clearly, the objectives of the research were not adequately defined or inappropriate methods were chosen. As for most activities, market research projects need to be planned with care before work actually starts.

ELEMENTS OF A MARKET RESEARCH PLAN

The main elements in an effective research plan are summarized below and discussed in this chapter:

- the decisions to be made and problems to be solved;
- research objectives;
- information coverage;
- accuracy levels;
- research methods;
- resources;
- timetable; and
- quality issues.

INFORMATION FOR DECISION MAKING

A market research project should ultimately contribute to market decision making or to identifying or solving problems which will entail decisions being made. Keeping to this principle throughout a project will avoid many problems. The output of the research may well be interesting but it should not just be interesting; it should meet a relevance test – how can this be used to make a better decision?

In some cases the link of the research to decision making is clearcut and direct. A choice has to be made between two options – eg product formulation A or B – and the research is carried out to increase the chance of taking the best decision – the formulation with the highest level of consumer acceptance. However, often, before any decision can be taken, the possible options need to be identified – eg the types of new products to consider for the range. In some cases the problems or opportunities facing the business are by no means obvious and need diagnosing – eg the existing product range is too narrow or it lies mainly on the down part of the product life cycle curve. Research can, therefore, contribute to the decision-making process at the various stages indicated in the framework given in Table 3.1. The decision stages can be loosely thought of as lying on a strategic (what are the problems) to tactical (which decision) policy continuum.

Table 3.1   *Research and decision-making stages*

Decision stage	Research style
What are the problems/opportunities?	Exploratory
What are the options (to solve a problem)?	Diagnosis
What should the decision be?	Testing

As suggested in Table 3.1, for each stage of decision making there is an appropriate research style. Where the problems or opportunities facing the business have not been defined, exploratory research is required and it is likely that the methodology will be 'open' and as much concerned with identifying issues or hypotheses as solving or testing them. On the other hand, at this stage high levels of accuracy are not likely to be required. At the other end of the spectrum the research is likely to be highly focused and concerned with only a very narrow range of issues. Also accuracy levels may now need to be much higher – eg is the product preference indicated among the research sample indicative of the position among all consumers? The qualitative/quantitative classification of research and information also can be linked to the above; exploratory research is often qualitative and testing is nearly always quantitative. However, there is not a perfect fit here by any means; sometimes research techniques which are regarded as quantitative are appropriate for the exploratory stage. Desk research too can be a valuable tool at this stage.

The techniques of market research rest on scientific method. However, uncovering the problems that need solving, defining the decision options and choosing appropriate research tools have a strong creative element. The organizational context in which the work is carried out also has an important bearing on the value of the outcome. Too often the research expert is brought in only at the third stage of the decision-making sequence and after the problems and options have been diagnosed or more likely simply assumed. Research is well placed to assist at these stages through various techniques (eg of qualitative research), applying the results of other research studies or importing research based tools such as 'brainstorming' to assist managers in uncovering the issues of their business. A number of writers have covered, in different ways, this creative contribution of market research, including Smith and Dexter (1994) and Weinman (1991).

RESEARCH OBJECTIVES

Every research project should have a defined and explicit objective which succinctly states *why* the research is being carried out – see Chapman (1989). All other aspects of planning and carrying out the research flow from this objective; in other words, if they do not contribute towards achieving this objective they almost certainly should not be undertaken. The objective should relate to the marketing decision which will have to be made or the problem that needs a solution (and decision) eg:

> Identify and quantify the opportunity for the company to enter the Spanish market and provide information relevant to planning how to do this.

Research objectives should be brief and should not be confused with a listing of the information required to meet them (sometimes referred to as detailed objectives). Unless the researcher is the person responsible for making the decisions, it is essential that the objective is agreed with the 'client' – whoever will make the decision; it is no use carrying out an extensive project and then discovering the marketing manager is considering entering the Portuguese as well as the Spanish market.

There is a certain art in drafting effective objectives (see Smith and Dexter, 1994) and this is not just a matter of words – badly thought-out objectives will lead to poor or less than optimum research. Two traps to avoid are the global, all-encompassing objectives and those which prejudge the problem or decisions to be made. An example of a global and too ambitious objective might be:

> Examine the position of the company in its marketplace and identify new opportunities.

At the stage of uncovering the business's problems or opportunities, such vague objectives may lie behind exploratory research. However, even at this stage, the researcher will very soon need a more focused approach and delimited objectives, since choices will have to be made about where to look for the potential problems or opportunities; you cannot carry on being completely open-minded indefinitely. At the option identification/diagnosis or decision-making/testing stages, the objectives certainly must be sharply focused if the research data is going to be relevant to the decision-making process.

Prejudgement is the opposite of over-ambition. Assumptions are made which ought to be tested through research. Faced with falling sales, for example, the temptation may be to research customer acceptance of the product and its features. But quite possibly this is not the problem at all; maybe the distribution system just does not get the product to customers. In terms of the framework set out earlier (in Table 3.1) this and similar problems arise through mistaking the level reached in the decision process and possibly the style of research needed. As previously mentioned, the organizational position of market research can be a contributory factor to such poorly planned research – the researcher is brought into the decision-making process too late, after questionable assumptions have been made and not critically examined.

Where the starting point for the research is a problem (or potential problem/opportunity) rather than a clear-cut decision to be made, an effective approach is to think of and list as many explanations as possible. In other words, develop alternate hypotheses. This may be done by the researcher but better still at a 'brain-storming' of all the key staff involved. The researcher may make a specific contribution to this process based on the results of previous research in related areas. He or she may also usefully act as facilitator to the meeting.

With only a little effort, the list of hypotheses generated is likely to be quite extensive and probably more than can be sensibly covered in any one research project. In this case some selection will have to be made of the hypotheses which are to be covered in the research project. This is likely to be based on a judgement of which is the more likely explanation of the problem; evidence that is already available – including from previous research as well as from more informal sources – may enable some hypotheses to be discounted confidently. With this done, the hypotheses which do seem worth researching will be the basis of a valid research objective.

INFORMATION COVERAGE

To meet the defined objective, a range of information will be required and will in turn be an input into the decisions that eventually will be made. For a given objective the information list, with only a little thought, will soon be quite long; possibly too long. In the case of the 'Spanish' project for example the list might be as follows:

Identify and quantify the opportunity for the company to enter the Spanish market and provide information relevant to planning how to do this.

1. The size of the market for the company's products with breakdown by:
   ● product grouping;
   ● customer group; and
   ● region.
2. Trends in market size over the last five years and prospects for the next five with breakdown as per number 1.
3. Existing suppliers to the Spanish market, shares held with breakdowns as per number 1.
4. Basis of competition between suppliers, eg product differentiation, service, pricing.
5. Pricing levels in the market; use of discounts, etc.
6. Distribution structures and links to primary suppliers.
7. Customer satisfaction with existing suppliers/products and their relative standing in the market. Any unsatisfied customer needs.

This list is by no means exhaustive and other information headings also may be considered important. There is no such thing as an absolutely right or wrong coverage although the effectiveness of the research will be shaped by what is included or left out; the list will be more or less useful. Often the problem is not so much that headings are left out but that the coverage is too comprehensive in relation to the research resources – organizational, budgetary and timetable – available.

The example given above for instance is likely to involve quite a major research project and it is very possible that the resources available are insufficient to cover all that seems useful. The initial 'wish list' of headings may, therefore, need pruning or separating into what is absolutely vital to know and what is of lesser importance.

Another approach to meeting an objective which appears to entail an extensive research coverage and major research input, is staging. In the example of the Spanish market, it is possible that coverage of the market size (without detailed breakdowns) and suppliers' shares may indicate a limited or nil opportunity of market entry. If this is the case, other information would be of no practical use. In other words, there is a hierarchy of relevant data with the relevance of some conditional on others in the list. It may be sensible, therefore, to establish such critical data – eg market size and suppliers' shares – in a first stage project and on the basis of the outcome of this to then decide whether further research is required. Quite possibly this first stage research can be carried out quickly and at low cost (eg through desk research). Staging is particularly advantageous in in-house (rather than commissioned) research and even if there is no apparent basis for staging the information coverage – eg all data seem equally vital – carrying out desk research before planning any fieldwork is to be recommended to minimize effort and costs; Smith and Dexter (1994) express it as working on the assumption that the data already exist until a search reveals otherwise.

A final aspect of defining the information coverage is to set boundaries or limits to the research. These may be geographical (eg the market in Great Britain excluding Northern Ireland), by product range (eg high density polystyrene) or by market or application (eg use in the construction industry, for trade use etc). Again these boundaries should be explicit and agreed with the 'client' and should at least initially be based on the decision-making needs of the business rather than research convenience or practicality. However, as in other aspects of information coverage, it may be necessary to compromise from the ideal in this respect and set limits for reasons of research resources. What is important is that this is done consciously and that a choice is not made without considering alternatives or the potential consequences of limiting the project to particular boundaries.

Taking time and effort in defining the coverage of the research is essential if the results are truly to assist the decision-making process. In addition, however, a well defined research coverage is of practical value in later stages of the project and particularly at the questionnaire design stage. With the coverage defined and listed, much of the work involved in developing a questionnaire is effectively already done.

ACCURACY

Another aspect of initial research planning is deciding on the level of accuracy that should be sought. This has a strong bearing on the choice of research methods not only at the detailed level such as sample size, but also in terms of the basic approach including the choice between quantitative or qualitative methods. When professional market researchers ask their clients how accurate any data should be the answer is often 'very accurate' or 'as accurate as possible'. However, accuracy, at least where fieldwork is involved, has a price and, as a general rule, increases in accuracy not only cost more but disproportionately more.*

Nor is a high level of accuracy always needed to meet the overall research objective. If in the Spanish example the company would consider sales of £500,000 pa to be worthwhile, it might not matter if the total market size was £40 million or £50 million (an accuracy of +/– 25 per cent). However, in other cases a more closely defined level of accuracy may be essential to meet the research objectives. If, for example, in an advertising research study the objective was to measure the impact of a campaign on brand awareness through comparing before and after campaign measures, the accuracy must be at least commensurate with the anticipated increase in awareness. If this is 10 per cent, a sampling method with results within +/– 5 per cent accuracy at the two measurement stages would not be capable of yielding reliable evidence on the effectiveness of the campaign. This accuracy level might imply an awareness level before the campaign of between 35 per cent and 45 per cent if the sample result was 40 per cent, and between 45 per cent and 55 per cent after the campaign if the sample result was 50 per cent. In other words, the data might imply that the campaign was very successful or it had no effect at all.

The required accuracy must, therefore, be linked to how the resulting data will be used – the nature of the decisions that the research will guide. Even if precise definition of accuracy levels is not practically possible (this is often the case) some judgement should still be made on the reliability sought from the information. This may be as simple as a contrast between an attempt at measurement (quantitative research) compared to just description and explanation (qualitative research). Both approaches can contribute to effective marketing decisions but it is important that neither is used for the wrong application. Like information coverage, accuracy levels need to be considered before deciding on appropriate research methods.

---

* If a sample of 500 is statistically likely to be accurate to +/– 5 per cent, what size of sample will be needed to increase the accuracy to +/– 2.5 per cent? It is not 1,000 but nearer 2,000 and the costs involved possibly more than twice as high. Diminishing returns very much apply.

RESEARCH METHODS AND DESIGN

Research methods concern how the required information will be collected, and effective planning presupposes an understanding of the alternatives and how and when each can be effectively used. The issues are covered in detail in later chapters and for now the reader should take some things on faith.

Figure 3.1 is a framework for developing a research design with the choices driven by the objectives and information requirements of the project.

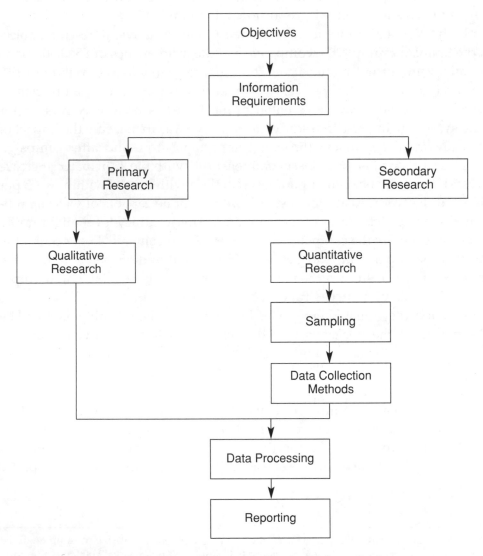

Figure 3.1 *Market research methods*

The most fundamental choice in research methods is between secondary or desk research and primary research or fieldwork. As we will show in the next chapter, the potential and scope of desk research is enormous and the objectives of many research projects, whether undertaken in-house or through commissioning an outside supplier, can be largely or wholly met from data that is already 'freely' available. A difficulty at the planning stage, however, is that there is often some uncertainty of the likely outcome of desk research – what will be found or not. Also there are some types of information which in principle cannot be obtained in this way (eg usually attitude type data such as how a particular company is regarded in its marketplace). In many projects, however, carrying out an initial desk research stage is strongly recommended as a way of gaining the maximum benefit from the research budget. Desk/secondary research is nearly always far cheaper (and quicker) than primary research/fieldwork and there is no point in spending time and money interviewing to find out what is already available and accessible at little cost. Too often money and time is spent 're-inventing the wheel'. One reason why secondary research sources are often omitted is institutional. Most research is carried out by market research agencies which for various reasons find problems in offering desk research as a profit earning service. In this respect in-house research can have an edge over buying-in.

Once desk research is completed (and assuming it does not yield all the information required for the project) primary research or fieldwork can be planned to fill in the gaps. The choices involved – the elements of the primary research design – include the following issues (these are expanded in later chapters):

- Whether the nature of the information sought is primarily quantitative or qualitative.
- Sampling issues including:
    - the universe to be covered eg: all adults, housewives, buyers of specific products in consumer markets and comparable aspects of industrial markets;
    - sectors or subgroupings of the whole universe which are of specific interest and need to be considered in sampling design;
    - sampling method and size (number of interviews).
- Data collection methods – eg face-to-face or phone interviews, postal survey, observation etc.
- How the resulting data will be analysed – particularly relevant for more sophisticated techniques such as conjoint analysis.

The basis of the decisions made in each of the above areas should relate to the research objectives, the planned information coverage and the accuracy sought. Or at least this should be so in theory. In practice other factors have to be taken into account and especially the resources available including the budget. Quite possibly the ideal may be face-to-face interviews with a sample of 250 decision makers in consuming industries but for practical reasons a postal survey has to be used instead. In commercial market research such compromises are inevitable whether the project is carried out in-house or bought-in; research methods are seldom to a theoretical optimum and may fall well short of the ideal with some trade-off in terms of coverage and accuracy against the budget. However, there is some point beyond which compromises are a danger; if the affordable or practical methods are not capable of yielding the required data to adequate accuracy levels, it will be better not to do the research at all; decisions based on hunches may be better than using fatally flawed and spurious research.

RESOURCES

As just suggested, research methods are in practice inevitably shaped by available resources and largely this is a matter of money; with enough cash, any shortcomings in existing resources can usually be overcome.

What budget should be made available for the research project? The methodologically pure researcher would argue that the budget should be whatever is needed to meet the research objectives, provide the information required and to finance the methods needed to produce that information to the defined accuracy level. However, in practice, it is more a question of what funds are available or can be afforded for the project relative to other calls on business expenditure. Furthermore, even if cash is freely available, there are other considerations and especially the amount at risk in the decision which the research is to guide. If the decision may entail capital expenditure of £1 million, a research budget of £10,000 may be well worth spending – if the research indicates that the planned expenditure is a poor investment, only the research cost will be lost rather than most or all of the £1 million investment. However, if the decision has much lower cost implications, the value of doing the research will be less; obviously there is no point to spending £10,000 on research to decide whether to invest in a project entailing only this level of expenditure. This is often the case with advertising research, which is relatively expensive compared to the advertising budget. For example, a business-to-business advertising campaign of £50,000 may cost £30,000 to research if 200 companies are interviewed in a pre-campaign study and a matching sample of a further 200 are interviewed 'post' the campaign.

However it is done, research planning should, therefore, include making a budget available for the work. Monitoring of actual expenditure against this budget can then be carried out so that the latter is kept to or at least only exceeded for good reasons. With in-house projects, the true costs include both the real and the notional. The former includes items such as travel costs and materials while the latter is mainly the cost of the research staff's time. This time has a cost and if there is a diversion from other work, it is the 'opportunity' cost that matters – revenue lost from not doing routine or normal work. It all depends on the systems and culture of the organization whether or not such notional costs are identified, measured and set against the research activity. Regardless of whether they are measured, however, these costs exist. Buying-in research can sometimes be a cheaper option.

Apart from a cash budget, the major resource required for a research project is suitably qualified people. Who is available for the work and the time they can set aside affects not only how quickly the project can be carried out but also the methods that can be practically used. One in-house researcher can realistically carry out a programme of say 20 key decision-maker interviews (in an industrial market) or a limited number of deep, qualitative interviews (in a consumer market) but he or she probably cannot even contemplate a nationwide visit programme to 100 respondents. Such limitations may necessitate a switch to other methods such as phone or post or force a reduction in sample size (but with thought given to the effect on accuracy levels).

Where research is bought in from an outside supplier, the problem of limited people-resources will be far less of an issue; the ability of an agency to provide the resources needed is an important criterion in selecting it for the particular project. Similarly, limitations of in-house research resources can be overcome by buying-in specific services from a professional research agency – eg on a 'field and tab' basis (see Chapter 14).

TIMETABLE

A research plan needs a timetable. Even if there is neither a real deadline nor constraint on the input, it is better to be committed to a finish date otherwise the project is likely to drag on forever. The two determinants of a timetable are the deadline and how long the planned research activities will take to carry out. Resources determine the latter and experience of the intended methods will enable realistic estimates to be made of how long each stage will take. The deadline, on the other hand, is likely to be driven by external events and time-frames; the research results may be needed to fit the lead time in installing plant, or by the time the next year's business plan is developed or by the end of an accounting period. To an extent it may be possible to speed up the research to fit such exterior constraints or the method itself may be trimmed. Certainly good research can be carried out within a short timetable but, beyond some point, quality will be compromised. Some deadlines have to be met but many are not as fixed as are made out.

MAINTAINING QUALITY IN RESEARCH

While good research can guide decision making, poor research can mislead. For any research project there needs to be confidence that the results are within agreed parameters of reliability. Quality issues relating to ensuring data are adequate to their purposes are, therefore, an important concern in research planning and execution. Research design is one dimension of quality; the choices made in areas such as qualitative or quantitative approaches, sampling size, fieldwork methods etc need to be appropriate to the research objectives and coverage. However, in addition, quality is also an organizational issue – how the research is managed and controlled. Deficiencies in these areas may not inevitably reduce the reliability of the data but they are certainly likely to do so. Four key areas of the organizational aspect of quality in research are:

1. competence;
2. working practices;
3. verification; and
4. validation.

Competence relates to the people carrying out the research task; do they have the skills necessary to design and carry out the project? This is relevant at both professional and support levels. Effective research designs, as well as the interpretation of the results, demand skills and experience at the professional level. This should be obvious. However, support staff, especially those involved in data collection, also need skills; errors resulting from poor fieldwork practice are very likely to exceed any theoretically calculated sampling error. Assuring staff competence will require effective recruitment and training programmes by the research supplier or in-house organization.

To produce consistently high quality research, staff not only need skills and training, they also need the discipline of effective working practices. What these are depends on the size, structure and nature of the organization in which they work; what is appropriate for a one-man research consultancy is very different to that needed in a 'top ten' agency. Also such practices do not have to be formalized into 'systems' although the larger the organization the more likely that this becomes essential. Working practices, it should also be said, provide a framework for effective design and creativity and not a barrier to these essentials.

Verification issues are concerned with establishing whether a research plan is fully translated into practice and may require the working practices to build-in various types of checking; checking the research design against the objectives, the questionnaire against the information coverage and whether interviewers carried out interviews as the design intended (eg asked the questions as framed). The extent of verification is related to the level of division of labour and the number of project team members. Most market research agencies, for example, use teams of part-time interviewers employed as more or less casual labour and this requires formal methods of verifying fieldwork, based on check-backs to respondents (see also Chapter 14).

In most sciences, validation is a matter of replicability. Experimental results can be and are checked through repeating the experiment (usually by different groups of scientists). Quantitative market research at least is theoretically replicable in this way. A survey using the same methods should produce the same (within sampling error) results although the elapse of time may well have produced changes in whatever is being measured – eg in the case of opinion polls, changes in voting intentions – and in practice this means that validation through replication is not a real option. Furthermore, for practical and budgetary reasons such validation is very rarely carried out – *ad hoc* research (in contrast to continuous or tracking studies) is in this sense a one shot. Another approach to validation is by comparing the outcome of the decision made on the basis of the research with what the research predicted. However, by then it is too late to validate – the research has been 'used'. Also for various reasons 'real world' outcomes often do not prove or disprove the research findings. The research may have been 'right' but the practical implementation of the resulting marketing decisions may have been at fault. Similarly the research results often can be a self-fulfilling prophecy – on the basis of the data, one formulation is selected or given most marketplace support and, therefore, inevitably succeeds. Validation of research is, therefore, seldom possible in any rigorous way although comparison of the data output with other and independent sources, such as previous research in an area, may provide some indications. Because validation is often so problematical there is an increased need to focus on other parts of quality control and assurance.

PREPARING A WRITTEN PLAN

Whether research is carried out in-house or by an outside agency, a formal and written plan is essential for projects of any size and complexity. In the case of research by an outside agency, such a plan is prepared as part of the commissioning process; the agency prepares a 'proposal' before commission and this is very largely a research plan. The format of such a plan can vary considerably but the following are the major research plan headings which should be covered or at least considered:

- Analysis of the problems or issues the research addresses.
- The research objectives.
- The research covering the information required; scope, boundaries and limits and accuracy levels.
- Research methods/design including the role of secondary/desk research versus primary methods; qualitative or quantitative approaches; sampling issues; data collection methods and any implications of the data analysis techniques to be used.
- Reporting (how the research results will be communicated to decision makers).
- Timetable broken down by main stages and activities.
- Costs by element.
- Quality assurance issues.

We recommend that a formal written plan for the research should always be prepared and cover each aspect of the work discussed in this chapter. This may seem over-formal where the researcher and user are one and the same but even in this case efficient research is more likely if an explicit plan is drawn up. In such a case, its format is immaterial and as long as it is legible, neatness and presentation quality carry no premium. Where the plan is to be presented to others, such as an internal client – perhaps before the budget is sanctioned – presentational quality is, however, important. The message may be the same, but high standards will enhance credibility. (See also Chapter 13 for a more detailed explanation of writing briefs.)

4

How to get information for next to nothing

WHY RE-INVENT THE WHEEL?

There is no point reinventing the wheel and there are many metaphorical wheels available to the market researcher. The expert desk researcher can quickly and inexpensively dig out data from a wide variety of sources to answer many of the questions that have already been asked. So why do we spend so much on primary research? The reason, very often, is because we don't know how to locate the information. Or it may be that information is not in quite the shape we require and therefore it escapes our notice that with a little bit of reworking it could be very useful. It could be dated and we need something more current. Sometimes, desk research seems too easy. A big decision surely needs a lot of money spending on it and merits an original piece of research? It is not so. Information that is in the public domain has at least been subjected to the test of public scrutiny. This is not to say that it will definitely be correct, but it could have been challenged and that may in itself help the researcher judge its accuracy.

I once ran a training course that in the first instance was called simply 'Desk research'. There were very few takers. It seems such a boring subject. When the course was renamed 'How to get information for next to nothing' it became oversubscribed and has been run many times since. Desk research is information that costs next to nothing. It sits underneath our noses. It can easily be carried out by the do-it-yourself researcher. Moreover, for the do-it-yourself researcher, desk research is a very practical tool – in most cases he or she is not at any disadvantage compared to the resources of a professional agency. A couple of days of desk research has a very big yield and the benefits of spending much more time searching quickly diminish.

Desk research is a term that is used loosely and it generally refers to the collection of secondary data or that which has already been collected. To most people it suggests published reports and statistics and these are certainly important sources. In the context of this chapter the term is widened to include all sources of information that do not involve a field survey and, in addition to the more traditional sources, this could include speaking to someone at a trade association or carrying out an interview with an expert.

RESOURCES

Until the advent of the Internet and online databases, access to libraries was the only important resource needed to carry out desk research. Despite the marvels of the information highway, some data are easier to access from hard copy and off the library shelves. Indeed, the Internet for all its value is still not as comprehensive in its coverage of statistical data as it is in product and company information. The desk researcher should acquaint himself or herself with the nearest commercial library.

All major cities have at least one good municipal or university library and few researchers will be more than an hour's travel from such a resource. From time to time the reference books in the main body of the library will be useful, but for the most part it is the commercial section that is of greatest interest.

There are also some important national libraries open to a desk researcher, including a range of services from the British Library and two important government resources: the Central Statistical Office and the DTI Export Marketing Information Centre, a major source of international market research. There are also many specialist libraries run by industry bodies and others; these can best be located through ASLIB.

SOURCES OF SOURCES – THE HIGH-LEVEL VIEW

Before exploring some of the popular sources of information to market researchers, it is worth pointing out that there are some useful 'sources of sources'. These range from inexpensive books such as *How to Find Information – Business: A Guide to Searching in Published Sources* ('How to Find Series') by Nigel Spencer (available from Amazon.com) through to the much more expensive *Croner's A–Z of Business Information Sources or Croner's European Business Information Sources* (www.croner. cch.co.uk). Croner's A–Z lists some of the best Web sources and the European guide provides a starting point for gathering information from European countries. Both are available on CD ROM.

There are also other, general guides which can be used to track down sources of data, including those covering published research, the press, directories and statistics; examples of all of these have been mentioned above. For international markets there are comparable 'sources of sources', including *European Directory of Marketing Information Sources* and *Directory of International Sources of Business Information*. Some or all of these 'sources of sources' will be found in a good library, together with other indexes, eg *Research Index*, which lists articles published in the press. The library's own cataloguing and indexing systems also provide a means of systematically searching out data. With experience, sources likely to be relevant to a particular field will become familiar and provide short cuts, though a full search technique is also recommended.

Encyclopaedias are useful storehouses of information for the market researcher, either to check out a technical issue or to obtain a closer definition of the subject and its associated terminology. Now that *Encyclopaedia Britannica* is on line (www.britannica.com) it has become universally accessible for browsing alphabetically, by subject, or for a quick word search.

The United States has led the field in the collection and dissemination of business information for many years. The Central Intelligence Agency (CIA) uses its expertise on our behalf to bring together basic intelligence that began as the National Intelligence Survey and is now an on-line *Factbook* that can be easily examined country by country (www.cia.gov/cia/publications/factbook/). The whole database can be downloaded, though this requires either considerable patience or a broad-bandwidth connection. Virtually every country in the world is covered . The Factbook gives geographical statistics of countries, the demographic breakdown of their population, economic overviews (in some detail), transportation, government, and maps galore. Another route to similar information is www.geographic.org.

INDUSTRY EXPERTS

Another means of locating data sources is through direct contact with organizations and individuals who have knowledge of a particular field. Trade associations and the publishers of information are examples. This sort of approach strays outside desk research in the strictest sense. However, a two-way traffic between sources (which identify potential contacts) and expert interviewing (to identify sources) is a means of getting the most value from desk research at little extra cost (possibly at a saving if sources are identified more efficiently).

You could also try FIND/SVP, which has a Quick Consulting and Research Service that aims to answer questions on markets through a fixed-fee retainer system and deliver the results by phone, fax or e-mail at a quite modest cost.

THE INTERNET

Accessing information via the Internet is the modern alternative to hours spent in libraries. The Internet is a global interconnection of networks that link servers (computers housing information and so connect businesses, academic institutions, trade associations, government agencies, medical facilities, scientific establishments and private individuals). Using browsers such as Microsoft's Internet Explorer or Netscape's Navigator, it is possible to access the sites or user groups of the many millions who are now linked through the Net.

Accessing the Internet requires the user to have a computer with a modem and a subscription to an Internet service provider (ISP) such as America On Line (AOL), Demon or BT Internet. Thereafter, it is a matter of dialling up the service provider to log on to the Internet and possibly the payment of a local telephone charge.

For market researchers, the Internet has two important sources of information:

1. the sites that companies, organizations and individuals have created to promote or communicate their products, services or views;
2. user groups, which are made up of people who have an interest in a particular subject.

Web sites are recognized by the prefix 'www'. Companies operating in the UK typically have sites with citations such as www.companyname.co.uk, while those aiming at an international audience are more likely to be referenced as www.companyname.com. A non-profit making organization would have the suffix 'org' after its name as in www.charity.org and a university or academic institution would be completed by the initials 'ac' as in www.university.ac.

The World Wide Web is estimated to contain over 2 billion pages of publicly accessible information. The problem is not the volume of information but finding that tiny bit that you need in this enormous ocean. Fortunately for researchers, search engine technology has increased by leaps and bounds and an appropriate word-string in a search engine such as Google, Alta Vista or Yahoo will usually deliver thousands of hits. This too is a researcher's problem, for who ever looks beyond page three of these?

Search engines use programmes based on a spider or a crawler, which look for key words or a word string in those billions of pages. The results are copied into a huge database (an index or list of information) and you are presented with the summary contents of the search at each site together with a hyperlink, from which a click will take you to the reference. Meta search engines such as Dogpile or Metacrawler use several search engines all at once, and then blend the results into a convenient form, such as listing the references in declining order of appropriateness to the search request.

In this massive sea of information it may be difficult to find what we require because:

1. We are using the wrong search strategy – a different word or arrangement of words may yield more precise hits.
2. We are using the wrong search engine – even the very best search engines do not cover all the pages on the Net, so the vital piece you are looking for may never be uncovered. A different search engine could produce a different result.
3. We are using the wrong word – the use of the British spelling of tyres would miss out on Web references to the American spelling of tires.
4. The information we are looking for may not be available in precisely that form. A search for the volumes of tyres bought as original equipment by Ford may come to naught, but it would be easy to derive the figure by finding out the number of Ford cars produced per year and multiplying by five (one per wheel plus the spare).

A search strategy with a suitable arrangement of words may well hit the bullseye and locate the information that is being sought. When typing in the search string it may be helpful to use double quotation marks to enclose the phrase so that "world health organization" will only deliver references to those three words in that combination. Without the quotation marks, most search engines look for each of the three words separately and would deliver hundreds of thousands of irrelevant references to world, to health and to organizations. (Note that the Internet is indifferent to capital letters.)

Thinking laterally is certainly the first principle of desk research using the Internet. Avoid using very common terms (eg Internet or people), as this will lead to thousands of hits but irrelevant results. Where possible, use a phrase (in double quotation marks) or proper name to narrow the search and therefore retrieve a smaller number of more relevant results. If too many results are generated, it is easy to refine the word string in the search box and carry out an advanced search or simply renew the search, since the speed of delivery of new results is such that they will be on the screen in a fraction of a second.

More often the search will start a trail that follows the links between related sites. The searcher must learn to surf from one site to another, bookmarking those that are useful for downloading or copying into a work file. Here it is worth emphasising that a crucial rule of desk research is always to note the reference of the data. Referenced data allows the credibility to be judged and it facilitates re-examination.

Lewis Endlar, a leading expert on the Internet at Manchester Metropolitan University, makes the claim that it is possible to find out almost anything via the Net. His claim, though bold, is based on the fact that the Internet provides access to millions of knowledgeable people through user groups, so that a question thrown into the pool will sooner or later be answered. Of course, it may not be necessary to tap into this bottomless resource of knowledge, as the information may already be out there, posted on a Web site.

There are over 10,000 user groups (also called news groups or discussion groups) on the Internet covering almost every subject. They are roughly organized by topic, ranging from hobbies and recreation (prefixed by rec) through to computers (comp), science (sci), culture, religion, as well as 'alternative' subjects (alt). A question posted within an appropriate user group by a researcher may well find an answer from one of the millions of Internet users. An easy way to access user groups is through a search engine such as Deja News.

At the time of writing, the best search engine for market researchers appears to be Google. It offers speed and consistent high quality hits through a programme built on algorithms. Northernlight is another highly recommended search engine because it parcels up its hits into folders with common themes. Each search also has a 'Special Collection' folder which contains links to articles that may well have a market commentary so valued by researchers.

ONLINE DATABASES AND MARKET DATA

Many databases of articles and reports can now be accessed via the Internet. Sometimes the information required by market researchers is available from commercial providers, who charge significantly for access either as an up-front figure or on a pay-as-you-use basis – eg Dialog/Data-Star and FT Profile. The user of such sources has to become a subscriber and must learn how to carry out searches efficiently (to minimize costs). Free or low-cost training is offered to new subscribers. In comparison to the Internet, searching online databases is more costly and typically could cost between £5,000 and £10,000 per year to a serious user. This is because the databases house collections of valuable reports, which, even though available on a page-by-page basis, still have a hefty price tag. For those who want access to online databases but cannot justify signing on, it is possible to employ the services of skilled desk researchers through an organization such as the British Library.

A database such as Profound from Dialog (www.dialog.com) provides access to a range of business and economic information, including news archives from over 5,000 publications, financial reports from over 4.5 million companies, market research reports, country data, economic data and broker reports.

However, this begs the question of which database should be accessed in the first place – no one 'host' provides a direct gateway to all cyber-data. To fill the gap there are a number of database source books published, including _On Line Business_ and _Company Databases_ and _Directory of On Line Databases_ – the latter is published twice a year by Gale Research and has 4,900 publicly accessible online databases. The major hosts (eg Reuters, Data-Star) also publish their own guides.

The major benefit of any sort of online database is the speed of locating material using key word searching to match what is available to what is sought. This is particularly of benefit in searching press files (manually looking through the past few months' issues of even one paper is a daunting task).

There is an increasing number of Web sites that offer archive material to researchers without their having to sign up, though there usually is a fee for the report or part of it. The table of contents is available free and there are many synopses of reports, which may be sufficient for those requiring just an overview. The charges made for bought-in reports and similar sources range from the nominal to levels comparable to commissioning _ad hoc_ research. Most fall within the £500 to £5,000 bracket.

A good source of market research data, offering full or part reports, is www.marketresearch.com, which allows access to a collection of over 40,000 publications from over 350 research firms.

One of the best general databases of commercial and financial news is ft.com – the _Financial Times'_ web site. It is also worth looking on www.findarticles.com, whose archive of articles may contain a synopsis of the data you are looking for.

SPECIALIZED INDUSTRY DATA

Material such as abstracts, statistics and large directories are increasingly available on CD ROM or by password from an Internet site. For example, information on the chemical and rubber industry can be obtained from RAPRA – the Rubber and Plastics Research Association – on CD ROM on a subscription basis. Where such a source is going to be consulted frequently, such formats may be the best way of accessing data. Searching and abstracting data is as convenient as online and once the initial cost has been met (this may be substantial but often no more than buying traditional hard-copy versions), there is no marginal cost of access (unlike pay-as-you-use online databases). As more researchers gain access to broad bandwidth, the speed of access to the Internet will increase and the delivery of archived material on CD ROM will decline in favour of constantly updated information on the Web.

COMPANY DATA

Researchers need company data for competitor benchmarking, sourcing suppliers or building profiles of customers and potential customers. Only a few years ago company literature was a mainstay of such searches. Sales literature is prepared for the public domain and will be sent readily on request. Today company Web sites are brimming with useful information. They contain pictures of products, maps of distributors, data sheets, company histories, press releases, and sometimes financial background. The information is nearly always more extensive and current than printed brochures and it is available in an instant. A request from the CEO for a product search could be put together in couple of hours and contain an impressive amount of material.

Financial data on companies is available in the United Kingdom from Companies House (www.companieshouse.gov.uk). Companies House's WebSales offers the searchable Company Names and Addresses Index free of charge and enables the searcher to look up information on more than 1.5 million companies. Of these about 11,000 are public companies (PLCs) which issue shares, and of the PLCs, about 7,000 are quoted on the Stock Exchange. Smaller companies file only limited information and this can reduce the value of company accounts in niche markets. Searching for a company can be carried out using its name or its unique company registration number.

Details that can be obtained free from Companies House online include:

● the registered office address of the company;

- dates for the last accounts and annual returns;
- date of incorporation;
- country of origin (original country of registration);
- status, eg live, dissolved, etc;
- insolvency details;
- previous names;
- company type;
- nature of business;
- branch details;
- overseas company information.

In addition to the free basic company details, certain company documents and reports can be purchased for very modest sums by credit card and delivered electronically. These include scanned image documents of the latest company accounts, annual returns, current appointments and outstanding mortgages.

Another source of financial data is EXTEL, which offers information on over 30,000 companies worldwide, and about 10,000 based in the United Kingdom. In addition to basic directory information, EXTEL provides a range of financial information for each company:

- accounts for five years: balance sheet, income statement, cash flow, etc;
- daily share prices back to 1988;
- financial ratios.

It is possible to search for an individual company, or to select a group of companies that meet certain criteria; for example, companies in a particular industry with a specified financial criteria such as turnover, price/earnings ratio, etc.

The US Securities & Exchange Commission (SEC) requires all US public companies (except foreign companies and companies with less than $10 million in assets and 500 shareholders) to file registration statements, periodic reports, and other forms electronically and anyone can access and download this information for free from its Web site (www.sec.gov).

GOVERNMENT STATISTICS

In most projects, the desk researcher will seek 'hard' statistical data and sooner or later this will point towards a government source. These cover most areas of business and social life.

In the United Kingdom, the National Statistics Web site (www.statistics.gov.uk) contains a vast range of official UK statistics and information about statistics, which can be accessed and downloaded free. The site allows searching by themes such as agriculture/fishing/forestry, commerce, energy, industry, education, crime and justice, the labour market, the population, etc.

The *Annual Abstract of Statistics* is an easy way into the major series of statistics and is available in hard copy from The Stationery Office (TSO). There is also a free catalogue of the main publications from the same government bookshop, which is well worth picking up. However, the bible is the *Guide to Official Statistics*, a substantial volume that is regularly revised.

One of the cornerstones of the Government's statistical service and a massive source of data for market researchers (see Market Research Society, 1993) is the decennial Census of Population (the most recent of which was carried out in 2001, with data becoming available in 2003. Marketers use census output for segmentation by demographics and survey planning (eg setting quota samples). The census is also the basis of geodemographic analysis systems.

The UK Government is not, of course, unique in providing a statistical service. Governments of most developed countries provide as good or better data covering their own territories – the United States, for example, is very well documented. A visit to US Department Of Commerce site on www.doc.com offers a treasure trove of information from industry sector statistics to economic analysis to demographic data and research publications. There is a good search engine to help navigate through this very large site.

There are also international bodies collecting and publishing statistics. For the EU the office responsible is Eurostat, and this source will increasingly be important in projects covering the whole single market of the EU. Two other major publishers are the UN and the OECD.

As with other sources, government statistics can increasingly be accessed online as well as from hard copy. Data-Star is one online host providing access.

TRADE AND INDUSTRY BODIES

Every trade, no matter how obscure, nearly always has some collective body to represent its interests (and also usually spawns several trade publications – see below). To meet members' needs, and for PR purposes, most of these bodies publish or can make available (sometimes to members only) considerable information about their industry. The organization and sophistication of these bodies and the volume of the information offered varies enormously. Some do no more than publish an annual report, while others are the recognized source of detailed industry statistics (eg the SMMT for the motor vehicle industry). There are various directories of these organizations (eg _Directory of British Associations_) and a desk researcher should not only seek out publications of relevant bodies but also contact them directly; information that is not published may be obtained in this way.

MARKET RESEARCH REPORTS

A number of specialist market research companies speculatively carry out studies, which are then sold as publications – albeit relatively expensive, measured against the price we are used to paying for more conventional reference books. However, compared to privately commissioned studies these are incredibly good value. Often referred to as 'multi-client reports', these publications cover every subject imaginable from A to Z. There are over 30,000 multi-client reports available and they can be located through several sources. _Marketsearch_ lists 20,000 published reports from 700 firms. The database can be searched in hard copy or from the company's Web site (www.marketsearch-dir.com). Another directory of published market research is _Findex_ from Euromonitor. This directory, also known as _The Worldwide Directory of Market Research, Reports, Studies and Surveys_, provides details on 9,000 market reports.

THE PRESS

The general, business and trade press are key sources for the desk researcher. As well as 'news', these sources include much background material, including special supplements on industries and markets. The general press includes the quality dailies and Sundays – _The Times, Independent, Guardian, Telegraph_, etc – and periodicals such as _The Economist_. Of the business press, _The Financial Times_ is a major reference source in its own right.

There are several press indexes (eg _Research Index_), but searching the general press is now better done online. Research Index has indexes of over 300 UK newspapers, trade journals and 'popular' business periodicals. The two sections are arranged by company and industry. It is published every two weeks, so it is easy to find current information. Each entry gives the title/headline of the article, newspaper or periodical title and date, and page number. The industry section is cumulated quarterly. There is also a Web version of _Research Index_ which covers the most recent 14 months (www.researchindex.co.uk).

In industrial markets the trade press is a very important source of market research information. Every industry and trade has regular journals which can be identified in publications such as *BRAD* and *Pims*. While much useful data is in these sources, finding material can be quite laborious. Many publications have a poor or no index and some are not available online, so there may be no alternative to reading through hard-copy back issues.

DIRECTORIES

Directories are the staple diet of market researchers. They provide details of companies that either supply or consume goods and they are the usual source for preparing sample frames (list of companies or people to be interviewed). The directories may also provide a profile of a company, detailing its size by giving the number of employees, or whether it is an agent or producer.

One of the most comprehensive general directories is *Yellow Pages* (www.yell.co.uk), since every company in the United Kingdom with a telephone number is given a free entry. These directories form the most comprehensive listing of small and medium enterprises (SMEs). Within the Yell Group, The Business Database supplies data on around 1.5 million UK businesses sourced from the free-line entries in the *Yellow Pages* printed directories. From its Web site it is possible to run counts and download lists for sample frames.

Every country has its *Yellow Pages* on the Internet (www.gelbe-seiten.de, www.goudengids.nl, www.paginegialle.it, www.paginas-amarillas.es), from where it is possible to locate companies in the detailed product groupings used by the directory. For relatively modest sums, researchers can order lists of companies' addresses and telephone numbers (in hard or soft copy) filtered by Standard Industrial Classification, company size (number of employees) and geographical region.

Other general directories, which comprise larger companies than those in *Yellow Pages*, include *Kompass* and *Dun & Bradstreet's Key British Enterprises*. These sources can be found in almost any library and they are now available for the whole of Europe and the United States on CD ROM or on the Internet. The online facility allows entries to be abstracted using filters such as location, size of company and industry specialization.

As well as these general sources, most industries have their own specialized directories, which may have a better listing of suppliers and buyers. Specialized directories can be located through guides such as *Current British Directories*.

THE RANGE OF INFORMATION AVAILABLE FROM DESK RESEARCH

Sources such as those outlined above can be used to obtain data on the majority of subjects likely to be covered in a market research project. These include those mentioned below.

The marketing environment

Markets do not exist in isolation and are shaped by environmental factors such as the state of the general economy, demographic trends, the legislative framework and various social factors. An understanding of these external factors is likely to be part of any full analysis of a market. The marketing environment is generally well documented and desk research (rather than primary research) is the only practical source available. The economy, demographics and key social variables are all well covered by the Government's statistical service and the many publications it produces. Other sources in this area include special reports (government and private), and press commentary.

Geodemographics

This is a subject in its own right with quite an extensive literature. Geodemographics is also a specialized commercial service with several UK companies (with opposite numbers in other countries) offering such data systems for marketing applications. Leventhal (1990) loosely defines geodemographics as 'the classification of small areas according to the characteristics of their residents'. Leventhal also identifies two underlying principles:

1. People living in the same neighbourhood are more likely to have similar characteristics than a similar number of people chosen at random.
2. Neighbourhoods can be usefully classified on the characteristics of their residents; two geographically separate neighbourhoods of the same classification are likely to contain similar types of people.

UK geodemographics systems are all based on the output of the Census of Population (using the output data at the smallest geographical level, Census Enumeration Districts) and provide classifications based on a number of typologies as given in Table 4.1.

Table 4.1   *Example of area classification (Pinpoint)*

A	Rural
B	Armed forces
C	Upwardly mobile young families
D	Affluent households
E	Older people in small houses
F	Suburban middle aged or older
G	Working people with families
H	Poor urban areas
I	Low status areas with flats
J	Inner city bedsits
K	Poor multi-ethnic areas
L	Crowded council neighbourhoods
X	Unclassified or unmatched

Source: Leventhal (1990)

Although the geographical basis of the input data is Census Enumeration Districts, suppliers of geodemographic systems can provide area classifications to map grid references or postcodes and also complete files of individually classified households.

Applications of geodemographics include customer profiling (through correlation with sales records or via market research surveys) and customer targeting; having profiled customers in geodemographic terms, they can be reached very effectively through finely targeted direct marketing. Geographical information systems (GIS) also use this geodemographic data for retail planning and site location by bringing together different information sources to measure overlap and gaps in the data. A simple example would be the overlaying of three databases, a map of main roads, a population database and a database of car dealer showrooms, in order to see where there is potential (subject to land availability) for new dealer sites.

Geodemographics is now used extensively as an input in research survey sample planning (many large continuous surveys are planned and produce output on a geodemographic basis). Where marketing planning is based on geodemographics, there is an obvious need to have the neighbourhood classifications as a variable in the research data.

Market structure and size

The structure of most business and industrial markets can be fully analysed through desk research. Sources include the general and trade press, directories, company financial data, published reports, trade association output and government statistics. The latter source includes _UK Markets_ (formerly _Business Monitor_), which provides, for all industries, details of production, imports and exports with detailed product breakdowns on an annual basis. Government statistics such as _UK Markets_ go back into long time series and provide a basis for historical and future trend analysis. This source or others may not provide market size estimates of the specific category of interest, but with ingenuity reasonable approximations can usually be derived from top-down (making estimates from a wider classification which includes the one of interest) or bottom-up (aggregating sub classifications). The skill in this sort of work includes bringing together disparate pieces of data from separate sources, eg _UK Markets_ plus press reports and company accounts analysis. A useful additional type of source to mention for market sizing and analysis is various compendiums such as _Market Assessment of Top Markets_ and _Market Size Digest_.

Suppliers and brands

Data on suppliers and brands can be thought of as an extension of the sort of market structure analysis considered above and may include profiles of major suppliers and their brands, marketing methods and advertising tactics, and factors making for success. The press (including trade journals), directories, company accounts and published reports are all potentially useful sources. So is advertising and trade literature (especially in technical markets) and such material can usually be collected free. One important area of information, which is usually outside the scope of desk research, is consumers' attitudes to and satisfaction with suppliers. Generally this can be obtained only through primary research, though in some industries published reports may have relevant data.

Distribution and retailing

In most businesses, distributors are playing an increasing role, as they provide a cost-effective means of supplying and servicing small (and sometimes not so small) accounts. Distribution structures can vary considerably, with many tiers ranging from importers, through to main distributors, local dealers, etc. Sources that provide an analysis of these structures are much the same as those just discussed for primary suppliers. Consumer markets are generally retail markets and retailing generally is very well documented, including in the press and in published reports.

Products

Desk research can provide detailed product information. Trade publications in some markets compare products from alternative suppliers. Mail-order catalogues are another source of product details. Product literature is often particularly relevant in technical markets and is a valuable source for analysing product features. Visits to exhibitions and trade fairs to collect this literature are an example of 'near' desk research, which can be used before moving into primary research. Pricing information may also be available from the sources just mentioned, although the difference between list prices and what is actually paid may reduce the value of such information.

Desk research is not usually thought to have a role in new product evaluation and certainly consumer reaction to a new product has to be established through primary research. However, the fate of other new launches can provide very useful information and can be accessed from the trade press and other sources.

International marketing

The low cost of desk research is even more evident in international marketing. In the United Kingdom there are libraries and online databases that are readily accessible and stacked with information on overseas markets. The different types of sources available and the range of topics are much the same as those for markets in the United Kingdom. However, the consistency and comparability of data is often a problem. For EU markets there are a number of pan-Europen sources, including the output from Eurostat, which has already been mentioned. Two important and inexpensive sources of European data from Eurostat are *Eurostat Yearbook 2001* (*the statistical guide to Europe*) and the *Panorama of European Business*. Both are available on CD ROM (www.europa.eu.int/comm/eurostat/).

PLANNING, RECORDING AND EVALUATING DESK RESEARCH

A plan is needed if the search for published data is to be efficient. A written plan is a help to desk research, whether it is utilizing library or online sources. Before visiting a library or logging-on, the information sought should be specified in some detail, though flexibility and some ingenuity are also needed (eg looking for relevant data under wider or narrower classifications and creatively making connections). Likely sources including 'sources of sources' can also be planned in advance, particularly as experience is gained. In the case of online database searching, a planned approach is particularly vital if log-on costs are to be kept to a minimum; the search strategy should be planned offline, not online.

The desk research plan should also include a timetable. How long should be spent on the desk research part of a project? This will depend on the breadth of the information sought, the type of data and the resources to be used. It is difficult to generalize. However, what can be said is that diminishing returns apply and after quite a short time the extra information gained falls in proportion to the time spent searching.

Once found, data needs recording in the form of notes or photocopies. In the case of online searches the equivalent is downloading into files. The source of any data should always be recorded, so that its accuracy can be evaluated and, if necessary, retraced. The sources should also be recorded, as they may need to be attributed. In long projects and repeat work, this will provide useful short cuts to the most valuable sources and ensure that the same blind alleys are avoided.

Information needs not only collecting but also evaluating. In part this is a matter of making judgements about its validity. We are often fooled into trusting data that are published. Once in black and white, we assume that it must be correct. The experienced desk researcher learns that market size figures that are published need to be cross-checked by two or three sources, and frequently there are some serious anomalies.

All secondary data accessed through desk research were originally generated through primary research. Thorough validation requires going back to the source and understanding the methodology used: was it based on some sort of census, on a sample survey, on some crude formula using a ratio or merely on anecdotal evidence? Where possible, two or more sources for the same data can be compared (though make sure that they are different). However, some sense of proportion has to be kept. It is simply not possible to thoroughly validate in such ways all the data, nor is it necessary to do so – as previously mentioned, market researchers can work within quite wide bands of accuracy for practical purposes.

As well as validating the data, evaluation also includes its integration into a meaningful whole. Looking for linkages and patterns can and should be part of the desk research process, with initial material often pointing to other sources and subjects. That is why it was stated earlier that although planning is needed in desk research, flexibility should be retained. Subsequent analysis and integration of data will be facilitated by good note and record keeping when the material is collected and, if this is voluminous, by reasonably organized filing.

THE LIMITS OF DESK RESEARCH

Desk research can be very fruitful. However, it has its limits and it may only provide part of the information sought in a project. As previously suggested, where a mix of desk and primary research is likely to be required there is everything to be gained by carrying out desk research first and then filling the gaps through interviewing. In this way, the more expensive primary techniques are used only where essential.

One limit of desk research is its unpredictability. At least for the novice or where the subject area is unfamiliar, there can be no certainty of what the desk research will yield and what gaps will remain. This is partly the reason why desk research is not a major service supplied by market research agencies. It would be difficult for an agency to quote for carrying out desk research, carry out the project and deliver a scant report at the end saying that despite a thorough search, nothing was found. For this reason, much desk research is carried out in-house by internal researchers. At least a short desk research exercise will involve only modest costs and may save on much more expensive fieldwork. Unlike an agency, a 'do your own' researcher can live with little to show for the desk research stage.

Some information is also in principle not available from desk research and with a little experience this is obvious from the start. Generally this includes most attitude-type data, especially where the subject of consumer attitudes is particular rather than general opinions – of your own and competitor companies, of a novel product, of a specific advert, etc.

Between desk research and conventional fieldwork there are some useful hybrid activities. These include simple observation as a means of data collection (see page 62) and 'overview' or 'expert' interviews, both techniques within the resources of any 'do your own' researcher.

LIST OF CONTACTS

Annual Abstract of Statistics, The Stationery Office Ltd, 123 Kingsway, London WC2B 6BQ (tel: 020 7873 0011).

ASLIB, The Association for Information Management, Staple Hall, Stone House Court, London EC3A 7PB (tel: 020 7903 0000).

BRAD, Maclean Hunter Ltd, Chalk Lane, Cockfosters Road, Barnet, Herts EN4 0BU (tel: 020 8242 3000).

British Library, 96 Euston Road, St Pancras, London NW1 2DB (tel: 020 7412 7677; fax: 020 7412 7794).

Companies House, Crown Way, Cardiff CF4 3UZ (tel: 08703 333636; fax: 02920 380900).

Croner.CCH Group Ltd, 145 London Road, Kingston upon Thames, Surrey KT2 6SR (tel: 020 8547 3333; fax: 020 8547 2638).

CSO Newport Library and Information Service, Cardiff Road, Newport, Gwent NP10 8XG (tel: 01633 812973).

Current British Directories, CBD Research (see The Stationery Office).

Dialog/Data-Star (part of Dialog Corporation), 3rd Floor, Palace House, 3 Cathedral Street, London SE1 9DE (tel: 020 7940 6900).

Directory of British Associations, CBD Research, Chancery House, 15 Wickham Road, Beckenham, Kent BR3 5JS (tel: 020 8650 7745; fax: 020 8650 0768).

Directory of International Sources of Business Information (Ball), Pitman Publishers, 128 Long Acre, London WC2E 9AN (tel: 020 7379 7383).

Directory of On Line Databases, Gale Research International, 110 St Martin's Lane, London WC2N 4BA (tel: 020 7257 2930; fax: 020 7257 2940).

European Directory of Marketing Information Sources, Euromonitor, 60–61 Britton Street, London EC1M 5UX (tel: 020 7251 1105; fax: 020 7608 3149).

Eurostat Data Shop Luxembourg, 4, Rue Alphonse Weicker, B.P. 453, L–2014 Luxembourg (tel: +00 352 43 35 22 51; fax: +00 352 43 35 22 221) and in the UK, Data Shop Newport, Room 1.015, Government Buildings, Newport, Gwent NP10 8XG (tel: 01633 813369; fax: 01633 813333).

Eurostat, Statistical Office of the European Communities, Jean Molinet Building, Rue Alcide de Gaspari, L-2920 Luxembourg (tel: +00 352 43 01 33 444 Fax: +00 352 43 01 35 349).

Findex, available through Euromonitor, 60-61 Britton Street, London EC1M 5UX (tel: 020 7251 1105; fax: 020 7608 3149).

Financial Times, Business Research Centre, Fitzroy House, 13-17 Epworth Street, London EC2A 4DL (tel: 020 7970 0100).

FT Interactive Data, 13 Epworth Street, London EC2A 4DL (tel: 020 7251 3333).

FT Profile, Financial Times Information Ltd, Fitzroy House, 13–17 Epworth Street, London EC2A 4DL (tel: 020 7825 7902; fax: 020 7825 7988).

Guide to Official Statistics (see The Stationery Office).

IRN SVP United Kingdom, Vigilant House, 120 Wilton Road, London W1V 1JZ (tel: 020 7808 7107; fax: 020 7808 7108).

Key British Enterprises, _Dun & Bradstreet_, Holmers Farm Way, High Wycombe, Bucks HP12 4UL (tel: 01494 422000).

Kompass, Reed Business Information, Windsor Court, East Grinstead, West Sussex RH19 1XA (tel: 01342 326972).

Market Assessment of Top Markets, Market Assessment Publications, 5th Floor, 110 Strand, London WC2R 0AA (tel: 020 7836 5111).

Market Size _Digest_, Mintel International Group, 18 Long Lane, London EC1A 9HE (tel: 020 7606 4533).

Marketsearch, Arlington Publications, 1 Hay Hill, Berkeley Square, London W1J 6DH (tel: 020 7495 1940).

OECD, 2 Rue Andre-Pascal, 75775 Paris CEDEX 16, France (tel: 00 33 01 45 24 82 00; fax: 00 33 01 45 24 85 00; publications also available from The Stationery Office).

On Line Business and Company Databases (Parkinson), (see ASLIB).

Pims, Pims UK Ltd, Mildmay Avenue, London N1 4RS (tel : 020 7226 1000).

Profound, The Dialog Corporation, Palace House, 3 Cathedral Street London SE1 9DE (tel: 020 7940 6900).

Research Index Ltd, Becor House, Green Lane, Lincoln LN6 7D (tel: 01522 524212).

Rubber & Plastics Research Association (tel: 00 1 330 972 7197).

SMMT, Society of Motor Manufacturers and Traders, Forbes House, Halkin Street, London SW1X 7DS (tel: 020 7235 7000 fax: 020 7235 7112).

The Stationery Office, PO Box 29, St Crispins, Duke Street, Norwich NR3 1PD (tel: 0870 600 5522; fax 0870 600 5533).

Trade Partners UK, 66–74 Victoria Street, London SW1E 6SW (tel: 020 7215 5444).

UK Markets, Office of National Statistics, Cardiff Road, Newport, Gwent NP10 8XG (tel: 01633 815696).

United Nations Information Centre, 21st Floor, Millbank Tower, 21–24 Millbank, London SWIP 4QH (tel: 020 7630 1981; fax: 020 7976 6478).

5

Qualitative research

The terms 'qualitative' and 'quantitative' are frequently used by market researchers to divide the methods of investigation into those which are concerned with obtaining an understanding of a subject (the former) and those which are involved in measuring things (the latter). Qualitative research accounts for just over a tenth of the value of the market research commissions in the United Kingdom. However, the importance of qualitative research belies this spend as it very often precedes quantitative work and therefore guides its direction. Sometimes the outcome of the qualitative research is so convincing, it stands alone in guiding business decisions.

In this chapter we:

- consider the differences between qualitative and quantitative research;
- look at areas where qualitative research can help in decision making; and
- examine focus groups and depth interviews – the two most important methods of data collection in qualitative research.

THE DIFFERENCES BETWEEN QUALITATIVE AND QUANTITATIVE RESEARCH

The roots of the words 'qualitative' and 'quantitative' imply that one is based on quality and the other on quantity. There is some truth in this. Qualitative researchers would argue that they may not interview many people, but those they speak to really do count. This is because qualitative research is centrally concerned with the understanding rather than the measurement of things – see Sampson (1967). The trouble is, the lack of measurement means that it is never possible to be absolutely sure that the findings are correct.

Qualitative research borrows many methods from clinical psychology and uses ideas founded in sociology and anthropology. This association with other intellectual traditions suggests a rigour in the research methods. However, it is the inability to validate qualitative research that causes some consternation in the market research camp. The government, for example, has until recently commissioned little qualitative research as it is worried that the findings would not stand up to public scrutiny. More recently though, since the 1997 General Election, interest by government in focus groups and similar has become a news item.

This focus on quality and small numbers of respondents allows the research consultants to collect much of the data themselves in contrast to quantitative surveys where the numbers of interviews are too great for any single person to make more than a dent. One of the strengths of qualitative research is that it deeply involves experienced and skilled practitioners in the subject who can lift data and turn it into creative research findings. Here too there are problems as well as advantages. A single idea mentioned by one respondent, and picked up by a qualitative researcher, could result in the Yorkie bar – or it could be a red herring. So much depends on the skills of the practitioner.

Small numbers of respondents and just one or two people carrying out the interviewing allows more open-ended questions than in quantitative surveys. Whereas it would be highly problematic to deal with 1,000 open-ended responses to the question 'What makes you happy?', the qualitative researcher can cope with 20–30 responses and parry with prompts such as 'Tell me more', or 'Why is that?' Open-ended questioning is the fabric of qualitative researchers.

There is no hard and fast rule as to the break in sample size between qualitative and quantitative research. Most researchers would agree that 30 or fewer respondents would certainly constitute qualitative work. Others would argue that any sample much below 200 interviews is verging on the qualitative because such low numbers produce findings with extremely large bands of error.

According to Goodyear (1990), qualitative and quantitative research differs in four important ways:

1. in the type of problem that each can solve;
2. the methods of sampling;
3. the methods and style of collecting information; and
4. the approach to and techniques of analysis.

This provides a useful structure for examining the subject. First we look at the different problems that can be solved by qualitative research. Then we explore the different means by which qualitative research is carried out – observation, focus groups and depth interviews. Finally we discuss how projective interviewing techniques are used by qualitative researchers to dig deep and obtain insights that cannot be achieved by ordinary questioning.

PROBLEMS THAT CAN BE SOLVED BY QUALITATIVE RESEARCH

Qualitative research can be used as an 'exploratory' tool. Where there is uncertainty about a subject, and the researcher does not know what detailed questions to ask, a few depth interviews or groups may be sufficient to provide an understanding and explanations that answer the problem. Imagine that you are a manager of a hospital, eager to improve the standard of patient care. Your 'clients' include the young, the mentally ill, the old and the very poorly. What they think of your service is decisive in guiding how you develop in the future – but how do you find out what they think? The very young, the very old and the mentally ill clients may be unable to tell you. And when do you interview them? If you do so while they are in the hospital, it could bias the result as their treatment may not yet be over and, in any case, they may find it hard to be critical while feeling vulnerable and in care. Interviewing them after their treatment is problematical as they would have to be contacted at home and so be widely scattered.

Designing a quantitative study for checking on standards of patient care is likely to be complicated and costly. It may be better to consider a qualitative approach, focusing not on the patients themselves but a group of respondents who can speak on their behalf. Group discussions with general practitioners (GPs) in the hospital's territory could provide a distilled view of the strengths and weaknesses of the hospital and of individual departments. Focus groups with GPs could be convened quickly and the results available within a couple of weeks. A couple of focus groups is not a sizeable study but they could provide a signpost as to where the real problems lie and give focus to any subsequent quantitative research.

In the same vein, researchers may be faced with a marketing problem which needs investigation. Problem solving requires an understanding of the cause and effects and these could be flushed out by discussion in groups or depths. When used in this capacity, qualitative research is a 'diagnostic' tool. Typical subjects for analysis could be a downturn in sales, a loss of market share or an increase in complaints. A major UK manufacturer of domestic heating boilers looked at the latest trade association figures and saw that it had suffered a loss of share. This had not been apparent from the company's sales figures which were holding up quite well in a market which was buoyant. Four focus groups with plumbers who install boilers were sufficient to show that a major competitor was heavily discounting and using direct mail to promote its boilers – a method of promotion that was concealed from the competing suppliers.

Very often, qualitative research is used for 'creative' inspiration and guidance. For example, if an advertising agency wants ideas for a new campaign it may get these from the interaction of thoughts arising in focus groups. The creative power of qualitative research need not be confined to teasing out ideas for advertising; it can be used to guide all types of innovative work such as new product development and branding. A manufacturer of crisps was concerned that the health food trend eventually would affect his market and wanted to know in which way he could respond. Qualitative research was commissioned to find out if, with some modification, crisps could be positioned as a health food.

Qualitative research also can be used to 'evaluate' ideas. Focus groups or depth interviews can be used to find out what people think of a different presentation of an advert or pack design. Of course, there will be no large numbers to substantiate the evaluation but the views of the small number of respondents may be sufficiently convincing. A cable manufacturer wanted to steal a march in the competitive field of house wiring and designed a pack which looked very different to the conventional reels which electricians had used for years. Although the pack offered a number of advantages, electricians are very much driven by habit and focus groups showed if there would be any resistance to the new product.

METHODS OF QUALITATIVE RESEARCH

Observation

Qualitative researchers use any means they can of obtaining information themselves. This allows them to link the data collection and interpretation closely. Qualitative researchers feel that they know the answer because they have got the information firsthand. We should not forget that it is only in the last 50 years that market researchers have collected information by questioning. Prior to this it was considered normal to find out what was going on by observation. The London based market research agency, Mass-Observation, carried the legacy of this method in its title until absorbed by BMRB in the early 1990s.

Today, observation is used wherever watching is thought preferable to speaking to people. It plays an important role in researching children, whose powers of expression may not allow them to articulate exactly what they think. Observation is used in shopping surveys, especially in-store, when the customer is looking at the shelves and deciding what to buy. It is used to answer how things are done in practice. The way that people open packs of biscuits and their reading of instructions sometimes can be answered more honestly by observation than by questioning.

The results of observation may be recorded in note form, as was the case during the Second World War when the government commissioned researchers to go into the streets and pubs and observe and record what was going on. Today, the camera offers an excellent means of capturing observations and videos of group discussions provide insights, beyond the spoken word, from the body language of respondents. Videos in stores are used to watch people at the point of sale and give a perspective which could not be obtained by interviewing. (It should be noted that the market research industry has some concerns about the use of hidden cameras for observation purposes.)

Focus groups

Group discussions (or focus groups) are the most widely used qualitative research technique in Europe and the United States. This is a tool borrowed from psychotherapy where it has long been realized that people can be encouraged to open up if they are asked to share their views as part of a small group. Within the group there is a brainstorming effect so that a comment from one person sparks ideas from another. In this way groups can yield more than one-to-one interviews. After a warming up period, the group may gel and a bonding between members acts as further encouragement to disclosure.

In Europe, groups usually comprise six to eight respondents (Cooper, 1989) rather than the 10 to 12 which is more typical of the United States. In Europe it is generally accepted that the purpose of groups is to obtain insights and understandings whereas in the US there is a tendency for moderators who run the groups to measure a split of opinion by a show of hands.

Respondents are recruited to groups if they are relevant to the study. For example:

● they are in a target group of sex/age/social class and could be buyers of a product or service that is being studied;
● they are already buyers of a certain product;
● they are drawn from a particular occupation or profession (usually relevant in business-to-business research).

Correct recruitment, of the desired type of respondents – eg by demographics, by their product usage etc – is an important quality issue in qualitative research (whether using groups or depth interviews). The general practice in agency organized qualitative research is to use interviewers to recruit the required respondents and the professional researcher only becomes involved, as the moderator, once the group meets (the practice in depth interviews is often similar in this respect). This division of labour requires that the recruiters are given precise instructions on whom to recruit and a recruitment questionnaire that establishes that the respondent qualifies is generally considered essential. There is also the need to validate respondents to ensure they really are who they claim to be (see Marks, 1993).

Having been persuaded to attend, the group members meet at a viewing centre. A researcher acts as group leader or moderator, drawing out those who are shy and keeping in check those who wish to dominate, all the time maintaining a relaxed and easy manner to stimulate open discussion. The meetings last an hour or more and the proceedings are recorded on audio tape and/or video.

One group is hardly enough as the results could be atypical. In any project there are usually a number of groups, perhaps covering between them a spread of respondents and geographic areas. Typically four groups are sufficient to cover a single respondent type.

In order to obtain any real feedback, respondents in groups need some information. This would be fed to them in a controlled manner by the moderator who unfolds the subject, almost always working from the broad to the particular. It may only be towards the end of a group that it becomes obvious to respondents what is the real subject under review. During the course of the group the moderator may provide descriptions, illustrations, samples, packs or adverts, to stimulate the discussion and obtain perceptions and reactions.

As well as standard groups, many variations are in use or have been tried at one time or another. This includes mini groups (consisting of up to five respondents only), extended groups lasting several hours, iterate groups which reconvene (eg to consider development work carried out on designs after the results from initial groups) and groups where people such as designers participate and engage in dialogue with respondents – see Glen (1998). 'DIY' groups have even been tried without moderators present – see Yelland and Varty (1997).

There are some drawbacks and limitations to groups.

First, to mention the most obvious, groups are a qualitative and not a quantitative research technique. If we need to ask 'how many' type questions we should almost certainly be using another technique.

In a project we may need both qualitative and quantitative research. In the example of the new cable pack, we may perhaps find that the new pack is acceptable to all electricians except those who handle existing reels in a certain way – rolling them along the floor when laying out the cable, for example. During the groups it became apparent that only one or two electricians laid out cable in this way. How common is it generally, however? Perhaps a follow-on quantitative survey is required.

The reason why groups are not capable of yielding quantitative information is really twofold. The samples are inevitably small. For example, four groups are typical for a study and this covers only 30 or 20 respondents. Second, the actual form of a group does not lend itself to precise quantification of data – there is a general discussion, perhaps even boisterous argument, and this is difficult to translate into measurable responses. Attempts to make recording more rigorous, and thus facilitate a more quantitative analysis, include using self-completion questionnaires during the groups (these may also stimulate subsequent discussion) and more recently the introduction of IT (see Sweeney *et al*, 1997). However, more precise recording alone does not make small sample qualitative research a basis for quantification.

Another feature of groups is the high element of subjectivity in handling them and in their interpretation. The outcome depends very much on the group leader and how he or she:

- structures the discussion;
- conducts the meeting;
- analyses and interprets the results.

There is some element of subjectivity in all research but it is particularly strong in group discussion work. If the same brief is given to two experienced group researchers there is a chance that the outcome will differ to some extent. This is obviously far from the scientific approach to quantitative research where the interviewer's personality is expected to have no effect on the result. A client commissioning group discussions should recognize that the outcome will reflect the views of the respondents and the researcher in some uncertain mixture. Therefore, there has to be every confidence in the ability and skill of the researcher. It is not only important that clients recognize this point, but that the researcher does so as well. The point of 'DIY' groups, mentioned above, was partly to lessen or obviate moderator effects.

The small sample, coupled with this subjectivity, makes the group discussions very suspect to some more quantitative-minded researchers. However, the 'number jocks' too must recognize the limitations of their own techniques, particularly the impossibility of answering the many 'how' and 'why' questions which are vital in marketing.

Depth interviewing

In second place in popularity as a qualitative research technique, behind group discussions, are depth interviews. The term 'depth' or 'in-depth' is bandied around by market researchers without a precise meaning but implies somehow that the interview is longer rather than shorter, unstructured rather than structured and face-to-face rather than over the telephone. Because the subject is covered in depth, there is a suggestion that the respondent digs deeper for answers, talks more freely and so the true facts, perceptions and motivations are discovered. Very often the interview is tape recorded rather than written down on a questionnaire.

Depth interviews are used where it is important that there is no 'contamination' of respondents' views, one with the others, as happens in group discussions. Also, depths may be preferable to groups when the subject is highly sensitive because it is about sexual practices, personal hygiene or financial planning.

In a depth interview, each respondent has the opportunity of speaking for most of the duration which is often between half an hour to an hour. In a group discussion, all other things being equal, the discussion time is shared between the respondents and the moderator and each person only has the chance to speak for around eight to ten minutes. This means that the output from eight depth interviews is (say) eight hours of taped discussion – much more than the one and a half hours arising from the same number of people in a group. Depth interviews, however, do not benefit from the interaction and 'dynamic' which is so important in groups.

In business-to-business markets depth interviews may be the only option because it simply is not possible to recruit people to groups if they are too thinly scattered. It is necessary to have a pool of around 50 respondents within a tight geographical area (say where time to travel to the venue is within an hour) to successfully achieve eight or nine recruits at the appointed hour. Pulling people from a wider area would need a subject of riveting interest or a very attractive incentive.

Incidentally, the nature of business or industrial markets often leads to the use of small samples just because the universe (the number of all potential respondents) is so small. In this situation there may be little point in using structured interviews and regardless of subject matter all fieldwork may be 'depth'.

Respondents targeted in depth interviewing have to be chosen carefully. Just as in group discussion recruitment, they are likely to be chosen on the basis of their age, sex, social class or because they are buyers (or not buyers) of a product or service.

Fundamental to depth interviewing is listening. To listen carefully to a respondent is to show interest and this is an encouragement to say more. Furthermore, only through listening will an understanding be built up from which there could be a deeper line of questioning – the very substance of depth interviewing.

Listening and asking questions, or stimulating discussion, may be enough but if the nut is a hard one to crack or the subject well buried beneath the surface, some help may be required. For this qualitative researchers turn to projective interviewing techniques.

Projective interviewing techniques

Projective interviewing techniques are used in both focus groups and depth interviews to overcome the barriers of communication between the informant and the interviewer which may be the result of embarrassment, sensitivity or simply not being able to articulate the answer.

When barriers exist, direct questioning could draw a blank or invoke an answer given in ignorance but which is believed to be correct. Worse, direct questioning on some of the sensitive subjects could create an obstruction which mars subsequent co-operation.

Indirect question

The indirect question is probably the most common of all the projective interviewing techniques. The interviewer asks a question about what other people think or do and so removes the subject from the respondent. For example, in order to get a buyer to talk about the prices they are paying for products, a question may be asked such as:

> Thinking about… (*state type of product*), what would be a typical price paid by someone in this industry who was buying about 10,000 units per year?

The price which the respondent gives may not be precisely that which he or she pays but, by speaking the words, the taboo is broken and the interviewer can gauge the mood of the situation. It could easily lead to further questions:

> And from your own company's point of view, would the price you pay be higher or lower than this figure?

Instead of asking outright, 'How much do you pay for "x"?', the indirect approach creeps up on the subject so that the respondent gives away bits at a time until all is revealed.

This approach is also called the 'third person test' as respondents are asked to describe what other people (the third persons) would do in certain circumstances.

Word association/sentence completion/story completion

A very simple projective technique is to ask respondents to think of words which are associated with a product or brand. Equally, the questions could focus on a product and the respondents are asked what feelings or words come to mind. In a group discussion about hot drinks of various kinds, the words coffee, tea and hot chocolate produced the following list of words. Just looking through them gives a feel for the positioning of the drinks and their strengths and weaknesses.

Coffee	**Tea**	**Hot chocolate**
Perky	Afternoon	Bedtime
Morning	Refreshing	Winter
Aroma	Morning	Family
Black	Weak	Story time
Strong	Cheap	Sweet
Filter	Ladies	Children
Palpitations	Biscuits	Friendly

Sentence completion is a development of word association. The interviewer reads out or shows the beginnings of sentences and asks the respondent to add an ending. As with word association, this is done in rapid tempo to ensure that instantaneous replies are obtained and the answers are spontaneous rather than too considered.

The sentences can vary from being open in format to those which are more focused and constrain the replies and it can be useful to have both types in a battery. For example:

If only there was a hot drink which…

When I have a cup of tea I think…

The nicest thing about coffee is…

Analogy/symbolic analogy

Some projective techniques extend people's imaginations laterally. Thinking about a subject in another context can be a means of opening up the mind. Respondents may be asked to think of a brand as people or an object.

If the car was a person, what sort of person would it be?

The resulting answers may give many clues as to the views people hold on the car. Is the nominated person male or female? Young or old? Classy, stylish or boring? What would the car do for a living? Where would the car go on holiday? What type of books would the car read? Through the conversion of an object to a person the personality of the object could be made clearer.

By way of example, a study was carried out into people's perceptions of organizations which carry out market research. These included market research companies, management consultancies and academic institutions. A large number of respondents in the study suggested that the consultancies were typified by one or other of the 'big cat family' implying such organizations were powerful, fast, perhaps even predatory. The academic institutions were positioned as owls and elephants; the one clever, the other with a long memory though also characterized by being large and slow. Market research companies on the other hand had no distinct image as an animal of any kind suggesting that they lacked a positive identity.

Projective questioning of this type could be used to draw out feelings about a brand or a product which may not be uncovered in conventional questioning.

What colour or colours come to mind when you think of…?

What music comes to mind when you think of…?

Fantasy

This is another of the projective techniques which encourages lateral thinking. In fantasy questioning, respondents are asked to imagine a very different world, perhaps one where the start of the fantasy has been mapped out for them by the interviewer. They then take over, involving the product or brand in some way or another. Getting people to think in fantasies is one way of removing the shackles of normal thinking, and perhaps uncovering hidden angles.

The subject need not be a weird fantasy; it could be a simple story which the respondent has to complete.

Future scenario

Another lateral thinking device is the future scenario. As the name suggests, the respondent is asked to describe the future, including the position and role of the product at that time. The way it fits into society, the uses to which it is put, the modifications to the product itself, may all give clues as to its strengths and weaknesses.

Obituary

Respondents may be asked to write an obituary for a product, bringing out its good and bad points and saying why it eventually disappeared.

Cartoons

Projective techniques can use pictures as well as words. These include cartoons, picture association, psychodrawing and modelling.

In cartoon tests the respondent is faced with a picture depicting a situation. The situation is deliberately vague with balloons rising out of the characters ready to contain their words or thoughts. One of the balloons may be left blank for the respondent to fill in. Through the interpretation of the drawing, the respondent is projecting his or her own thoughts but doing so into a neutral environment, that is the picture.

The technique works well in both consumer and business-to-business interviews and is particularly suited to situations where the answers are not so obvious and need a little thought. The cartoon tests flush out the hidden feelings and thoughts and are not a substitute for open-ended questioning.

An extension of the cartoon drawings is the 'thematic apperception test'. This technique has been borrowed from clinical psychology and comprises deliberately indistinct and ambiguous drawings, the subject of which is not obvious at all. For the most part these are human figures in situations which the respondent has to describe and, in so doing, uncovers their own thoughts and prejudices. This is the type of technique that every marketing student learns about but is seldom used in everyday market research.

Picture association/interpretation

It is quite common in groups to show respondents a board (see Figure 5.1) on which there are many pictures of houses or people. The respondents are then asked to link the product under discussion with one of the pictures in an attempt to 'position' it more closely. For example:

> If the product was to live in any one of the houses shown on this board, which would it be?

> And if the product was a person, which of the people shown on this board would it be?

Figure 5.1   *Story board*

Psychodrawing

Respondents are given drawing materials and asked to create a picture which represents their view of a product or brand. The final drawing may show aspects that are hard to put into words. Moreover, the drawing may become a discussion point which allows the respondent to explain their thinking at the time and it is this which provides the insights. The subject and the respondents have to be right to achieve a successful result with psychodrawing. Respondents should be creative though not necessarily good artists as their artistic representation means far less than the colours and general theme of the drawing.

Modelling

This is another technique often quoted in textbooks but which is seldom if ever used. Reputedly people are given plasticine or modelling clay and asked to make a

representation of the product or subject under study. The approach is limited because it is heavily dependent on some level of modelling skill and the respondent's mind is focused on how to make an acceptable shape rather than communicating a subtle feeling.

Psychodrama

In this projective technique respondents are asked to role play, acting parts which have been ascribed to them by the moderator. For example, one person may be asked to play the role of a salesperson and the other the role of a buyer. The positioning of people in conflicting situations can be a powerful means of flushing out the arguments as each defends his or her position. Interesting results can be achieved by asking people who do not hold a particular view to argue its case in order to find out if and how this changes their opinion on the subject.

This type of research can only work if the respondents are sufficiently creative and of the right frame of mind. Role playing may be considered appropriate for an extended group and it could be something that the interviewer tries if the group has gelled and a good rapport has developed. Without this spark, the role playing would fall flat.

Analysis of projective techniques

Some way-out projective techniques may be fun but how will the findings be presented? Careful thought has to be given to this as the researcher's own interpretation and the way this is portrayed in the report and the presentation is always in danger of skewing the findings. In qualitative research especially, the 'facts' never speak entirely for themselves.

6

Quantitative research

Quantitative research is concerned with measuring aspects of a market or the population of consumers making up the market. This includes 'soft' phenomena such as consumer attitudes as well as the 'hard' things such as market size, brand shares, purchase frequencies etc. Some important quantitative techniques are discussed later in the book and the purpose of this chapter is to give an overview of all the important elements that make up a quantitative research design including sampling, data collection methods and research management issues. Our other aim in this chapter is to discuss some of the key considerations that should determine the choice and selection of methods and techniques; the type of data required, the level of a market for which measurements should be sought, the frequencies with which these measurements are needed and the nature of potential respondents. An even more fundamental driver of the research design than any of these, however, is the research objectives; this must be the starting point from which any methodological choices are made. The only reason this topic is not elaborated further here is because it has already been covered (in Chapter 3).

QUANTITATIVE RESEARCH AND SAMPLING

Quantitative data on a market or consumer group can be obtained through carrying out a census – obtaining the relevant measures from every single consumer or (in the case of business-to-business research) player in the market. In practice market research through a census is very rare; for one thing it is usually prohibitively expensive to obtain data from every individual (the government only carries out a population census once every 10 years) and even if the money is available the timescales involved are likely to be too long to meet commercial deadlines. Furthermore, a census is unnecessary since the alternative, sampling, can normally produce adequate and acceptably reliable data for a fraction of the cost.

Quantitative market research is, therefore, nearly always based on more or less rigorous sampling methods which have in common the assumption that the data from the samples can be taken to represent, within estimated levels of accuracy, the population or universe from which they are drawn. The resulting data, therefore, can be taken to stand for the population or to provide a basis for projecting it (eg by 'grossing up'). Because of its central importance in market research generally and particularly quantitative research, a separate chapter (7) is given over to sampling and the subject is, therefore, largely left until then except where implications of sampling need to be mentioned in relation to other aspects of quantitative research.

TYPES OF QUANTITATIVE DATA

The range of information which can be and is collected through quantitative research is enormous if not infinite. Earlier chapters (1 and 2) have given examples. However, in relation to deciding how data should be collected, all the possibilities can be slotted into a simple threefold classification:

1. market measures;
2. customer profiles or segmentation; and
3. attitudinal data.

Market measures quantify and describe a market. Common examples include: market and sector size; shares of the market held by suppliers or brands; penetration levels (what proportion of all potential consumers own or buy a product); purchase and consumption frequencies; patterns of consumption and seasonality. Also the retail/distribution structure of the market including the proportions of the total going through each type of outlet. Data of this type is essential for any manager developing or reviewing a marketing plan for a company, product group or brand. As we discuss shortly, market measures can be taken at various levels of the market; at the point of consumption (eg through interviews with consumers), but also at the point of manufacture or at the point of distribution. Market measures taken from a sample are generally projected or grossed up to the total market or population – eg the proportion of households in a sample found to be without a PC can be multiplied by available estimates of the number of total households to provide an indicator of untapped potential.

A vital concern in any marketing is knowing and understanding the potential customer base; what type of people or organizations are they? What other types of products or services do they own or use? What is required to meet this need is customer profiling or segmentation data and it is quantitative in nature because reliable breakdowns are needed for the whole market or population – if a survey indicates that among the sample interviewed the large majority of gas wall heater owners are in social classes D and E and live in older houses, we need to be confident, if we are to use the data in marketing planning, that this is the case for the whole population. Profiling data can take various forms: socio-demographics (age, sex, income and occupation group, education level, home tenure etc); geo-demographics (see Chapter 4); various business classifications such as company size, industry etc for business-to-business research or it can relate to consumer behaviour (ownership of various products, purchase or usage levels, media exposure etc). It can even include variables which are essentially attitudinal eg a classification based on attitudes to new products. Unlike market measures, consumer profiling data can be collected only from consumers (including organizations in the case of business-to-business research) although the distribution or manufacturing levels in the market may also need profiling.

Attitudinal data is used in a quite general sense to cover concepts such as awareness, perceptions, beliefs, evaluations, preferences and propensities. In other words they are, in their various forms, subjective and reside in the minds of individuals (attitudinal data is collected in business-to-business research but in the end it is still attitudes of individuals within organizations – companies, as such, do not have attitudes). Much market research is concerned with attitudes and attitude measurement because attitudes are assumed to influence if not determine behaviour; understand consumer attitudes and your marketing may mould consumer choice in your favour. Similarly, attitudes are taken to be a predictor of future behaviour; preferences between real products or concept bundles can, with appropriate analysis, lead to predications on what will actually happen in the market including the consequences if various elements in the marketing mix such as price are changed.

Attitudes are of course also very much the subject of qualitative research which is often concerned to identify relevant dimensions and categories of attitudes. In quantitative research, however, the focus is on establishing the degree to which specific attitudes exist among the market and population – qualitative research may have revealed some doubts about quality of a particular product but what proportion of potential consumers hold such negative views and how does this link to such things as purchase frequency? Various techniques are used to measure attitudes but in one form or another scalar measurement is the usual tool (see later in this chapter and Chapter 8).

LEVEL OF MEASUREMENT

Figure 6.1 represents the structure of a market. It happens to be the market for certain building products but with minor changes it would represent other markets operating through distinct levels – products go from manufacturers via distributors and/or a retail level to reach final buyers. Most markets operate in this way although the details vary considerably.

Market measures may be required at any level of the market; manufacturers' sales, distributors' sales, retail sales etc and they will be different because of the way the channels feed into each other, because of the effect of margins and mark-ups (if

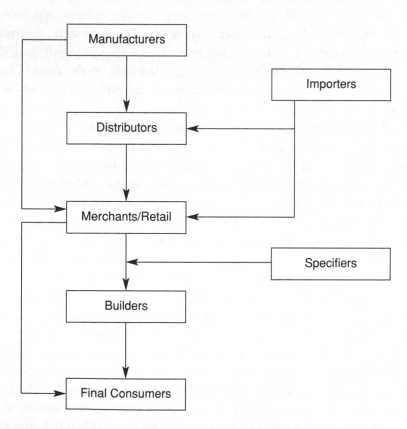

Figure 6.1   *Market levels*

the measurement is in value) and at least if short timespan variations are measured, because of the time taken for goods to pass through each level of the market and the effects of stock-holding. Depending on our interests, therefore, research measurements need to focus on particular market levels and use techniques appropriate to that level. Manufacturers' sales for example may be collected through a cooperative effort with each manufacturer passing on sales figures, in confidence, to a third party (eg a trade association) which collates them. Retail sales and brand shares are likely to be collected most accurately at the retail level through a retail audit (see page 80). Patterns of consumption and profiles of consumers, however, will require data collection at the final level through some type of interviewing programme. The market level from which data is required, therefore, has an important bearing on the research methodology.

Because market levels connect to each other (as illustrated in Figure 6.1), market measures for one level can often be inferred or estimated from data taken from another. The size of a market, for example, can be estimated by grossing-up the consumption levels among a sample to the total population within the market. With adjustments (eg for imported products, 'shrinkage' through the retail chain, etc) estimates also can be made of manufacturers' and distributors'/retail sales. However, in making such estimates various uncertain assumptions nearly always have to be made and this affects the reliability of the final data. Similarly the estimates made at the consumer level are within some range of error some of which cannot even be estimated. Often, because data from the higher (or lower) level cannot be accessed (eg manufacturers just will not cooperate), bottom-up or top-down estimates have to be made but this is nearly always a second best methodology; market measures are better taken directly from the level to which they relate.

Consumer profiling and attitudinal data can obviously only be taken from the appropriate level although in the case of the latter it is important to think about whose attitudes need to be considered. The views of the final consumer will in the long term shape a market but for a manufacturer a more immediate concern may be the views of decision makers at a distribution level; it is they who are the immediate customers.

FREQUENCY OF MEASUREMENT

Market research data is often required at only a single point in time; the current size of a market, the shares held now by each brand, the profile of current consumers etc. In such cases the research methodology is commonly designed as a one-off and the project is *ad hoc*. Possibly at some future date it may be decided to collect the same sort of data again and a similar research design may be used but at the time the first project is considered this is not a significant concern. Of all market research projects carried out, the majority in number are *ad hoc* and collect data for one point in time only. However, in terms of research expenditure (see Chapter 14) the reverse is true; most market research budgets are taken up buying repeat measures through continuous research.

Continuous data allows important measures to be tracked over time; movements in brand shares for example show progress (or decline) against competitors and changes in the trend provide an early warning to take action. Discrete trends also can be interrelated to other measures taken in the continuous research programme (eg media exposure) or independent variables such as economic indicators and all the data can be integrated into a model which allows for predictions to be made or enables 'what if' questions to be answered.

There are various well established market research techniques for continuous measurement but in all of them a common concern is that any trends identified in the data, over time, are 'real' and not just the effect of research variations such as sampling error (discussed in the next chapter) or the result of changing the measuring tools – eg questions and their wording. A consequence of this is usually a requirement for robust methodologies based on large samples (which are also needed to enable subsamples to be compared reliably) as well as standardization in how data is collected – eg once tested, questionnaire changes are kept to a minimum. Continuous data can be collected from matched samples (each made up of different respondents) and in some applications this is the preferred approach. However, for at least market measure data, panels – with the same sample used repeatedly – are generally agreed to provide more reliable data (see Blyth, 1990).

Whatever specific techniques are used for continuous research, one feature of them all is high costs; because the samples are large, because the set-up work for panels is considerable and because techniques need piloting, as well as because data collection is ongoing, the costs involved are generally very substantial and often more than most research users can afford or are willing to finance. Therefore, much continuous research is also syndicated with costs shared among a number of subscribers. Another sort of research where costs are shared is omnibus surveys. These too are in a sense continuous since they involve programmes of regularly repeated interviewing with samples to closely defined specifications. However, the primary purpose of these is to offer subscribers requiring only a limited range of data (eg which can be covered in two or three questions) a means of low-cost access to 'good' samples and although subscribers may choose to use the omnibus repeatedly to obtain trend data they may equally use these vehicles as an alternative to their own *ad hoc* research.

Between purely one-off *ad hoc* research and ongoing continuous programmes, there is often a need to carry out data collection in a number of 'waves' over a limited timescale. A common application of this approach is in advertising pre- and post-research. The objective of many advertising campaigns is to increase awareness of say a brand among a target population. The extent to which this is achieved is measured by establishing, through interviews, awareness levels before the campaign starts and after it finishes with any increase assumed to be the result of the advertising (a decline in awareness is rather harder to explain!). The same technique can be used to measure other effects than simple awareness such as movements in attitudes. As well as simple before and after measures, interviewing can be carried out regularly during the campaign to identify any build up of its effects.

In common with full-blown continuous research, a concern in developing pre- and post-research designs is that any effect measured is caused by external variables – eg the advertising – and is not just the result of research variations. One aspect of this is that the samples have to be large enough so that the changes measured are 'real' and not within the range of sampling variation – the anticipated change sought from the campaign should be considered in deciding what sample size is large enough. Another problem area is the question of cause and effect; awareness may have increased over the campaign period but possibly this was partly a result of other factors such as stocking levels by retailers or even the activity of competitors. These sort of problems can be met through using control data. For example, research may be carried out in an area where there was no advertising campaign and any changes here used to adjust the data from the campaign areas.

THE NATURE OF THE RESPONDENT

Another aspect of what is being measured, and which should shape the research design if interviewing techniques are to be used, is the nature of the respondent: the methods appropriate for establishing financial directors' attitudes to merchant banks are different to those required for establishing children's toy preferences.

The location of potential respondents may, for example, influence any decision to use phone or visit interviewing. Other considerations may favour face-to-face methods but if the selected sample of 50 major buyers of an industrial material is spread all over Western Europe, phone interviewing may be the only practical option. Similarly street interviewing may be ruled out if an important part of the sample is seldom found there; eg older people.

Respondents' personal attributes may also influence the research design. Self-completion surveys are not appropriate among an illiterate or semi-literate respondent group or where interest in the subject of the research is likely to be low. Similarly the wording of questions may need to reflect respondents' language skills and familiarity with terminology: computer jargon may have a place in a survey of IT workers but not among the general population. Where, as is common, the sample is mixed in these respects, the design must usually work from 'lowest common denominator' assumptions.

Access to communications and the status of respondents are also relevant to an appropriate design. While most business-to-business respondents can be contacted by phone this will be less the case where shopfloor attitudes need to be established or where workers are very mobile. In such cases respondents may need to be recruited away from their place of work. Differential ownership levels for telephones are also still a factor limiting the use of phone research in consumer research. The exclusion of no-phone homes may not be considered important (possibly the subject of the research is less relevant to lower income groups) but if it is, the phone may have to be ruled out as a research tool. At the other end of the scale, prior appointments may have to be set to interview senior managers by phone.

METHODS OF DATA COLLECTION: DIRECT MEASUREMENT

Interviewing is often assumed to be the 'standard' method of quantitative data collection. However, interviewing is in reality a method of collecting hearsay evidence; what people say they do rather than what they actually do. The respondent, for example, says that, on average, he or she buys ten pints of milk a week, but is this the actual consumption level? Data drawn from interview responses has inevitably many intrinsic limitations (see Semon, 1994) and for some market measures it is better to take more direct readings. AGB's* Superpanel, for example, now uses in-home barcode readers to establish panel members' purchase levels rather than relying on interview responses or even self-recording in 'diaries' – see Blyth (1990). Forms of direct data collection, briefly discussed below, include retail audits, television audience research and mystery shopping as well as its use in panels of the type carried out by AGB. Because these techniques are commonly used in large scale continuous research programmes they are, in terms of research spend at least, very important to the 'industry'.

Manufacturers and especially manufacturers of FMCGs need regularly to measure the position of their brands at the retail level and this is carried out through retail audits. A representative sample of relevant retail outlets is taken (including

---

* AGB Taylor Nelson is one of the UK's largest market research companies – see Chapter 14.

different types and sizes of outlet with the final data broken down between these classifications) and their sales established for relevant brands and products. The data from outlets is then aggregated and grossed up to represent the whole retail market. The classic method of measuring sales at each outlet was to physically count stock levels of products and compare these counts at two points in time; the difference plus deliveries (taken from delivery notes etc) equated to sales over the period (allowance is needed for 'shrinkage') – see McCarthy (1990). Although simple in concept, this work is clearly very labour intensive and may be disruptive to the retail outlet (retailer co-operation is obviously essential in such audits). Over the last decade or so, however, stock counts in retail auditing have been increasingly replaced by access to electronic point of sale (EPOS) data (see Mason, 1990).

At least all large FMCG outlets now use EPOS techniques at their tills with equipment such as bar code readers recording data for each and every product bought and thereby providing information to tightly control stock levels, purchasing, shelf space, etc as well as facilitating efficient checkouts. EPOS data, however, is also a substitute for the methods previously used in retail audits and offers increased accuracy (eg no more lost delivery notes), more frequent measurement (hourly if need be) and many other benefits (eg cross-relating items purchased). Much retail auditing is, therefore, now based on EPOS data with the major research companies involved (eg Nielsen) securing access to retailers' own databases. The older methods, however, still have a role to play in establishing non-sales data such as in-store promotion activities. Retail audits, while not conceptually complex, are a major organizational undertaking, complicated in some respects by EPOS. Consequently, they are carried out by only a few specialized companies. The costs involved are inevitably very high and the data is very largely syndicated. Retail audits are also ongoing and, therefore, continuous in the sense we have discussed.

As already mentioned, direct measures based on EPOS type techniques are also now used in home panels which offer measures of purchases (mirroring retail sales) together with consumer profile data – not only are sales levels established but the data can be linked to and segmented by consumer groupings. These techniques, therefore, overcome a limitation of retail audit data; sales can be measured but we do not know who is buying the products. The use of 'store cards' and 'loyalty cards' by some supermarkets is changing all this. These swipe cards link the purchases made by a consumer to consumer profiling data from another source. So, if you have recently purchased nappies from Tesco, don't be surprised if you are mailed with a promotion introducing you to their new range of babies' clothes.

Another sort of research panel which uses direct data measures is for TV audience research. Various sorts of meters can be fitted to a panel member's television set and record which programmes are watched. However, just as EPOS data do not show who buys, simple audience meters cannot record who in the household watches specific programmes and, until fairly recently, meter data had to be supplemented by self-completion diaries of viewing. Some of these limitations of metering are now though being overcome by true 'peoplemeters' – see Buck (1990).

A final sort of direct measurement to mention and which has grown in use recently, is mystery shopping. Aspects such as service levels in retail outlets can be measured by interviewing customers but the data can have reliability problems through limitations of respondent recall. An alternative is to observe and record what actually happens in the outlets and this is done by research staff posing as customers. For further details of this technique see Chapter 9. Arguably this technique, which relies on researcher observation, is less 'direct' than methods such as retail audits which deal in data with no real subjective element at all. Other sorts of observation are also used occasionally in market research – eg traffic counts – and in poster research.

METHODS OF DATA COLLECTION: INTERVIEWING

Although the direct methods of data collection have an important role in some types of quantitative market research and may be capable of yielding better market measurement data, most of the information required in research projects can be obtained only through questioning respondents; through interviewing.

There are a number of methods of interviewing but what they all have in common is that the data produced is totally dependent on the questions asked. Nor is this just a matter of the substance of the questions. The form of the question put and especially its wording affects the nature of the response and, therefore, the final data.

To obtain attitude data, scales are often used; respondents, for example, are asked to indicate their evaluation of an aspect of a product by selecting a point on a scale. The scale might be numeric (from 1 = very poor to 10 = excellent) or semantic (very poor... fairly poor... neither good nor poor... fairly good... very good). Also the number of scale points might be increased or reduced, or the wording on the semantic scale changed or the positive and negative ends transposed, etc. Whatever the specific form of scale used it will certainly affect the data produced; in the case of evaluative scales the average rating for the product feature will be higher or lower depending on the type of scale. Does this matter in practice? In day-to-day research the answer is probably not a great deal. For one thing the differences in data through such variations are usually small. Furthermore, scales are generally used to produce comparisons from one data set to another; in the case of product feature evaluation, for example, what is sought is a comparison of the ratings given for all the features (or all the products) measured and the absolute 'score' levels may be of no real interest. Providing, therefore, the same scales are used throughout, which types are used may be irrelevant. However, the need for such comparability is why in continuous research (or for that matter before and after research) it is important to use the same form of scales or questions so that changes in data reflect 'real' shifts and not just changes in the tools used.

The use of different types of scales is only one example of the effect of the form of question employed. Others include the way questions are phrased, the use of words that may have variable meanings (both to the researcher and respondent) and the way the questions are asked; eg where the stress is placed in a sentence. All introduce additional variables or potential bias into the data and can significantly affect the research outcome. Minimising any such bias is an aim of effective questionnaire design and this subject is covered in Chapter 8.

In developing questionnaires one aim is standardization. The same questionnaires are used for all respondents in a sample and the carefully framed questions are meant to be asked as set out in the questionnaire. Standardization is also a requirement in other aspects of quantitative interviewing. These include how the questionnaire is administered, selection of respondents in a defined way (decided in the sampling plan) and standardized methods of recording responses. Again, these topics are discussed in more detail elsewhere.

An aspect of the research design, which needs deciding at an early stage, is the method of interviewing. There are three main options: face-to-face, phone and self-completion and these are all discussed in some detail in Chapter 9 (also see Table 6.1). The choice between these methods should be determined in the light of the nature of the data sought (some methods are better than others for certain types of data), who is to be interviewed (which may favour or require say face-to-face and not phone interviewing) and any need to expose respondents to stimuli such as products. Consideration of costs and budgets and the timescale available also, in the commercial world, affect the choice – in practice often to a greater extent than any theoretical considerations.

Table 6.1 *Methods of interviewing*

Face-to-face	Phone	Self-completion
Street	Stand alone	Postal
In-home	With other techniques	Other
Place of work		
Venue		

Face-to-face interviewing is very widely used in market research and apart from its generally high cost and sometimes the extended timetable needed, there are few disadvantages to this method compared to phone or self-completion. Face-to-face interviews are used in both consumer and business-to-business research (for cost reasons rather less in the latter) and may be carried out in 'the street' – any public place – in respondents' homes, at places of work (particularly relevant for business-to-business research) or special venues – eg where products can be shown as part of the interview (often referred to as 'hall' tests).

The main alternative to face-to-face interviewing is phone research and the use of this technique has grown rapidly in commercial market research over the last decade. The technique is particularly widely used in business-to-business research – all business respondents are contactable by phone and familiar with communicating this way. Certain sorts of data, however, cannot be collected as successfully (eg extensive attitude data) or at all (eg where products or other stimulus need to be shown) by phone. However, some of these limitations can be overcome partly by using a combination of phone and other techniques.

Self-completion data collection may be coupled with other techniques including phone interviewing or as part of a face-to-face interview, but its most common form is the postal survey which, although it uses standardized questionnaires, is not strictly speaking a form of interviewing at all. Postal research certainly has a role but is less suitable for some types of data (see Chapters 8 and 9). Also, non-response and the consequent bias can be a particular problem. Similar to using the traditional post as a means of distributing self-completion questionnaires to respondents, are alternatives such as the fax – which works very well as an adjunct to phone interviewing – or even e-mail (as yet a novel technique but possibly with long-term potential – see Schuldt and Totten, 1994). To date, the penetration of equipment limits these forms of communication to business-to-business research.

For those with a particular interest in the topic, self-completion is documented frequently in the literature – probably because it is relatively easy to mount postal surveys to produce publication data.

PRODUCT AND STIMULUS EXPOSURE

This aspect of quantitative research design has already been touched on in discussing face-to-face interviews. To collect data at all, or as a means of stimulating effective responses, respondents may need to be exposed to material. At its simplest this can be just 'show cards' used to supplement questions; scale points on a semantic scale for example are better shown as each scale dimension is covered and this is why this sort of questioning is less effective by phone; respondents have problems remembering more than three scale points if they are not constantly in front of them. Similarly, in face-to-face interviews simple illustrations may be shown to respondents – eg a photograph of two bottle shapes being compared. The illustrations may be of products or packs or can be pictorial or word representations of product concepts and these may be married to data analysis techniques such as conjoint or SIMALTO (see Chapters 9 and 12).

Beyond some point it is impractical to show even illustrations in normal interview locations – in the home, street or place of work. This applies to most advertising testing involving finished or roughs of artwork and, of course, even more so to video material. In these cases venue interviewing is normally required. Respondents are recruited and brought into a 'hall' where the material can be displayed adequately. It also can be exposed in a controlled and sequential way where this is appropriate.

Venue research is also a common requirement where respondents need to be exposed to actual products and where the responses sought require them not only to see the product but also handle, taste or smell it. Again the exposure to the product can be controlled. Some products, however, cannot be researched in this way. Responses may for example be sought after the product has been used for some time or in the case of more intimate items exposure or if use in the venue may not be acceptable. In these cases home (or place of work) placement is used and this usually requires interviewers to deliver the product and give instructions about its use and then return later to carry out the interview. Postal distribution sometimes can be an alternative and this can be linked to two-stage phone interviewing. There is more detailed discussion of product research in Chapter 10.

DATA RECORDING AND DATA ANALYSIS

Because quantitative research involves collecting a standard range of data from a significant sample of respondents – typically hundreds or thousands – the method of data recording needs to be considered as part of the research design. The paper questionnaire is still the standard method of data recording in all types of interviewing and direct data collection also often employs equivalent data sheets – eg one per outlet covered in a retail audit. The potential for responses to be mis-recorded is, however, yet another type of bias which can distort data. Most questionnaires used in quantitative research involve a predominance of pre-coded or closed questions (see Chapter 8) and the layout of the response points (boxes to tick, codes to circle etc) can help to minimize problems of mis-recording. More problematical, however, is the recording of open-ended questions (eg – 'Why did you buy this product, then?'). Interviewers are instructed to record such responses 'verbatim' but in practice they usually do not – a lengthy or rambling response is summarized or abbreviated and there is no way of knowing whether what is recorded reasonably reflects the response given.* Even the recording of apparently simple responses such as numbers can lead to problems; zeros missed off or decimal places moved. Minimizing such problems is partly a matter of interviewer training and briefing although reducing the use of open-ended questions in a quantitative survey may be the more radical and sure solution.

Paper questionnaires and record forms are now not the only method of data recording available. The capture of computer data in processes such as retail auditing has already been mentioned. Electronic media is also now widely used in interviewing for recording responses and also (in place of questionnaires) to structure and control the interview (and interviewer). Computer data recording is used in both phone interviewing (CATI – computer aided telephone interviewing) and face-to-face (CAPI – computer aided personal interviewing). These techniques (discussed in Chapter 9) offer advantages in terms of turnaround speed through reducing the data processing task and sometimes interviewer efficiency. They may also reduce bias due to mis-recording of responses or the sequence of questions (the question next on screen is the one asked). They can also reduce some problems of fieldwork management (eg cheating or make it easier to spot cheating). Electronic data capture is, however, rather less suited to open-ended questions although the enforced discipline of having to use closed questions may improve the quality of the data.

Data analysis (discussed in Chapter 12) is often not thought about at the research design stage – it is assumed that whatever is recorded can be analysed. However, even where this assumption proves to be true, neglect of data analysis issues at an early stage will certainly increase costs and lengthen timescales. The way responses are recorded will, for example, make the data entry task easier or harder. Also certain analysis techniques (eg conjoint, SIMALTO) require data to be not only recorded in a particular way but obtained through special forms of questioning. Another linkage between data collection and analysis bringing us back to the problems of using open-ended questioning in quantitative research; not only is there potential bias from interviewer recording of responses to this type of question but the coding stage of data analysis can introduce another type of bias as well as addi-

---

* Problems of mis-recording of open-ended questions can be solved by audio recording. However, this creates additional problems and expense; for quantitative research every recording needs transcribing and then sorting or coding.

tional work, costs and time. At worst, the responses to open-enders are mis-heard by the interviewer, poorly recorded on the questionnaire and then further mangled at the coding stage.

RESEARCH MANAGEMENT ISSUES

The data required in quantitative research does not collect itself. On the contrary, the whole process is very labour intensive not only during the collection stage but before (eg drawing the interview samples) and afterwards (editing, coding and data entry). Commercial market research requires creative input from professional staff but is also very dependent on much larger numbers of less skilled workers (see also Chapter 14). This creates a need for a management element as part of any research design and this is not only a matter of keeping costs and timescales in control. The quality of the data will be strongly influenced by how interviewing and other tasks are controlled and managed. Some of the potential biases in data arising from poor interviewing techniques (eg not following questionnaire wording), mis-recording responses or at the coding stage have already been mentioned. In the next chapter sampling error will be discussed, but in much research, variability and error from other sources such as those already discussed can be equal or greater than the level of sampling error and often there is no way of estimating their magnitude. One type of such bias which has not already been mentioned is non-response.

Over time, average response rates in commercial research have fallen (see Brown, 1994; Meier, 1991) and where they are measured at all they can be as low as 60 per cent. If non-response was random the problem would be of little consequence but it is not. Typically certain groups of potential respondents are less likely to respond than others – some neighbourhoods, for example, are now effectively no-go areas for face-to-face interviewing – and although weighting methods (see Chapter 7) can partly compensate, the problem leads to quite significant levels of data distortion.

Good project management can at least limit the effect of some of these problems as well as keep research in tight financial and timescale control. The size of an interview team can, for example, be used to reduce the problems of one interviewer's bad practice significantly distorting the overall data although, conversely, the larger the team the greater the potential variability in working practices. Interviewers also need briefing adequately so that they know how to contact respondents and how to administer the questionnaire. Undoubtedly personnel briefings are best but for face-to-face interviewing these are often ruled out on cost grounds and well written briefing notes have to suffice (for phone interviewing carried out from one location, personal briefing is far more common).

The structure of the market research industry (see Chapter 14) generally requires fieldwork to be verified after completion. This usually involves a check-back, to say 10 per cent of respondents, with key questions re-asked. Also an issue is to establish that they have been interviewed at all; the incidence is not high, but outright cheating by interviewers is not unknown. Interviewers also need general training in how to work and this is a separate and prior issue to briefing for a particular job; the minimum accepted training duration for a raw recruit is considered to be two to three days with follow-on close supervision. The need for training, briefing and verification also exists at the data processing stage and wherever else labour-intensive tasks are carried out by staff not directly involved in the design of the research.

A final aspect of research management to mention is logistics. This may include questionnaire printing, delivery and collection of material to a dispersed interviewing team and where product testing is involved, the sourcing and handling of products. Misprinting – eg from a former version of a questionnaire – is not uncommon and needs quality control procedures to minimize the problem. Late or lost questionnaires to or from interviewers can lengthen timescales or result in interviewing beyond some date which is critical to the research design (eg in advertising research). It can also lead to a lower effective sample than planned with a consequent effect on data reliability. In product testing it is nearly always essential to

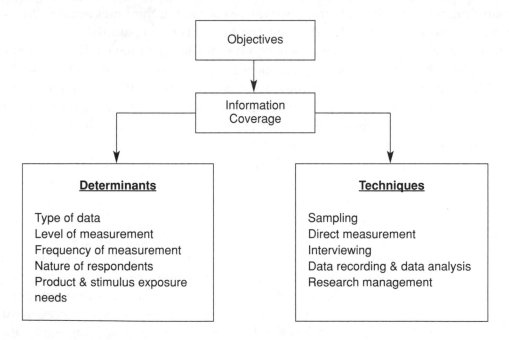

Figure 6.2 *Developing a quantitative research design*

expose respondents to controlled products; consistent batches, presented in a uniform manner (eg temperature) and quite often in a 'blind' or debranding form. Moving outside such defined product parameters can affect the resulting data and careful planning is, therefore, needed in sourcing, storing and handling research products. There is also, for food products at least, the need to avoid mass poisoning of respondents and the whole issue of test safety is increasingly moving into the public health and legal domain. These and other logistic at aspects of a research design are all potential sources of error which need controlling.

DEVELOPING THE RESEARCH DESIGN

Hopefully, this chapter will have shown the need for a quantitative research design to be carefully thought out. Starting with the objectives and required coverage of the project (as discussed in Chapter 3) the final design is a matter of selecting from the array of established techniques, after taking into account the determinants we have discussed (Figure 6.2 summarizes the process). Whatever the final choices made, they should always be set out in the written research plan (as discussed in Chapter 3).

However, as well as good research practice, methods are inevitably shaped by available budgets and timescales. In most commercial research this nearly always leads to a compromise with what is ideal. This is the way of the world and the researcher's responsibilities in this respect are to make clear the consequences of the constraints – eg lower accuracy and reliability – and sometimes to draw a line when what can be afforded just cannot produce the data sought.

7

Samples

As briefly discussed in the last chapter, quantitative research – and for that matter qualitative research – is nearly always based on samples. Some understanding of the basic principles of sampling, therefore, is required by anyone involved in market research as a subject or practical activity. This is true even for those who use rather than design research; a basic grasp is needed to avoid mistaken thinking and the abuse of the data when drawing conclusions.

Sampling is based on statistical theory which is a far larger subject than can be covered in this chapter. We shall, therefore, keep statistical concepts and formulae to an absolute minimum. However, the reader is urged to acquire some basic statistical literacy – there are many good books on this subject including those specifically written for market research applications (eg Hague and Harris, 1993).

SAMPLING SIZE, SAMPLING ERROR AND CONFIDENCE LEVELS

Confidence to use samples in market research (or in any application) is based on a branch of statistical theory which allows the accuracy levels of samples to be estimated within ranges of probabilities. Typically, in market research, 95 per cent probability levels – also referred to as 'confidence levels' – are taken. It might be said, for example, that if a measure from a sample (eg awareness levels of a brand) is 50 per cent, the accuracy level (or 'sampling error' or 'confidence limits') at 95 per cent probability of +/– 3 per cent. In other words we are confident that amongst the whole population there is a 95 per cent chance that the measure is between 47 per cent and 53 per cent (there is of course though a 5 per cent chance that the measure is outside these limits; complete certainty is not possible). The probability level – the chance of the sample measure being within the limits – does not have to be 95 per cent; it can be higher (eg 99 per cent) or lower leg (eg 90 per cent). At the lower probability the sampling error will be smaller (eg +/–1 per cent) but greater at the higher level (eg +/–5 per cent). Note, however, that the sample is not any more or less accurate; it is just that the level of accuracy (sampling error) is expressed in different ways for the same sample and we can choose with which probability level to work. In practice, market research normally works with the 95 per cent probability level and takes the sampling error at this level in drawing any conclusions from the data (eg whether any increase in consumption, from sample results at two points in time, is in the statistical sense significant).

In estimating the accuracy of a sample, or selecting a sample to meet a required level of accuracy, there are two critical variables; the size of the sample and the measure being taken which for simplicity we shall take as a single percentage – eg the percentage aware of a brand. A common mistake about sample size is to assume that accuracy is determined by the proportion of a population included in a sample (eg 10 per cent of a population). Assuming a large population, this is not the case and what matters is the absolute size of the sample regardless of the size of the population – a sample of 500 drawn from a population of one million will be as accurate as a sample of 500 from a population of five million.*

The relationship between sampling error, a percentage measure and sample size can be expressed as a formula or (for the mathematically challenged) in chart form – Figure 7.1.

$$\text{Sampling error} = \frac{1.96 \sqrt{p \% \, (100 - p \%)}}{n}$$

Where:

p = the measure taken;

n = sample size.

---

* This assumes that in each case the samples are truly random samples of the respective populations.

Note: the value 1.96 included in the formula is for a 95 per cent probability level; at other levels other values are substituted (eg 2.58 at the 99 per cent level).

Formula for calculating the sampling error of a single percentage measure (95 per cent probability level)

By applying the formula it can be calculated, for example, that from a sample of 500 respondents (n), a measure of 20 per cent (p) – eg aware of a brand – will have a sampling error of +/– 3.5 per cent at the 95 per cent probability level – ie:

$$\frac{1.96 \ \sqrt{20 \ (100 - 20)}}{500} = 3.5\%$$

This means, therefore, that based on a sample of 500 we can be 95 per cent sure that the true measure (eg of brand awareness) among the whole population from which the sample was drawn will be within +/– 3.5 per cent of 20 per cent, ie between 16.5 per cent and 23.5 per cent.

Sampling error also can be estimated from Figure 7.1 although not with the same precision. The dotted line A in Figure 7.1 intersects the 20 per cent sample measure on the left-hand column and a sample size of 500 on the right-hand column. The middle column shows the sampling error – it appears as somewhere just over +/– 3 per cent.

Figure 7.1 or the formula (whichever the reader is most comfortable with) can be used also to explore the effect on sampling error of different measures and of altering the size of the sample. In Figure 7.1 dotted line B passes through the same sample size as A (500) but the measure in this case is 50 per cent and it will be seen that the sampling error is now higher and about +/– 4.5 per cent. Using the formula it can be calculated more accurately as +/– 4.38 per cent. The sampling error is in fact greatest for a 50 per cent measure – this is best understood from the formula; try various values of p if you cannot grasp why this is the case from just looking at the formula.* The accuracy of a sample, therefore, depends on the measure taken and to speak of a sample being accurate to say +/– 5 per cent is, strictly speaking, misleading without reference to a particular measure.

The formula and chart also can be used to demonstrate the effect of sample size on accuracy levels. Line C in the chart also rests (as does A) rests on the 20 per cent

---

* The formula also explains why in Figure 7.1 the measure column only covers values up to 50 per cent – for a given sample size the sampling error of say 45 per cent is the same as of 55 per cent etc; if necessary, prove this by using different values of p in the formula.

measure but the sample size is now 1,000 (instead of 500 for line A). The accuracy in this case is shown to be somewhat above +/– 2.25 per cent and can be calculated more accurately from the formula as +/– 2.47 per cent. An increase in accuracy level, therefore, has been obtained by doubling the sample. Note, however, that the improvement is less than proportional; the accuracy of a sample is in fact proportional to the square root of its size and increases in accuracy are proportional to the square root of the increase (this should be apparent from the formula) and to halve the sampling error (ie double the precision) we need to make the sample four times as big. Costs of carrying out data collection are clearly related to the number of interviews (sample size) and, therefore, the extra costs of increasing the sample are always disproportionate to the gains in accuracy. As discussed elsewhere the accuracy needed from research depends on the use to which the results are put and there always need to be good reasons for increasing accuracy levels bearing in mind the cost penalties.

So far we have used the relationship between sample size and the measures taken to calculate sampling error. In practice it may be more useful to use the relationship to calculate the sample size required to achieve results within a defined accuracy

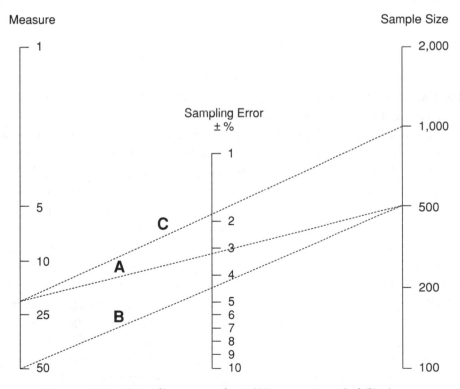

Figure 7.1 *Sampling error chart (95 per cent probability)*

level/sampling error. Using the chart will show that if a measure of 20 per cent is anticipated and the required accuracy is +/– 2.5 per cent, a sample size of 1000 will be required – the three values lie along line C. The previous formula also can be transposed to calculate sample size:

$$\text{Sample size} \quad = \quad \frac{3.84\,[p\,\%(100 - p\,\%)]}{se^2}$$

where:

se   = *accepted sample error;*
p   = *anticipated measure.*

Formula for calculating sample size (95 per cent probability level)

To calculate the required sample for a given sampling error level requires the measurement value (p) to be known. However, in practice, samples are selected before data is collected and, therefore, before the value of the measure is known. Possibly a reasonable estimate can be made – eg from previous research or published data – but if not, the 'worst case' can be assumed and the value of the measure taken as 50 per cent. The consequence of doing this, though, may be to pay the costs of a larger sample than necessary. The '50 per cent' assumption is also appropriate when, as is common, a whole range of measures is being collected; some are almost bound to be around 50 per cent.

An additional and important point about sample measures is that it is common to seek not only measures for the whole sample but for subsamples within it. A sample of 500 adults drawn randomly, for example, is likely to include around 250 men and 250 women. Quite possibly it will be useful to look separately at the results from each sex – such differences (as well as for other demographics – age, income group etc) may be vital in marketing planning. However, in looking separately at say men, the effective sample is now 250 and the accuracy level is rather lower than for the whole sample of 500 and this needs to be borne in mind when comparing differences between the data for men and women – a small difference may not be 'real' and simply reflect the sampling accuracy levels. Too many market research studies, including those carried out professionally, discuss differences between subsamples where the numbers involved (bases) are just too small to allow inferences to be drawn with any reliability. The moral of this is that when planning samples it is important to think about which subgroups may be important and to seek sufficient numbers in each one. Subsamples should often determine total sample size.

SAMPLING SMALL POPULATIONS

It was stated earlier that sampling error is not dependent on the proportion of the population sampled. However, this is assuming the population is large – say over 100,000. For small finite populations common, for example, in business markets, special rules apply. The statistical theory involved in such cases is quite complex but the key point is that for a given level of accuracy, the required sample size from a limited population is smaller (and therefore cheaper to research) than would be required using the calculations relevant to large populations. The table below shows sample sizes required for different sized small populations in order to be 95 per cent confident that the sampling error is no more than 5 per cent for a 50 per cent measure (as discussed above, the 'worst case position').

Table 7.1   _Table for determining required sample size with a 5 per cent sampling error at 95 per cent confidence (assuming a sample measure of 50 per cent)_

Population	Sample	Population	Sample
10	10	550	228
30	28	1,100	285
60	52	1,700	313
80	66	2,400	331
110	86	4,000	351
170	118	8,000	367
210	136	20,000	377
320	175	100,000	384

For a large population the required sample, given the other assumptions in Table 7.1, is 384 (using the formula given on page 94). In other words the special rules relating to sampling small populations cease to apply at populations of 100,000 + (ie 100,000 is a large population). Looking at the table it will also be seen that the special adjustment for small populations becomes really important for populations of less than about 2,000 and is more than proportionately greater as population size decreases.

STATISTICAL SIGNIFICANCE

In comparing the subsamples previously discussed we are effectively asking the question whether the differences between two samples are statistically significant.

The chart in Figure 7.1 or the previous formula can be used to give a rough and ready indication – eg if the measure in one subsample was 25 per cent and in another 20 per cent and in each case the size of the subsample was 250, the calculated sampling errors could be set out as follows:

Subsample	Measure (%)	Sample error* (+/-%)	Range within (%)
A	20	5.0	15–25
B	25	5.4	19.6–30.4

*95% probability level

It can be seen that the true measurement in the population represented by subsample A may be as low as 15 per cent and as high as 25 per cent – the level found in subsample B – while in the case of the population represented by subsample B, the true measure could be as low as 19.6 per cent or as high as 30.4 per cent. In other words the difference between the measures from the two subsamples overlaps with their ranges of sampling error and we can conclude the difference is not likely to be statistically significant. A better approach to the question of significance is to apply a formal significance test and an appropriate procedure for comparing two percentage, measures is as follows:

1. Calculate the 'standard error' of the difference between the two percentages (p_1 and p_2) by using the formula:

$$Standard\ error\ (p_1 - p_2) = \sqrt{pq \left[\frac{1}{n_1} + \frac{1}{n_2} \right]}$$

where n_1 and n_2 are the respective sample sizes, and where

$$p = \frac{n_1 p_1 + n_2 p_2}{n_1 + n_2}$$
$$q = 100 - p$$

2. Use the formula below to calculate z – a comparison of the difference between the two measures and the standard error of this difference:

$$z = \frac{p_1 - p_2}{Standard\ error\ (p_1 - p_2)}$$

3. If z is greater than or equal to 1.96 we can conclude that there is a 95 per cent probability that the difference between the two measures reflects true differences found in the populations from which the samples have been drawn. If, however, z is less than 1.96 the difference is not statistically significant at a 95 per cent probability level – it could reflect sampling rather than real differences likely to be found in the population (we can also work on other probability levels – for a 99 per cent level a significant difference is where z is equal to or greater than 2.58).

Using the above procedure, the value of z in the above examples of two sub-samples producing measures of 20 per cent and 25 per cent is 1.33 and since this is less than 1.96 we can say the difference between the two measures is not statistically significant at a 95 per cent probability (and obviously also at a 99 per cent probability).

RANDOM SAMPLING

The discussion of sampling (and sample accuracy) to this point, assumes that the sample is 'random'. Random in this context has a precise meaning – that every member of the population being sampled has a known probability (depending on the sampling design this probability may be the same for every member) of being included in the sample – another term for a random sample is a 'probability sample'. If this is not the case, if some members of the population have an unknown probability of being sampled and are perhaps in practice unlikely to be, the sample is not truly random; it is 'biased'.

In any random sampling design, the first step is always to define the population. The method of drawing the sample cannot be considered until this is done and done with some precision. Depending on the objectives of the research the population from which data is required may be a 'natural' one of individuals (eg all adults over 18) or individuals with defined characteristics (eg the person responsible for shopping for a household, or car owners or pizza eaters, etc), households or other small groupings or, in business-to-business research, companies and organizations – probably in defined industries or customers of a particular supplier (usually of the research sponsor). In almost all cases the population definition also needs to include some geographic boundaries – England and Wales, the South East, etc.

Once the population is defined a true random sample requires that a 'sample frame' (a listing – of all individuals making up the population) is available.* However, considering what this actually means in practice points to the difficulties in using true random samples in market research.

A hypothetical sampling frame for pupils at a particular school might be the school roll and if this has been well kept it is probably near enough a fully complete sampling frame. Selecting a random sample of say 200 from a school of 1,000 pupils could be carried out by taking the roll, numbering each pupil and using a table of 'random numbers' selecting 200 numbers in the range 1–1,000. If the roll is not already numbered this will be rather laborious work and it will be more practical to select the sample 'systematically' – taking every fifth name (the fraction from dividing the required sample by the total population) starting at a randomly selected point. The sample selected in either case should be truly random and free of bias. An important point about it is that it is 'preselected' – the interviewer does not select the respondents; they are chosen in advance and a potentially major source of bias is excluded.

Market research samples are not commonly drawn to represent such a well defined and recorded population as a school. Far more common is to seek a random sample of say all adults. Where can a complete sampling frame be found in this case? The source that immediately springs to mind is the electoral register. But is the electoral register a complete sampling frame of all adults? No. For a start it is at least four months out of date and in the meantime individuals will have moved, died, etc. Also, even on the day it was compiled, some individuals are intentionally never included (eg not British subjects) by the compilers or by the would-be electors – the short-lived poll tax is said to have significantly reduced the coverage of the register. Individuals are also just missed by accident. There are, therefore, significant omissions from electoral registers and samples of individuals drawn from them are consequently biased to some degree. However, for many research requirements the electoral register is as good a sample frame as can be found and its theoretical limitations are often regarded as not a significant practical problem. Some of the bias due to omissions can be corrected by formal procedures – the Kisk Selection Grid (see Hague and Harris, 1993) – used to select supplementary subsamples of individuals living at households of the randomly selected electors. The electoral registers can be used also as a sample frame of households as well as individuals since the arrangement of electors is in the household order.

Another important sampling frame for households is the Post Office postcode file. This is available as a computer file from which random samples can be easily

---

* In the case of multi-stage random sampling – see later – it is enough that a complete sampling frame is potentially available since only randomly selected parts of the frame will actually be used in sample selection.

selected electronically (various companies offer this service). Again though, there are inevitable omissions from the field and this introduces some bias.

Telephone interviewing, which entails no travel costs, is well suited to accessing a geographically dispersed random sample and systematic samples can be relatively easily drawn from A–Z phone books. Does this source, though, provide an unbiased random sample? Obviously phone interviewing can only reach homes with a phone and if a sample of the whole population is sought, phone interviewing is far short of the ideal method. However, even as a sample frame of phone homes, the A–Z directories are quite seriously deficient since a significant proportion of subscribers choose to be ex-directory and, therefore, will be excluded from any sample drawn in this way. Techniques developed to deal with this problem include random dialling, with a computer selecting contact numbers within phone code ranges and 'number plus one' – for a subsample, the number called is a random selection from the A–Z book plus one digit. Both these methods involve higher costs of 'wasted calls' – to non-residential subscribers, non-existing numbers etc. Also, since the reasons why people choose to be ex-directory undoubtedly include those that that do not want to be bothered by such as market research interviewers, response rates will be even lower than among listed households (response rates in consumer phone interviewing are low in any case). See Noble *et al* (1998).

Business-to-business research is concerned with populations not of individuals but organizations, companies, etc and often in defined sectors by industry, etc. Surprisingly there is no universal sample frame, or even comprehensive ones for most sectors, which is anywhere complete. Directories such as *Kompass* and *Dunn & Bradstreet* (available in various forms including CD ROM, computer files and in published volumes) for example, although widely used, miss out many smaller businesses. Also where research is of a sector, the definition of the sector relevant to the research objectives may not match the classifications used in sample frames. These comments may suggest that reliable sampling is not possible in business-to-business research but this is to overstate the problems. In practice, samples taken from sources such as directories, and often built from several such sources, while not completely free from bias, are good enough for most purposes. There are also other issues important in business-to-business research apart from sample frame limitations and particularly those relating to the fact that the units in the population, eg companies, are not of equal size – in fact they usually fit an 80:20 Pareto rule; 20 per cent of the units account for 80 per cent of the market being studied. To design a sampling plan that takes account of this, stratification or quotas are often used. More of this follows shortly.

A final sort of sampling frame to mention is customer lists. In recent years customer satisfaction research has become a common need and where individual customers are recorded as part of the normal business process, the lists – of individuals or organizations depending on the business – are often an effective frame for true random sampling. Some limitations and potential sources of bias, however, include that the list is out of date and, therefore, new customers are excluded, some customers are systematically left off the list (eg special accounts) and that 'accounts' rather than customers are listed or vice versa – see Semon (1994a) for a discussion of this particular problem. Some other aspects of customer list research are well covered by Dent (1992). It should of course be stressed that lists of customers are just that and if there is a need to include in the research the views of potential customers, a list of current customers alone will not produce this part of the sample (and lists of sales contacts, etc almost always have deficiencies). The methods used for drawing samples from customer lists also must be rigorous – do not leave it to the company's sales department which may, with the best intentions, not understand what is meant by random selection or deliberately exclude certain difficult customers.

While the electoral registers and sources such as the postcode files can be used as frames to draw near-random samples of all adults, consumer research often requires samples of particular groups of consumers; this may include ones defined by product usage. Research into microwave dinners, for example, needs to be carried out among owners of microwave ovens. In most cases, no sample frame of the required population is available and an approximation to a random sample can be achieved only through interviewing a sufficiently large sample of the wider population until the required sized sample of product users etc is found; in effect this is a subsample of a larger random sample. The number of 'wasted' initial contact interviews depends on the proportion of the wider population that qualifies – uses the product, owns the appliance etc. The costs of this sort of sample are in inverse proportion to the strike rate and can be prohibitive for minority samples. Practical means of reducing these costs include buying into omnibus surveys (see Chapter 14) and accessing respondent panels whose usage of the relevant products is already known.

MULTI-STAGE AND STRATIFIED SAMPLES

In our discussion of random sampling so far we have implied that the sample needs to be drawn from a complete sampling frame by using random numbers or systematic intervals. At least where we are concerned, with a large population spread over any sizeable area, this method is in practice impractical and virtually never used. Not only is the process of drawing the sample very laborious (eg from the electoral registers of all constituencies) but the resulting sample will be very dispersed and prohibitively expensive to contact and interview. The practical alternative is 'multi-stage sampling'. Where it is intended to select the sample from the electoral register, the procedure is commonly first to draw a random sample of constituencies (from a full listing) and then for the constituencies selected to draw a random sample of wards (again from a full listing). The final sample is then drawn randomly from the ward electoral register and will, as a result of this procedure, be clustered into small areas which can be far more economically contacted and interviewed. An in-built bias, however, can result from differentials in the number of electors in each constituency; a simple random sample from a listing will produce a sample biased against electors living in larger constituencies. The solution to this problem is a technique called 'sampling with probability proportional to size'. Briefly, this involves listing all constituencies and their number of electors together with a running cumulative total of electors. The sample is then drawn at systematic intervals from the latter (see Hague and Harris, 1993).

Because of its economy over simple random sampling, multi-stage sampling is widely used in market research wherever random samples of the whole population are sought. The technique can be used with other sample frames as well as the electoral register. A problem with the technique, however, is that sampling error is always increased. Effectively, additional sampling error is introduced at each stage of the sampling process and needs to be allowed for when selecting an effective size of sample. See also Harris (1977) for further discussion of the effects of clustering.

The value of stratified sampling is best illustrated in business-to-business applications. In research, for example, to establish the usage of a particular cable by telecommunications companies, a random selection from a complete listing of such companies may well not include BT (because it is only one out of say 500 listed). However, BT may account for 80 per cent of all the cable used and to miss the company would clearly produce results which could not be used to make estimates of the total market. This problem is a reflection that the population being sampled is not composed of 'equal' units and in fact is split into strata – in this case by size of cable spend (which probably correlates fairly well to size of company). The solution is, therefore, to use a stratified sample; the sample frame of companies is divided into say three strata of large, medium and small companies and samples drawn from each (in the example, BT might be taken as a stratum all on its own). The strata are unlikely to contain the same number of units – there are few large companies even though they account for a large proportion of consumption – and the sampling interval from each stratum to produce adequate numbers is likely to be different – eg one in two large companies, one in ten medium-sized companies and one in 25 small ones.

Stratified sampling can be used in various applications as well as business-to-business research. It is appropriate to use when the variable being measured (eg cable consumption) is known to be correlated with a variable available for sample stratification (eg company size) and will in these cases produce samples with lower sampling errors. The practical limitation of the technique is that data to use as a stratifying variable must be readily available for the population being sampled (eg telecommunication company turnover at least in broad terms, this is available from directories, etc).

RANDOM WALK SAMPLING

Random walk sampling is quite widely used in market research as a cheaper approximation to true random sampling. The sample is selected by taking small areas (eg selected as per multi-stage sampling), then selecting random starting-points within these areas and giving interviewers fixed routes to follow. The latter will specify the intervals of households to contact (eg every eighth house) and what to do at each street junction (eg turn alternatively left and right). Special rules will cover blocks of flats and what to do when buildings are non-residential. Whatever, the precise form of instructions, however, the main aim is to avoid the bias of inter-viewer respondent selection; the major limitation of quota sampling (see shortly). Theoretically, the resulting sample is not truly random but for most practical purposes it is treated as if it were, including in the calculation of sampling error. In market research applications random walk sampling is regarded as a relatively rigorous approach.

RANDOM SAMPLING AND NON-RESPONSE

The problem of non-response was briefly raised in the last chapter. From a sampling perspective non-response is a major source of bias in the achieved sample. For one reason or another it is in practice impossible to collect data from every individual making up a sample. Some will not be contactable, some may have moved away or died and some will certainly refuse to participate. If respondents live in certain parts of an inner-city it may be impractical even to approach them – interviewers increasingly will not go into some 'no go' areas. If for a random sample the response rate achieved is say 80 per cent (in practice now considered to be very high) then the 'achieved sample' from the 500 originally selected will be only 400 and possibly the accuracy levels with this smaller sample will be too low. Of course the problem can be apparently solved by 'sample replacement' – take a supplementary sample and make contact until the desired 500 interviews are achieved. However, we are back to problems of bias. The non-respondents may in some way or another differ significantly (in relation to the aims of the study) from those who were interviewed and the results may not, therefore, be representative of the whole population. Certainly some non-respondents differ to respondents in that they refuse to participate in surveys and this may well be very relevant in political polling or attitude research (ie non-cooperators may be a certain personality type that holds more critical attitudes in general).

Non-response is considered to be a significant practical problem by market researchers and particularly since average response rates to surveys are believed to be falling year by year (for further discussion of some aspects of non-response see Swan _et al_, 1991; Hahlo, 1992). One advantage of random and preselected samples in relation to non-response, however, is that at least the level of response achieved in a survey can be quantified – with a complete list of the sample the results of contact with each potential respondent can be logged. Also because of contact records, rigorous call-back procedures can be enforced to increase response; interviewers can be required to return up to three times at different times of day, to homes where there was no reply at the first call and the bias against respondents away from home a lot, consequently, can be reduced. Such procedures cannot be used in quota sampling (or at least their implementation cannot be assured); the subject to which we now turn.

QUOTA SAMPLES

In practical market research true random samples or even close approximations are used less often than is ideal from the perspective of sampling theory – in _ad hoc_ market research probably well under half of all interviewing is carried out amongst even approximations to random samples. Often it is impractical to draw a random sample (this includes that the cost of doing so is too high) or for one reason or another it is not appropriate – eg for selecting many minority samples including those of product users. The most widely used alternative to random sampling in consumer market research is 'quota sampling'. In effect the choice of respondents is left to interviewers (unlike the case with preselected random samples) providing they fill quotas to ensure the overall sample is representative, in key parameters, of the population being researched. In consumer research, demographics such as sex and social class are common quota parameters and they are often interlocked (eg age group quotas for each social class). Table 7.2 illustrates this. In research using these quotas respondents would be 'found' to match the characteristics of each cell (eg 12 respondents of social class C1 and aged 18 to 24), until all cells are filled. In Table 7.2 the quotas shown are for a total sample; where a number of interviewers are involved each is given their own individual sheet.

Table 7.2 *Example of interlocking quotas*

Age	Social class				
	AB	C1	C2	DE	**Total**
18–24	2	12	8	11	**33**
25–44	12	19	18	16	**65**
45+	17	24	25	36	**102**
Total	**31**	**55**	**51**	**63**	**200**

As well as simple demographics, quotas also can be set by geodemographic classifications. Quota samples are also common in business-to-business research; company size and industry classifications are standard quota classifications.

One practical problem with quota sampling is that the numbers required within a subgroup (eg higher income groups) may be sufficient to meet the needs of the total sample size but too small to provide reliable results about a subgroup which may be of particular interest. The common solution to this problem is to 'over-sample' the subgroup (eg instead of say 10 per cent of the sample being in the upper income group this is increased to say 25 per cent) and the results adjusted back to the true profile of the population at the data analysis stage through using weighting techniques (see Chapter 12).

Quota samples are very commonly used in market research. Their chief practical merit is low cost; there are no clerical costs of preselecting the sample, the interviewers' productivity (interviews per day) is higher because they are not following up initial non-responses and the technique can be used with low-cost street interviewing (where obviously preselection is a non-starter). The theoretical disadvantages are, however, considerable. First there is the bias of respondents being selected by interviewers who may consciously or otherwise reject potential respondents who appear 'difficult'. Also since initial non-responders are not followed up, there is a bias against those respondents who are less accessible – eg people working long hours. In fact the response rates – the scale of this problem – are unknown with quota sampling. Then there is the problem of non-computable sampling error. Quota samples like random samples are of course subject to sampling error but in this case there is no simple way of calculating what it is. Often the sampling error is calculated as if the sample was random but there is no theoretical basis for doing this. The likely sampling error of quota samples is subject to some dispute but some consider that the rule should be to assume that it is twice that of the same sized random samples. See Marsh and Scarborough (1990) for a further discussion of the bias of quota sampling.

As well as its application in quantitative research, quota sampling is widely used to recruit qualitative samples for group discussions etc. In a fairly loose sense the intention is to cover a sample which is broadly representative of the target population in terms of demographics, product usage or even attitudes to critical issues. However, since there is no attempt to quantify from the research in any rigorous sense, questions and problems of sampling error do not apply. Problems of interviewer bias in selection, however, still need to be considered.

In business-to-business research in particular, another term used is 'judgement samples'. In practice this means the researcher interviews a sample that he or she believes gives a true representation of the market. This can be linked to the concept of interviewing until the variation in aggregated key data is minimal from any additional interviews (applied properly this has some statistical validity) but more often it is just a matter of judgement – the researcher's feel – and while not 'scientific' may be the best that can be achieved in practice. In market research the need to compromise what is theoretically desirable with what is practically possible or can be afforded is ever present.

8

Questionnaire design

A questionnaire is a structured sequence of questions designed to draw out facts and opinions and which provides a vehicle for recording the data. This chapter begins with a discussion of the role of questionnaires and presents a fully formatted example with a variety of question layouts. A description of the different types of questions and questionnaires follows. We recommend procedures for designing a questionnaire and show the pitfalls to avoid. Finally, we discuss the special case of postal questionnaires.

THE FOUR PURPOSES OF QUESTIONNAIRES

Questionnaires fulfil four purposes. Their first and primary role is to draw accurate information from respondents. Secondly, they provide structure to interviews. In any survey of more than just a few people it is important that all respondents are asked the same questions in the same way. Without this structure it would be impossible to build an overall picture. The third purpose of questionnaires is to provide a standard form on which facts, comments and attitudes can be written down. A record of an interview is essential as, without it, points would be forgotten or distorted. Finally, questionnaires facilitate data processing. Answers are recorded in a common place on each questionnaire so that simple counts can be made of how many people said what. Without a questionnaire, a survey of 500 people would produce 500 jottings or free ranging interviews which would be impossible to process.

TYPES OF QUESTIONNAIRES

There are three different types of interview situations which in turn require three different types of questionnaire. These three classifications of questionnaire are summarized in Table 8.1.

Table 8.1 *A classification of questionnaires*

Type of questionnaire	Areas of use of questionnaire	Administration of questionnaire
Structured	Used in large interview programmes (typically over 200 interviews). Used where it is possible to anticipate the responses closely	Telephone/face-to-face/self-completion
Semi-structured	Used widely in business-to-business market research where there is a need to accommodate widely different responses from companies. Also used where the responses cannot be anticipated	Face-to-face/telephone
Unstructured	The basis of many studies into technical or narrow markets. Used in depth interviewing and group discussions. Allows probing and searching where the researcher is not fully sure of the responses before the interview	Group discussions/face-to-face interviews/depth telephone interviews

DIFFERENT TYPES OF QUESTION

Different types of question can be used to elicit information from respondents. Where a respondent is free to give any answer, and what is said is written down verbatim, the question is 'open'. When the respondent is free to give any answer, but the interviewer has a list of possible responses on the questionnaire, then this is an open-ended question with a closed response. The respondent would be unaware of the predefined responses which are there for the greater efficiency of completing the questionnaire and the subsequent data processing.

The second style of question is a 'closed or prompted question'. Here the replies are anticipated. They are read out or shown on a card and respondents are asked to choose whichever best indicates their answer. The predefined answers are worked out by common sense, as a result of earlier qualitative research or through a pilot study.

Structured questionnaires use closed questions and unstructured questionnaires use open questions. As might be expected, semi-structured questionnaires are made up of both types.

A further classification of questions is into their purpose which is threefold 'behavioural', 'attitudinal', or for 'classification'. The information which can be collected from these questions and their applications in different types of surveys is summarized in Table 8.2.

Table 8.2   *A classification of questions*

Type of question	Information sought	Types of surveys where used
Behavioural	Factual information on what the respondent is, does or owns. Also the frequency with which certain actions are carried out. Where people live	Surveys to find out market size, market shares, awareness and usage
Attitudinal	What people think of something. Their image and ratings of things. Why they do things	Image and attitude surveys, brand mapping studies, customer satisfaction surveys
Classification	Information that can be used to group respondents to see how they differ one from the other – such as their age, gender, social class, location of household, type of house, family composition	All surveys

Everyone is familiar with questionnaires. They sit underneath our noses in motorway cafes, they pour through our letterboxes on every subject imaginable. However, it may be helpful to view a questionnaire in its entirety when reflecting on the exercise of questionnaire design. A short telephone questionnaire is shown here; a larger, self-completion questionnaire can be found later in this chapter.

Customer Satisfaction Survey

Good morning/afternoon, I am phoning from B2B International in Manchester. We are carrying out research for Good Grub restaurants and are contacting all recent visitors to their restaurant.

Q1   Do you have 5 minutes to help us with this questionnaire?

Yes .... ☐ 1

No .... ☐ 2

Q2   Please enter today's date

☐

Q3   How often, on average, do you visit this restaurant?

Daily... ☐ 1

Twice a week... ☐ 2

Weekly... ☐ 3

Monthly .... ☐ 4

Q4   How many people were In your party today?

☐

Q5   Do you remember what you ordered?

Pasta .... ☐ 1   Ice cream............ ☐ 5

French fries......... ☐ 2   Coffee/tea .... ☐ 6

Pizza .... ☐ 3   Soft drink .... ☐ 7

Salad .... ☐ 4

What else did you order?   ☐

Q6   How much did you spend on {q5} in total?

☐

Q7   How do you rate the following?

	Very Poor	Poor	OK	Good	Very Good
Speed of service	☐	☐	☐	☐	☐
Cleanliness	☐	☐	☐	☐	☐
Parking	☐	☐	☐	☐	☐
Quality of food	☐	☐	☐	☐	☐
Choice of food	☐	☐	☐	☐	☐

Q8   How do you rate the overall performance of this restaurant, using a scale of 10 for excellent and 1 for poor?

☐

Q9   Are there any other comments that you would like to make?

☐

And finally....... a few questions about yourself

Q10   How old are you?

Under 18............. ☐ 1   45-60 .... ☐ 4

18-24 .... ☐ 2   Over 60.............. ☐ 5

25-44 .... ☐ 3

Q11   CODE male or female?

Male................... ☐ 1   Female................ ☐ 2

Q12   Enter the respondents postcode.

☐

Thank & Close

We now describe the three important classes of questions: behavioural, attitudinal and classification.

BEHAVIOURAL QUESTIONS

Behavioural questions are designed to find out what people (or companies) do. For example, do people go to the cinema?, how often do they go?, what type of films do they watch?, who do they go with? etc. They determine people's actions in terms of what they have eaten (or drunk), bought, used, visited, seen, read or heard. Behavioural questions record facts and not matters of opinion.

Behavioural questions address the following:

- Have you ever…?
- Do you ever…?
- Who do you know…?
- When did you last…?
- Which do you do most often…?
- Who does it…?
- How many…?
- Do you have…?
- In what way do you do it…?
- In the future will you…?

ATTITUDINAL QUESTIONS

People hold opinions or beliefs on everything from politics, to social precepts, to the products they buy and the companies which make or supply them. These attitudes are not necessary right, but this is hardly relevant since it is 'perceptions' that count. People's attitudes guide the way they act.

Researchers explore attitudes using questions which begin with Why?, How?, Which?, Who?, Where? and What? Also useful is the magical phrase, 'Would you explain…?'.

Attitudinal questions address the following:

- Why do you…?
- What do you think of…?
- Do you agree or disagree…?

- How do you rate...?
- Which is best (or worst) for...?

The purpose of rating scales

We can find out what people think of different companies, brands, products or services by asking in one of two ways:

1. Using an open-ended question which could be quite simple such as 'What do you think of...?' or 'Tell me the strong points of...' or 'Tell me the weak points...' etc.
2. Using a rating scale to measure the attitudes.

Open-ended questions are powerful in providing insights into what people think but they do not provide a benchmark by which we can see how we are improving. Measurements are crucial in determining how companies, products, and brands are seen in relative terms – one competitor to another – as well as how they are changing over time. Rating scales are the means by which these attitudes are measured.

Choosing the right rating scale

All rating scales offer the opportunity to measure attitudes. However, there are many different types of rating scales and they have their strengths and weaknesses. Let's first look at the different types of scales. A major division is:

- numeric scales;
- verbal scales.

Scales of one type or another have different purposes. They all measure attitudes, but some work better over the phone (eg numeric scales), some are better for indicating how to improve service (eg SIMALTO scales) and others are better for determining likelihood of buying something (eg semantic scales). Table 8.3 summarizes the advantages and disadvantages of the two main classes of scales – numeric and verbal.

Numeric rating scales

Numeric rating scales require respondents to express their feelings about a product, company, brand, or service by giving a number or score.

Table 8.3 *Advantages and disadvantages of numeric and verbal rating scales*

	Advantages	Disadvantages
Numeric scales	• Easy to administer over the telephone • Good for benchmarking different companies. • Can cover many attributes quickly.	• Don't have any specific meaning. • Don't relate to actions that must be taken. • Scores tend to be high (80 out of 100) and flatter.
Verbal scales	• Easy to understand. • Appropriate words make the results more actionable. • Easy to administer.	• Tedious when read out many times. • Adjectives may not translate exactly in multi-country studies. • Scale may be limited to a few levels.

A typical question using numeric rating scales could be as follows:

Q I would now like you to tell me what you think of XYZ Ltd for the quality of its products. Please give me a score out of 5 where 5 is excellent and 1 is very poor. Now, how would you rate it for the reliability of its deliveries on the same scale. And, finally, how would you rate it for its stock availability, again on a scale from 1 to 5 where 5 is excellent? Note: Score 6 for don't know and 7 for no answer/not stated.

Quality of products	1	2	3	4	5	6	7
Reliability of deliveries	1	2	3	4	5	6	7
Stock availability	1	2	3	4	5	6	7

In this particular example a scale from 1 to 5 has been used. The narrower the limits of the scale, the less discrimination required on the part of the respondent and therefore the easier it is to answer the question. Scales from 1 to 10 need a bit more consideration on the part of the respondent but they are perfectly acceptable and are widely used in market research. Some researchers like scales from 1 to 7 on the grounds that they make people think and perhaps increase the consideration.

Others prefer scales from 1 to 4 as they do not have a mid-point and so force a polarized result and prevent a clustering in the middle ground. On completion of the survey, the results from a question using a 5 point scale are tabulated and show the strengths and weaknesses of different suppliers (see Table 8.4).

Table 8.4   *Rating of companies (where 5 is excellent and 1 is very poor)*

Company	Quality of products	Reliability of deliveries	Stock	Number of respondents
A	4.3	4.0	3.1	62
B	4.2	4.0	3.3	50
C	4.0	3.6	3.6	45
D	3.7	3.5	4.0	37
Average	4.1	3.8	3.5	85

The distance between these companies may be easier to read if the scores are expressed out of 100. Of course, in such a table, the lowest score would be 10 not 0 (see Table 8.5).

Table 8.5   *Rating of companies (where 100 is excellent and 10 is very poor)*

Company	Quality of products	Reliability of deliveries	Stock	Number of respondents
A	86	80	62	62
B	84	80	66	50
C	80	72	72	45
D	74	70	80	37
Average	82	76	70	85

Verbal scales

Verbal scales have the advantage of 'meaning' something to a respondent. The words used in the scale may be more easily interpreted than simply using a score out of 5 or 10. The disadvantage of verbal scales is that they need to be read out to respondents (or shown to them on a card) and this takes time. In this respect it is easier to administer numeric ratings because once the concept has been explained to a respondent they can quickly give answers to a whole series of issues without the necessity of repeating the scale.

Likert scales

A typical verbal rating scale is called a Likert scale (after its originator). In a Likert scale respondents are asked to agree or disagree with a series of statements. There are usually five points on the scale. An advantage of such a scale is that the respondent can readily give answers to many statements using the same range of adjectives.

Q   I will now read out some statements that could refer to XYZ Ltd and I would like you to tell me if you agree strongly with the statement, agree slightly, neither agree nor disagree, disagree slightly or disagree strongly. The first statement is 'XYZ Ltd's products never break down'. Note: Read all statements. Circle 6 for don't know and 7 for no answer/not stated.

	Agree strongly	Agree slightly	Neither agree nor disagree	Disagree slightly	Disagree strongly	Don't know	Not stated
XYZ Ltd's products never break down	1	2	3	4	5	6	7
XYZ Ltd always delivers on time	1	2	3	4	5	6	7
XYZ Ltd always has stock available	1	2	3	4	5	6	7

Variable scales do not need to have number codes. They could be ungraded, using a line without divisions or marks, where respondents mark their feeling with a cross at an appropriate point. Clearly this type of scale is appropriate only for self-completion questionnaires.

Q   Please place a cross on the line to indicate if you agree or disagree that XYZ Ltd offers a full range of products.

Offers a full range of products   Disagree ●————————● Agree

Promptly resolves credit problems   Disagree ●————————● Agree

Semantic differential scales

A variation on this type of scale is a bi-polar scale in which pairs of opposite adjectives or adjectival phrases sit at each end. In the following example, adjectives have been chosen to represent each end of the spectrum.

Q   I would like to read out some words which describe people. You have to choose one word from each pair to describe yourself. If you think neither fits, you must choose the one which is closest. Would you say that you are:

Introverted	1	or extroverted	2
Traditionalist	1	or an experimenter	2
Stylish	1	or fashionable	2
Ambitious	1	or content	2
Independent	1	or gregarious	2
Intellectual	1	or practical	2

Perhaps the most common of the verbal rating scales have five points using two positive positions, two negative positions and one in the centre.

Q   Thinking of the range of products offered by XYZ Ltd, would you say it is very good, quite good, neither good nor poor, quite poor or very poor?
    And now would you say that its policy on the prompt resolution of credit problems is very good, quite good, neither good nor poor, quite poor or very poor?

	Very good	Quite good	Neither good nor poor	Quite poor	Very poor	Don't know	Not stated
Range of products	1	2	3	4	5	6	7
Resolution of credit problems	1	2	3	4	5	6	7

Verbal rating scales need not be read out. Indeed, they may work best in self-completion mode as they can quickly be scanned by eye and the answers circled or ticked without the tedium of reading out all the scales.

SIMALTO scales

SIMALTO is an acronym for simultaneous multi-attribute level trade-off (not many people know or can remember that!). It is a scale with specific positions that move in a hierarchy that may be of unequal steps but that mean something to both customers and to the supplier. As a result, the respondents can say what they want in terms of service levels (or product performance) and what they think they are getting at the present. Built into the SIMALTO question is the opportunity to say how much would be paid for an improvement by spending points in a trade-off question. An example follows:

Q   The table below shows a number of levels of service that you might receive from a supplier of widgets. Look through the table and write U in a box on each row to show what would be an unacceptable level of service.

   Looking at the same scales would you now indicate with an I the ideal level of service you would like to receive.

   I want you to think about XYZ Ltd and put an R in one box on each row to show what level of service you receive at the present from this company.

   Imagine that you had 20 points to spend to increase the service that XYZ Ltd provides to you. The figures in each box show how much it costs to move from one level of service to another. Now draw arrows from the level of service you receive at the present to the level you would like to receive from XYZ Ltd, adding up the points in each box until all your 20 points are spent.

Range of products	Always out of stock whenever I call. 0	Has what I want in stock 50 percent of the time. 5	Has what I want in stock 80 per cent of the time. 7	Always everything I want in stock. 15
Resolution of credit issues	Takes forever to solve credit problems and they always win. 0	Credit issues take a long time to solve but they get there in the end. 3	Credit issues get dealt with in an efficient but brusque manner. 7	They have a fair and fast resolution to credit issues. 9
Etc				
Etc				

Determining importance

Rating scales can also be used to assess the important of issues.

Q   I will now read a list of factors that some people have said influence their choice of a brand and I would like you to tell me how important this factor is to you. Read all factors. Circle 6 for don't know and 7 for no answer/not stated.

	Very important	Quite important	Neither important nor unimportant	Not very important	Not at all important	Don't know	Not stated
The products never break down	1	2	3	4	5	6	7
Delivery is always on time	1	2	3	4	5	6	7
Stock is always available	1	2	3	4	5	6	7

Though quite simple to administer, such a question may generate responses that indicate *all* the issues are important and so fail to discriminate between the key drivers. Attempts to achieve more discrimination include trade-off questions. These vary from points spend (as in the SIMALTO example shown above) through to simple ranking. In typical ranking questions the respondent is presented with a list and asked to state which is most important, which is second most important and so on. It becomes difficult for respondents to rank factors beyond the first three levels of importance.

Q   I will now read out some factors that other people have said are important influences on their choice of supplier. After I have read out the list would you tell me which is the most important factor in influencing your choice of supplier? Read list. Rotate start. Tick start.

   And what would be the second most important factor? And what would be the third most important factor? Obtain rank for three factors.

Factor	Rank
Products never break down	_____
Delivery is always on time	_____
Stock is always available	_____
Credit of three months	_____
Technical help-line	_____
Guarantee of two years	_____

In a telephone interview, it is necessary to limit the list to half a dozen or so factors. In a face-to-face interview it is possible to use a show card and so have a longer listing. However, even in a longer list, respondents find it difficult to rank more than three to five factors.

   Another approach is to use a points spend, as in the SIMALTO trade-off.

Q   I will now read out some factors that other people have said are important influences on their choice of supplier. To measure how important you think they are I would like you to allocate 10 points across these factors. The more important the factor, the more points you should give it. But the more you give to one factor, the fewer there are to give to the others. First I will read the list. Read list. Rotate start. Tick start. Now, how would you like to spend your 10 points?

Factor	Points out of 10
Products never break down	_____
Delivery is always on time	_____
Stock is always available	_____
Credit of three months	_____
Technical help-line	_____
Guarantee of two years	_____

CLASSIFICATION QUESTIONS

The third group of questions is those used to *classify* the information once it has been collected. Classification questions check that the correct quota of people or companies has been interviewed and are used to make comparisons between different groups of respondents. Most classification questions are behavioural (factual).

Typical classification questions are used to build a profile of respondents by finding out their age, sex, social class, where they live, their marital status, the type of houses they live in, the number of people in their family etc.

A number of standard classification questions crop up constantly in market research surveys. These are:

● *Sex.* There can be no classifications other than male and female.
● *Household status.* Most researchers classify adults into three groups which are:
  – Head of household ☐
  – Housewife ☐
  – Other adult ☐
● *Marital status.* This is usually asked by simply saying 'Are you…'
  – Single ☐
  – Married ☐
  – Widowed ☐
  – Divorced ☐
  – Separated ☐

● *Socio-economic Grade (SEG).* This is a classification peculiar to UK market researchers in which respondents are pigeon-holed according to the occupation of the head of the household. Thus, it combines the attributes of income, education and work status. In addition to social grades, researchers sometimes classify respondents by income group or lifestyle. In summary the socio-economic grades are:

A – higher managerial, administrative or professional
B – intermediate managerial, administrative or professional
C1 – supervisory, clerical, junior administrative or professional
C2 – skilled manual workers
D – semi-skilled and unskilled manual workers
E – state pensioners, widows, casual and lowest grade workers.

For most practical purposes these can be reduced to just four:
AB ☐
C1 ☐
C2 ☐
DE ☐

● *Industrial occupation.* Researchers often condense the many divisions of the Standard Industrial Classification (referred to usually as SIC) into more convenient and broader groupings. These could be as simple as:

Primary (farming, forestry, fishing, quarrying, etc) ☐
Manufacturing ☐
Retailing and distribution ☐
Service industries ☐
Public service ☐
Armed forces ☐
Education ☐
Professions (doctors, dentists, architects, etc) ☐

In surveys of the general public, it may be relevant to establish the level of employment of the respondent. For example:

Working full-time (over 30 hours a week) ☐
Working part-time (8–30 hours a week) ☐
Housewife (full-time at home) ☐
Student (full-time) ☐
Retired ☐
Temporarily unemployed (but seeking work) ☐

Permanently unemployed (eg chronically sick,
   independent means, etc) ☐

● *Number of employees.* The size of the firm in which the respondent works can be classified according to the number of employees:

0–9 ☐
10–24 ☐
25–99 ☐
100–249 ☐
250+ ☐

● *Location.* Depending on the scope of the survey, this can be according to one of the standard regions of the UK, ITV reception areas or even a simple split into North, Midlands and South.

● *Geodemographic.* People can be classified according to the type of neighbourhood in which they live (see also Chapter 4). These are often referred to as 'Acorn' or 'Pinpoint' classifications after the market research companies which devized them. They group people into neighbourhood types such as:

Agricultural areas ☐
Modern family houses, higher incomes ☐
Older houses of intermediate status ☐
Poor quality older terraced housing ☐
Better-off council estates ☐
Less well-off council estates ☐
Poorest council estates ☐
Multi-racial areas ☐
High status, non-family areas ☐
Affluent suburban housing ☐
Better-off retirement areas ☐
Unclassified ☐

PRINCIPLES OF QUESTIONNAIRE DESIGN

If questionnaires fail it is usually because they are dashed off with insufficient thought. Questions are missed out, badly constructed, too long, complicated and sometimes unintelligible. Questionnaire design is a refining process in which a rough draft is eventually converted to a precise and formatted document. It would be unusual (and dangerous) to design a questionnaire without at least three edits.

Ten rules guide the design of the questionnaire:

1. **Think about the objectives of the survey:** at the outset, the researcher should sit down with the research plan (the statement of what is to be achieved and the methods that will be involved) and list the objectives of the study. This will ensure that the survey covers all the necessary points and it will generate a rough topic list which eventually will be converted into more explicit questions.

2. **Think about how the interview will be carried out:** the way that the interview will be carried out will have a bearing on the framing of the questions. For example, open-ended questions usually result in poor replies in self-completion questionnaires.

3. **Think about the 'boiler plate' information and the introduction:** every questionnaire needs 'boiler plate' or standard information such as the name and address of the respondent, the date of the interview and the name of the interviewer. Write an introduction at the very beginning of the questionnaire. Make sure that it gives the interview a purpose as cooperation is helped if people feel that the interview has a legitimate purpose.

4. **Think about the design:** the questionnaire should make effective use of white space so that it is clear and easy to read. Questions and response options should be laid out in a standard format and if the questionnaire is to be administered on a doorstep in winter, the typeface should be large enough to read. Where appropriate, there should be ample space to write in open-ended comments.

5. **Think about the respondent:** questions should flow easily from one to another and be grouped into topics in a logical sequence.

7. **Think about the types of questions:** texture in the interview can be achieved by incorporating different styles of questions. The researcher can choose from open-ended questions, closed questions and scales.

8. **Think about the possible answers at the same time as thinking about the questions:** the whole purpose of a question is to derive answers and so it is essential that some thought is given to these since, in turn, they may influence the shape of the question. For example, it is no good asking wholesalers of vehicle clutches how many they sell each year if their time horizon is a week or a month.

9. **Think about how the data will be processed:** a coding system should be used which suits the way in which it will be analyzed – for example, on a

spreadsheet or using proprietary market research software. In a survey involving more than 30 respondents, analyzing the free-ranging (open-ended) responses is laborious and thought should be given to using pre-coded answers.

10. **Think about interviewer instructions:** questionnaires are usually administered by someone other than their designer and so the interviewer (or the respondent in the case of self-completion questionnaires) needs clear guidance in what to do at every stage. These instructions need to be differentiated from the text either by capitalized, emboldened or underlined type.

THINGS TO BEWARE OF WHEN DESIGNING QUESTIONNAIRES

Below are some tips on what to do and not to do when designing questionnaires:

- *Ensure that questions are without bias.* Questions should not be worded in such a way as to lead the respondent into the answer.
- *Make the questions as simple as possible.* Questions should not only be short, they should also be simple. Those which include multiple ideas or two questions in one will confuse and be misunderstood.
- *Make the questions very specific.* Notwithstanding the importance of brevity and simplicity, there are occasions when it is advisable to lengthen the question by adding memory cues. For example, it is good practice to be specific with time periods.
- *Avoid jargon or shorthand.* It cannot be assumed that respondents will understand words commonly used by researchers. Trade jargon, acronyms and initials should be avoided unless they are in everyday use.
- *Steer clear of sophisticated or uncommon words.* A questionnaire is not a place to score literary points so only use words in common speech. Colloquialisms are acceptable if they will be understood by everybody (some are highly regional).
- *Avoid ambiguous words.* Words such as 'usually' or 'frequently' have no specific meaning and need qualifying.
- *Avoid questions with a negative in them.* Questions are more difficult to understand if they are asked in a negative sense. It is better to say 'Do you ever…?', as opposed to 'Do you never…?
- *Avoid hypothetical questions.* It is difficult to answer questions on imaginary situations. Answers may be given but they cannot necessarily be trusted.
- *Do not use words which could be misheard.* This is especially important when the interview is administered over the telephone. On the telephone, 'what is your opinion of sects?' could yield interesting but not necessarily relevant answers.

- *Desensitize questions by using response bands.* For questions which ask people their age or companies their turnover it is best to offer a range of response bands. This softens the question by indicating that a broad answer is acceptable. Since the data will almost certainly be grouped into bands at the analysis stage, it may as well be collected in this way.

- *Ensure that fixed responses do not overlap.* The categories that are used in fixed response questions should be sequential and not overlap otherwise some answers will be caught on the cusp.

- *Allow for 'others' in fixed response questions.* Pre-coded answers should always allow for a response other than those listed. It should be noted that these 'other' responses will always be under-recorded.

GETTING THE QUESTIONNAIRE TO WORK

Before giving the questionnaire to the interviewing team, the researcher should at the very least read it out aloud. Better still, ask a colleague to play the role of respondent. Bringing the questionnaire into the spoken word exposes weaknesses in wording or phraseology and highlights inconsistencies.

If someone else will be carrying out the data processing, they should be given a draft of the questionnaire to see if they can spot any coding or routing problems.

Finally, the questionnaire is ready for piloting. In many surveys, half a dozen to 20 interviews will be sufficient to establish if the questionnaire really does work.

POSTAL QUESTIONNAIRES

A questionnaire with a poor layout and some inadequacies can still be made to work if it is administered by a skilled interviewer. However, a questionnaire which arrives through the post has to stand alone with no one at hand to provide advice, answer queries or ensure that the respondent understands what really was meant by the question. Postal questionnaires must be as near perfect as possible with clear questions, clear instructions and adequate room to write in answers.

Postal questionnaires should begin with easy questions. Once respondents have answered the first question there is a good chance that they will complete the rest. A difficult question at an early juncture is off-putting.

Ideally, the questionnaire should be desktop published and of good print quality. The more professional the production, the greater will be the response. The use of colour, an attractive layout and interesting use of white space will all encourage replies. (There are exceptions and questionnaires that look as if they have been knocked up on an old typewriter have been known to yield high responses because they look hand crafted and not part of a mass mailing.)

We have emphasized that successful postal questionnaires should be easy to complete. Wherever possible questions should have pre-coded answers simply requiring a box to be ticked or a number circled. Pre-coded questions are suited to postal questionnaires as they save the respondent time in writing in answers. Scalar questions are highly applicable to postal questionnaires because they can be completed quickly by ticking boxes.

The researcher needs to have a good background in a subject to design a workable self-completion questionnaire with sensible pre-coded answers. It would not be possible to construct the following question without some previous knowledge of who makes pipe lagging products (and this question is as complicated as should be used in a postal questionnaire).

Which of the companies listed below would you say has the widest range of pipe lagging products? TICK <u>ONE COMPANY ONLY</u> IN COLUMN A.

And which company has the smallest range? TICK<u> ONE COMPANY ONLY</u> IN COLUMN B.

	Column A **Widest Range**	Column B **Smallest Range**
Jiffy	☐	☐
Climatube	☐	☐
Jetlag	☐	☐
Tublite	☐	☐
Armaflex	☐	☐
Insultube	☐	☐
Don't know	☐	☐

Open-ended questions are badly answered in postal surveys. Questions that ask for free-ranging explanations get inadequate (and often illegible) answers. Typical responses are, 'because it is good', 'we have always bought it', 'it does its job' etc and there is no opportunity to find out why it is good, why they always buy it or in what way it does its job.

Nor is it possible to ask complicated questions in postal questionnaires. It is no good asking builders' merchants for a detailed breakdown of their purchases of pipe lagging products over the last year because such information will almost certainly need respondents to dig in their files. Such effort cannot be assumed from the respondents. The researcher stands some chance if lists of pre-coded answers are provided as this indicates to respondents that an approximation is all that is required.

Finally, about how much did your company spend on all types of pipe lagging in the last complete year?

Under £1,000	☐
£1,000 to £20,000	☐
£20,001 to £50,000	☐
Over £50,000	☐

In a postal questionnaire it is not possible to disclose information in a controlled fashion as in a telephone or visit interview because respondents probably will read ahead and become aware of forthcoming questions. In an administered questionnaire, the name of the sponsor may be disclosed towards the end, sometimes with special questions to find out more about attitudes to that company. Such unveiling cannot be used in a self-completion questionnaire.

Complicated routing must be avoided in postal surveys. Skipping questions creates confusion and leads to errors in completion.

Everything should make it easy for respondents to reply. A strong relationship between the person or organization sponsoring the research and the respondent will generate a high response. Where there is no relationship between the researcher and respondent the response will be very low. Table 8.6 provides an indication of response rates for different postal surveys. A reply paid envelope will raise response rates. Reply envelopes, affixed with stamps, yield a higher response than those using a business reply service as respondents hate throwing away unused stamps and steaming them off is too much trouble.

Postal surveys that offer anonymity usually have a higher response than those where respondents must identify themselves, although much depends on the circumstances. In many business-to-business surveys respondents may be happy to be identified as long as they are confident that the research is bona fide and not a surreptitious attempt at selling. So too, householders like to be assured that their names will not be sold on to a mailing house and that there will be no sales pressure to follow.

The cover letter accompanying the questionnaire is as important as the questionnaire itself. Wherever possible the name of the respondent should be used on the letter to create a sense of ownership and build the relationship which is crucial to a

Table 8.6 *Indications of response to different postal surveys*

Sponsor	Nature of relationship	Expected response rate from postal survey (per cent)
Survey of attitudes to financial services by insurance company.	Random sample of public therefore no strong relationships.	5 per cent – perhaps 10–15 per cent with a good incentive.
Survey of attitudes to a specific brand of truck.	Sample of operators of the brand of truck being researched.	25 per cent rising to 50 per cent if preceded by a phone call.
Survey of new car buyers.	Sample of people who have bought a new car in past six months.	50 per cent with no or small incentive.
Survey by new house buyers.	Sample of people who have moved into new house in past six months.	70 per cent with no or small incentive.

good response. Some words of caution. Unless there is absolute certainty about the name and position of the respondent, it is better to address the letter to 'The householder' or, in the case of business-to-business surveys, a functional title such as 'The Production Manager' or 'The Office Equipment Buyer'. Misspelling a name or using the name of someone who has long since left the company is worse than having no name at all.

Rules for writing good cover letters are as follows:

● Explain the purpose of the survey and why the respondent has been selected.
● Give the respondent a reason for wanting to complete the questionnaire – offer a benefit of one kind or another.
● Give clear instructions as to what should be done – how to fill it in, and how to send it back.
● Give an assurance that completing the questionnaire is easy.
● If it is possible to do so, give an assurance that replies will be confidential.
● Thank the respondent.

An example of a cover letter for a postal survey together with a sample self-completion questionnaire (which was handed out, not posted) is provided on the following pages.

 *Sheffield Hallam University*

student eXperience SURVEY 2000

HOW TO COMPLETE THIS QUESTIONNAIRE

This questionnaire is made up of two sections. The first section is about your experience as a student here at Sheffield Hallam University. The second section asks questions about you, which will help us to classify the information you have given us.

This questionnaire is designed for all Undergraduate and Postgraduate students enrolled on full and part time courses at SHU. You will find some questions are for certain groups of students (eg. Postgraduate students/part time students), this is indicated on the question. Please answer all the questions unless you are asked not to. If you feel the question is not relevant to you, please tick the **'not applicable'** box.

We are asking you to rate how satisfied you are with each of the issues by circling a number on the **SATISFACTION** scale, where:

7	**=**	**totally satisfied**
4	**=**	**neither satisfied nor dissatisfied**
I	**=**	**totally dissatisfied**

and then please also rate how important each of the issues are to you, by circling a number in the **IMPORTANCE** scale, where:

7	**=**	**very important**
4	**=**	**neither important nor unimportant**
I	**=**	**not at all important.**

For example:

Please rate the extent to which you are satisfied with the following in relation to public transport to and from University and then rate how important it is to you

		SATISFACTION	**IMPORTANCE**
Not applicable		Totally Dissatisfied — Neither Nor — Totally Satisfied	Not at all Important — Neither Nor — Very Important
a) ☐₁	convenience of public transport to and from University	I 2 ③ 4 5 6 7	I 2 3 4 ⑤ 6 7
b) ☑₂	cost of public transport to and from University	I 2 3 4 5 6 7	I 2 3 4 5 6 7
c) ☐₃	punctuality of public transport to and from University	I 2 3 4 ⑤ 6 7	I 2 3 4 5 6 ⑦

It should take you about 20 minutes to complete the whole questionnaire. This is **YOUR** chance to tell us what we do well and how we could improve.

Please note:
Ignore all the small numbers in brackets as these are for coding and analysis purposes only.

Please can we assure you that **ALL** the information in this survey is **confidential** and completely anonymous in accordance with the Market Research Society Code of Conduct and the requirements of the Data Protection Act.

Thank you for taking part and giving your time to complete this survey.

student eXperience

SECTION I *This section looks at your experience of studying at Sheffield Hallam University.*

If you feel there are any questions which are not relevant to you, please tick the 'not applicable' box.

1. YOUR PROGRAMME OF STUDY

Year of your course: I ☐₁ 2 ☐₂ 3 ☐₃ 4 ☐₄ 5 ☐₅ 6 or more ☐₆ (6)

Type of course: Full time ☐₁ Part time ☐₂ (7)

Does your work involve a work placement? Yes ☐₁ No ☐₂ (8)

The award you are studying for: (9)

Foundation ☐₁	BEng. ☐₄	BSc ☐₇	BEd ☐₀
HND/HNC ☐₂	BA ☐₅	MSc ☐₈	MA ☐ₓ
PGD/PDC ☐₃	PG Credit ☐₆	MBA ☐₉	Other ☐ᵥ *(please state)* _____

Title of your course: _____ (10-11)

On average, how many days per week do you come into the University? *(please circle)*

0   I   2   3   4   5   6   7   (12)

Please rate the extent to which you are satisfied with the following issues in relation to your <u>programme of study</u> <u>(course)</u>, and then rate how important it is <u>to you</u>.

(12) **Course Organisation**

	SATISFACTION	IMPORTANCE
Not applicable	Totally Dissatisfied — Neither Nor — Totally Satisfied	Not at all Important — Neither Nor — Very Important
a) ☐₁ course induction	I 2 3 4 5 6 7 (13)	I 2 3 4 5 6 7 (23)
b) ☐₂ information about your course (eg. course handbook/modules)	I 2 3 4 5 6 7 (14)	I 2 3 4 5 6 7 (24)
c) ☐₃ spread of workload across the academic year	I 2 3 4 5 6 7 (15)	I 2 3 4 5 6 7 (25)
d) ☐₄ amount of lecture time you have	I 2 3 4 5 6 7 (16)	I 2 3 4 5 6 7 (26)
e) ☐₅ amount of seminar/tutorial time you have	I 2 3 4 5 6 7 (17)	I 2 3 4 5 6 7 (27)
f) ☐₆ amount of workshop/practical time you have	I 2 3 4 5 6 7 (18)	I 2 3 4 5 6 7 (28)
g) ☐₇ way the timetable is spread across the week	I 2 3 4 5 6 7 (19)	I 2 3 4 5 6 7 (29)
h) ☐₈ notification of alterations to the timetable	I 2 3 4 5 6 7 (20)	I 2 3 4 5 6 7 (30)
i) ☐₉ attention given to students' views on your course	I 2 3 4 5 6 7 (21)	I 2 3 4 5 6 7 (31)
j) ☐₀ how you are kept in touch with what is happening on your course	I 2 3 4 5 6 7 (22)	I 2 3 4 5 6 7 (32)

(33) **Course Content**

	SATISFACTION	IMPORTANCE
Not applicable	Totally Dissatisfied — Neither Nor — Totally Satisfied	Not at all Important — Neither Nor — Very Important
a) ☐₁ your awareness of the course aims	I 2 3 4 5 6 7 (34)	I 2 3 4 5 6 7 (43)
b) ☐₂ content of your course	I 2 3 4 5 6 7 (35)	I 2 3 4 5 6 7 (44)
c) ☐₃ amount of choice and flexibility you have within your course	I 2 3 4 5 6 7 (36)	I 2 3 4 5 6 7 (45)
d) ☐₄ opportunity for work related placements	I 2 3 4 5 6 7 (37)	I 2 3 4 5 6 7 (46)
e) ☐₅ availability of placements	I 2 3 4 5 6 7 (38)	I 2 3 4 5 6 7 (47)
f) ☐₆ extent to which your course motivates you to study	I 2 3 4 5 6 7 (39)	I 2 3 4 5 6 7 (48)
g) ☐₇ extent to which your course meets your needs	I 2 3 4 5 6 7 (40)	I 2 3 4 5 6 7 (49)
h) ☐₈ extent to which your course prepares you for work	I 2 3 4 5 6 7 (41)	I 2 3 4 5 6 7 (50)
i) ☐₉ professional recognition of your course	I 2 3 4 5 6 7 (42)	I 2 3 4 5 6 7 (51)

student eXperience

If you feel there are any questions which are not relevant to you, please tick the 'not applicable' box.   **CARD 2**

(6) The Teaching Staff

		SATISFACTION	IMPORTANCE
Not applicable		Totally Dissatisfied — Neither Nor — Totally Satisfied	Not at all Important — Neither Nor — Very Important

a) ☐1 reliability of the academic staff (ie. don't cancel classes, punctuality) .... 1 2 3 4 5 6 7 (7) 1 2 3 4 5 6 7 (17)
b) ☐2 teaching ability of the academic staff .... 1 2 3 4 5 6 7 (8) 1 2 3 4 5 6 7 (18)
c) ☐3 knowledge and skills base of the academic staff .... 1 2 3 4 5 6 7 (9) 1 2 3 4 5 6 7 (19)
d) ☐4 appropriateness of learning and teaching methods used ..... 1 2 3 4 5 6 7 (10) 1 2 3 4 5 6 7 (20)
e) ☐5 availability of teaching support staff (eg. technicians) .... 1 2 3 4 5 6 7 (11) 1 2 3 4 5 6 7 (21)
f) ☐6 helpfulness of the teaching staff .... 1 2 3 4 5 6 7 (12) 1 2 3 4 5 6 7 (22)
g) ☐7 supervision of your dissertation .... 1 2 3 4 5 6 7 (13) 1 2 3 4 5 6 7 (23)

(21) Assessment

a) ☐1 information about when and where assessments take place .. 1 2 3 4 5 6 7 (22) 1 2 3 4 5 6 7 (30)
b) ☐2 flexibility of dates for handing in assessments .... 1 2 3 4 5 6 7 (23) 1 2 3 4 5 6 7 (31)
c) ☐3 information about assessment criteria .... 1 2 3 4 5 6 7 (24) 1 2 3 4 5 6 7 (32)
d) ☐4 consistency of marking standards .... 1 2 3 4 5 6 7 (25) 1 2 3 4 5 6 7 (33)
e) ☐5 methods of assessment used (eg. essay, exam, practical, etc.) . 1 2 3 4 5 6 7 (26) 1 2 3 4 5 6 7 (34)
f) ☐6 speed of return of course/assessment results .... 1 2 3 4 5 6 7 (27) 1 2 3 4 5 6 7 (35)
g) ☐7 usefulness of lecturers' feedback about assessments .... 1 2 3 4 5 6 7 (28) 1 2 3 4 5 6 7 (36)
h) ☐8 information about dissertation submission .... 1 2 3 4 5 6 7 (29) 1 2 3 4 5 6 7 (37)

(38) The Teaching Resources

a) ☐1 provision of course material (ie. handouts, technology based material) .... 1 2 3 4 5 6 7 (39) 1 2 3 4 5 6 7 (44)
b) ☐2 equipment available for learning and teaching purposes ..... 1 2 3 4 5 6 7 (40) 1 2 3 4 5 6 7 (45)
c) ☐3 state of the teaching rooms you use .... 1 2 3 4 5 6 7 (41) 1 2 3 4 5 6 7 (46)
d) ☐4 size of the teaching rooms for the size of group .... 1 2 3 4 5 6 7 (42) 1 2 3 4 5 6 7 (47)
e) ☐5 extra workspace (rooms) available to you eg. for group work . 1 2 3 4 5 6 7 (43) 1 2 3 4 5 6 7 (48)

(49) Academic and Pastoral Support

a) ☐1 your access to academic staff for assistance outside lecture time .... 1 2 3 4 5 6 7 (50) 1 2 3 4 5 6 7 (58)
b) ☐2 personal guidance and support from academic staff .... 1 2 3 4 5 6 7 (51) 1 2 3 4 5 6 7 (59)
c) ☐3 level of support whilst out on placements .... 1 2 3 4 5 6 7 (52) 1 2 3 4 5 6 7 (60)
d) ☐4 support for learning disabilities (eg. dyslexia) .... 1 2 3 4 5 6 7 (53) 1 2 3 4 5 6 7 (61)
e) ☐5 support for disabled students (eg. physical disabilities) .... 1 2 3 4 5 6 7 (54) 1 2 3 4 5 6 7 (62)
f) ☐6 assistance from the Learning Support Unit .... 1 2 3 4 5 6 7 (55) 1 2 3 4 5 6 7 (63)
g) ☐7 assistance from the English Language Support Unit .... 1 2 3 4 5 6 7 (56) 1 2 3 4 5 6 7 (64)
h) ☐8 support for part time students .... 1 2 3 4 5 6 7 (57) 1 2 3 4 5 6 7 (65)

2. STUDENT ADMINISTRATION

Please rate the extent to which you are satisfied with the following issues in relation to <u>student administration</u> both before and since you arrived at the University, and then rate how important it is <u>to you</u>.

(12) Before you arrived at the University

		SATISFACTION	IMPORTANCE
Not applicable		Totally Dissatisfied — Neither Nor — Totally Satisfied	Not at all Important — Neither Nor — Very Important

a) ☐1 open day/postgraduate recruitment fair .... 1 2 3 4 5 6 7 (67) 1 2 3 4 5 6 7 (73)
b) ☐2 information contained in the prospectus .... 1 2 3 4 5 6 7 (68) 1 2 3 4 5 6 7 (74)
c) ☐3 course information you received before starting at SHU (eg. timetables) .... 1 2 3 4 5 6 7 (69) 1 2 3 4 5 6 7 (75)
d) ☐4 admission process .... 1 2 3 4 5 6 7 (70) 1 2 3 4 5 6 7 (76)
e) ☐5 information through clearing .... 1 2 3 4 5 6 7 (71) 1 2 3 4 5 6 7 (77)
f) ☐6 availability of courses delivered part time at SHU .... 1 2 3 4 5 6 7 (72) 1 2 3 4 5 6 7 (78)

student experience

If you feel there are any questions which are not relevant to you, please tick the 'not applicable' box. **CARD 3**

(6) **Student Administration since you arrived at University**   **SATISFACTION**   **IMPORTANCE**

		Totally Dissatisfied			Neither Nor			Totally Satisfied			Not at all Important			Neither Nor			Very Important
Not applicable

a) ☐1 student handbook .... I 2 3 4 5 6 7 (7) .... I 2 3 4 5 6 7 (17)
b) ☐2 efficiency of the enrolment process .... I 2 3 4 5 6 7 (8) .... I 2 3 4 5 6 7 (18)
c) ☐3 timeliness and accuracy of invoicing for your course fee ..... I 2 3 4 5 6 7 (9) .... I 2 3 4 5 6 7 (19)
d) ☐4 method of payment of the course fees (ie. instalments) ..... I 2 3 4 5 6 7 (10) ...... I 2 3 4 5 6 7 (20)
e) ☐5 handling of your enquiries by the finance department .... I 2 3 4 5 6 7 (11) ...... I 2 3 4 5 6 7 (21)
f) ☐6 administration of student loans .... I 2 3 4 5 6 7 (12) ...... I 2 3 4 5 6 7 (22)
g) ☐7 availability of administration staff .... I 2 3 4 5 6 7 (13) ...... I 2 3 4 5 6 7 (23)
h) ☐8 handling of general enquiries within your school/department . I 2 3 4 5 6 7 (14) ...... I 2 3 4 5 6 7 (24)
i) ☐9 procedure for handing in assignments/assessments .... I 2 3 4 5 6 7 (15) ...... I 2 3 4 5 6 7 (25)
j) ☐0 complaints and appeals procedure .... I 2 3 4 5 6 7 (16) ...... I 2 3 4 5 6 7 (26)

3. COMPUTING FACILITIES

Which <u>University</u> computing facilities do you **MOST** frequently use?

(Please tick only ONE box. If you use more than one facility, please tick the area you want to rate in the following questions.)

City Campus	(27)	**Collegiate Crescent Campus**	(28)	**Psalter Lane Campus**	
Adsetts Centre - Level 2	☐1	Adsetts Centre - Level 2	☐1	A Block CIS Rooms	☐6
Adsetts Centre - Level 3	☐2	Learning Centre - Ground Floor	☐2	B Block CIS Rooms	☐7
Adsetts Centre - Level 5	☐3	Learning Centre - First Floor	☐3	Learning Centre	☐8
Adsetts Centre - Level 6	☐4				
Owen Building - Floor 3	☐5				
Owen Building - Floor 5	☐6	**Other Usage**			
Harmer Building - Floor 2	☐7	Other SHU facilities	☐4	(state location) _____	(29)
Eric Mensforth Building - Floor 2	☐8	I do not use any of these	☐5		
Surrey Building - Floor 2	☐9				
Howard Building - Floor 2	☐0				

Do you have access to a computer at home?   Yes ☐1   No ☐2   (30)
If yes,   is it connected to the Internet?   Yes ☐1   No ☐2   (31)
          is it a portable computer?   Yes ☐1   No ☐2   (32)

Please rate the extent to which you are satisfied with the following issues in relation to the <u>University computing facilities</u> you most frequently use, and then rate how important it is <u>to you</u>.

(33)   **SATISFACTION**   **IMPORTANCE**

| | Totally Dissatisfied | | Neither Nor | | Totally Satisfied | | Not at all Important | | Neither Nor | | Very Important |
Not applicable

a) ☐1 availability of computers at a time you want to use them .... I 2 3 4 5 6 7 (35) .... I 2 3 4 5 6 7 (48)
b) ☐2 how 'up to date' the computers are .... I 2 3 4 5 6 7 (36) .... I 2 3 4 5 6 7 (49)
c) ☐3 range of software packages available on the computers ...... I 2 3 4 5 6 7 (37) .... I 2 3 4 5 6 7 (50)
d) ☐4 training in the use of computers .... I 2 3 4 5 6 7 (38) .... I 2 3 4 5 6 7 (51)
e) ☐5 helpfulness of the computing support staff .... I 2 3 4 5 6 7 (39) .... I 2 3 4 5 6 7 (52)
f) ☐6 reliability of the computer network .... I 2 3 4 5 6 7 (40) .... I 2 3 4 5 6 7 (53)
g) ☐7 availability of internet/email services .... I 2 3 4 5 6 7 (41) .... I 2 3 4 5 6 7 (54)
h) ☐8 monitoring of the use of computers for legitimate work ..... I 2 3 4 5 6 7 (42) .... I 2 3 4 5 6 7 (55)
i) ☐9 availability of printing facilities .... I 2 3 4 5 6 7 (43) .... I 2 3 4 5 6 7 (56)
j) ☐10 remote (off site) log-on facility .... I 2 3 4 5 6 7 (44) .... I 2 3 4 5 6 7 (57)
k) ☐11 your access to web based learning materials .... I 2 3 4 5 6 7 (45) .... I 2 3 4 5 6 7 (58)
l) ☐12 postgraduate web page .... I 2 3 4 5 6 7 (46) .... I 2 3 4 5 6 7 (59)
m) ☐13 SHU web pages .... I 2 3 4 5 6 7 (47) .... I 2 3 4 5 6 7 (60)

student
eXperience

If you feel there are any questions which are not relevant to you, please tick the 'not applicable' box. **CARD 4**

4. THE LEARNING CENTRE (LIBRARY)

Which learning centre do you MOST frequently use? *(Tick ONE box only.)*

City campus (Adsetts) ☐₁   Collegiate campus ☐₂   Psalter Lane ☐₃   Other ☐₄   None ☐₅   (6)

Please rate the extent to which you are satisfied with the following in relation to the Learning Centre you most frequently use and then rate how important it is to you.

(7) **Materials**		SATISFACTION			IMPORTANCE		
Not applicable		Totally Dissatisfied	Neither Nor	Totally Satisfied	Not at all Important	Neither Nor	Very Important
a) ☐₁	information available about the Learning Centre services	1 2 3 4 5 6 7 (8)			...... 1 2 3 4 5 6 7 (14)		
b) ☐₂	availability of up to date books	1 2 3 4 5 6 7 (9)			...... 1 2 3 4 5 6 7 (15)		
c) ☐₃	range of journals/periodicals	1 2 3 4 5 6 7 (10)			...... 1 2 3 4 5 6 7 (16)		
d) ☐₄	availability of core course materials	1 2 3 4 5 6 7 (11)			...... 1 2 3 4 5 6 7 (17)		
e) ☐₅	speed the Learning Centre recovers overdue books	1 2 3 4 5 6 7 (12)			...... 1 2 3 4 5 6 7 (18)		
f) ☐₆	ease of locating books on shelves	1 2 3 4 5 6 7 (13)			...... 1 2 3 4 5 6 7 (19)		

(20) **Services**							
a) ☐₁	self service renewals or reservations	1 2 3 4 5 6 7 (21)			...... 1 2 3 4 5 6 7 (28)		
b) ☐₂	renewal of materials by telephone/fax/email	1 2 3 4 5 6 7 (22)			...... 1 2 3 4 5 6 7 (29)		
c) ☐₃	arrangements for loans from other SHU campus Learning Centres	1 2 3 4 5 6 7 (23)			...... 1 2 3 4 5 6 7 (30)		
d) ☐₄	efficiency of the inter-library loans service	1 2 3 4 5 6 7 (24)			...... 1 2 3 4 5 6 7 (31)		
e) ☐₅	helpfulness of the Learning Centre staff	1 2 3 4 5 6 7 (25)			...... 1 2 3 4 5 6 7 (32)		
f) ☐₆	opening hours	1 2 3 4 5 6 7 (26)			...... 1 2 3 4 5 6 7 (33)		
g) ☐₇	availability of photocopying facilities within the LC	1 2 3 4 5 6 7 (27)			...... 1 2 3 4 5 6 7 (34)		

(35) **Information Sources**							
a) ☐₁	range of information sources available	1 2 3 4 5 6 7 (36)			...... 1 2 3 4 5 6 7 (41)		
b) ☐₂	training sessions on how to use the Learning Centre	1 2 3 4 5 6 7 (37)			...... 1 2 3 4 5 6 7 (42)		
c) ☐₃	availability of the electronic databases	1 2 3 4 5 6 7 (38)			...... 1 2 3 4 5 6 7 (43)		
d) ☐₄	help and guidance to use electronic information services	1 2 3 4 5 6 7 (39)			...... 1 2 3 4 5 6 7 (44)		
e) ☐₅	availability of networked PC's in the Learning Centre	1 2 3 4 5 6 7 (40)			...... 1 2 3 4 5 6 7 (45)		

(46) **The Environment**							
a) ☐₁	availability of quiet working space in the Learning Centre	1 2 3 4 5 6 7 (47)			...... 1 2 3 4 5 6 7 (51)		
b) ☐₂	availability of group working space in the Learning Centre ...	1 2 3 4 5 6 7 (48)			...... 1 2 3 4 5 6 7 (52)		
c) ☐₃	general noise levels	1 2 3 4 5 6 7 (49)			...... 1 2 3 4 5 6 7 (53)		
d) ☐₄	cleanliness	1 2 3 4 5 6 7 (50)			...... 1 2 3 4 5 6 7 (54)		

student experience

131

If you feel there are any questions which are not relevant to you, please tick the 'not applicable' box.   **CARD 5**

5. SERVICES AND FACILITIES PROVIDED BY THE UNIVERSITY

Please rate the extent to which you are satisfied with the following in relation to the <u>general services and facilities</u> provided at the University, and then rate how important it is <u>to you</u>.

(6) **Student Services**	**SATISFACTION**			**IMPORTANCE**		
Not applicable	Totally Dissatisfied	Neither Nor	Totally Satisfied	Not at all Important	Neither Nor	Very Important
a) ☐₁ careers guidance service	1 2 3 4 5 6 7 (7)			1 2 3 4 5 6 7 (16)		
b) ☐₂ chaplaincy and spiritual welfare	1 2 3 4 5 6 7 (8)			1 2 3 4 5 6 7 (17)		
c) ☐₃ personal counselling	1 2 3 4 5 6 7 (9)			1 2 3 4 5 6 7 (18)		
d) ☐₄ pre-school childcare provision	1 2 3 4 5 6 7 (10)			1 2 3 4 5 6 7 (19)		
e) ☐₅ school age childcare provision	1 2 3 4 5 6 7 (11)			1 2 3 4 5 6 7 (20)		
f) ☐₆ medical care services	1 2 3 4 5 6 7 (12)			1 2 3 4 5 6 7 (21)		
g) ☐₇ student financial support	1 2 3 4 5 6 7 (13)			1 2 3 4 5 6 7 (22)		
h) ☐₈ educational guidance services	1 2 3 4 5 6 7 (14)			1 2 3 4 5 6 7 (23)		
i) ☐₉ international/overseas student support	1 2 3 4 5 6 7 (15)			1 2 3 4 5 6 7 (24)		

(25) **General Services / Facilities**						
a) ☐₁ sports facilities	1 2 3 4 5 6 7 (26)			1 2 3 4 5 6 7 (33)		
b) ☐₂ availability of car parking	1 2 3 4 5 6 7 (27)			1 2 3 4 5 6 7 (34)		
c) ☐₃ provision of cash machines	1 2 3 4 5 6 7 (28)			1 2 3 4 5 6 7 (35)		
d) ☐₄ availability of food/drink vending machines	1 2 3 4 5 6 7 (29)			1 2 3 4 5 6 7 (36)		
e) ☐₅ availability of common room space	1 2 3 4 5 6 7 (30)			1 2 3 4 5 6 7 (37)		
f) ☐₆ availability of space to eat your own food	1 2 3 4 5 6 7 (31)			1 2 3 4 5 6 7 (38)		
g) ☐₇ security and personal safety	1 2 3 4 5 6 7 (32)			1 2 3 4 5 6 7 (39)		

Postgrads only: Do you have any designated Postgraduate common rooms within your school? Yes ☐₁   No ☐₂ (40)

Do you think Postgraduate facilities should be separate from Undergraduate facilities? Yes ☐₁   No ☐₂ (41)

6. ACCOMMODATION PROVISION

Which type of accommodation do you presently live in during term time? *(Please tick only <u>ONE</u> box.)*

(42)

SHU Halls of Residence ....☐₁

SHU managed accommodation ....☐₂

Private sector accommodation allocated by SHU ......☐₃

Private sector accommodation you have found yourself . ☐₄   *Go to next section - (7. CATERING OUTLETS)*

Family/own home ....☐₅   *Go to next section - (7. CATERING OUTLETS)*

Please rate the extent to which you are satisfied with the following in relation to the **SHU accommodation provision you are currently living in**, and then rate how important it is <u>to you</u>.

(43) **Not applicable**	**SATISFACTION**			**IMPORTANCE**		
	Totally Dissatisfied	Neither Nor	Totally Satisfied	Not at all Important	Neither Nor	Very Important
a) ☐₁ assistance with finding accommodation through SHU	1 2 3 4 5 6 7 (44)			1 2 3 4 5 6 7 (52)		
b) ☐₂ criteria for allocation of accommodation	1 2 3 4 5 6 7 (45)			1 2 3 4 5 6 7 (53)		
c) ☐₃ information about accommodation in the private sector	1 2 3 4 5 6 7 (46)			1 2 3 4 5 6 7 (54)		
d) ☐₄ range of facilities in your accommodation	1 2 3 4 5 6 7 (47)			1 2 3 4 5 6 7 (55)		
e) ☐₅ location/convenience of your accommodation	1 2 3 4 5 6 7 (48)			1 2 3 4 5 6 7 (56)		
f) ☐₆ overall comfort of your accommodation	1 2 3 4 5 6 7 (49)			1 2 3 4 5 6 7 (57)		
g) ☐₇ security	1 2 3 4 5 6 7 (50)			1 2 3 4 5 6 7 (58)		
h) ☐₈ value for money	1 2 3 4 5 6 7 (51)			1 2 3 4 5 6 7 (59)		

student experience

If you feel there are any questions which are not relevant to you, please tick the 'not applicable' box. **CARD 6**

7. CATERING OUTLETS

Which catering outlet do you most frequently use? _(Please tick ONE box only.)_ (6)

Hub Grub (Nelson Mandela Building) .... □₁	The Howard Suite (Surrey Building, Level 6) .... □₇
Rollers Restaurant (Owen Building, Level 6) .... □₂	Millers Restaurant (Collegiate campus) .... □₈
Cutting Edge (The Atrium, Level 5) .... □₃	Turners Snack Bar (Collegiate campus) .... □₉
Heartspace Café (The Atrium, Level 2) .... □₄	Melters Snack Bar (Collegiate campus) .... □₀
Eric's (Eric Mensforth Building) .... □₅	Forgers Snack Bar (Collegiate campus) .... □ₓ
Stoddart Deli (Stoddart Building) .... □₅	Steeleys Restaurant (Psalter Lane campus) .... □ᵥ

Please rate the extent to which you are satisfied with the following in relation to the <u>catering outlet you most frequently use</u> (the one you have identified above), and then rate how important it is <u>to you</u>.

(7) Not applicable	SATISFACTION Totally Neither Totally Dissatisfied Nor Satisfied	IMPORTANCE Not at all Neither Very Important Nor Important
a) □₁ quality of the food	1 2 3 4 5 6 7 (8)	1 2 3 4 5 6 7 (18)
b) □₂ price of the food	1 2 3 4 5 6 7 (9)	1 2 3 4 5 6 7 (19)
c) □₃ range of food available on the menu	1 2 3 4 5 6 7 (10)	1 2 3 4 5 6 7 (20)
d) □₄ extent to which it caters for a range of dietary requirements .	1 2 3 4 5 6 7 (11)	1 2 3 4 5 6 7 (21)
e) □₅ ease of ordering the food	1 2 3 4 5 6 7 (12)	1 2 3 4 5 6 7 (22)
f) □₆ cleanliness of the place	1 2 3 4 5 6 7 (13)	1 2 3 4 5 6 7 (23)
g) □₇ comfort of the place	1 2 3 4 5 6 7 (14)	1 2 3 4 5 6 7 (24)
h) □₈ friendliness of the service	1 2 3 4 5 6 7 (15)	1 2 3 4 5 6 7 (25)
i) □₉ efficiency of the staff	1 2 3 4 5 6 7 (16)	1 2 3 4 5 6 7 (26)
j) □₀ opening times	1 2 3 4 5 6 7 (17)	1 2 3 4 5 6 7 (27)

8. THE STUDENTS UNION

Which campus bar do you most frequently use? _(Please tick ONE box only.)_ (28)

The Hub (The NMB - City campus) .... □₁	The Forgers (Collegiate campus) .... □₄
The Furnace Bar (The NMB - City campus) .... □₂	The Wham Bar (Psalter Lane) .... □₅
The Cooler Bar (The NMB - City campus) .... □₃	I have not visited a bar this academic year .... □₆

Please rate the extent to which you are satisfied with the following in relation to the <u>Students Union</u>, and then rate how important it is <u>to you</u>.

(29) Not applicable	SATISFACTION Totally Neither Totally Dissatisfied Nor Satisfied	IMPORTANCE Not at all Neither Very Important Nor Important
a) □₁ range of social activities provided in Freshers Week	1 2 3 4 5 6 7 (30)	1 2 3 4 5 6 7 (40)
b) □₂ promotion and publicity of SU activities and services	1 2 3 4 5 6 7 (31)	1 2 3 4 5 6 7 (41)
c) □₃ athletic union/clubs and societies	1 2 3 4 5 6 7 (32)	1 2 3 4 5 6 7 (42)
d) □₄ SU welfare services (eg. advice unit)	1 2 3 4 5 6 7 (33)	1 2 3 4 5 6 7 (43)
e) □₅ Student Union shop	1 2 3 4 5 6 7 (34)	1 2 3 4 5 6 7 (44)
f) □₆ events and entertainment programme	1 2 3 4 5 6 7 (35)	1 2 3 4 5 6 7 (45)
g) □₇ general appearance of the campus bar you most frequently use	1 2 3 4 5 6 7 (36)	1 2 3 4 5 6 7 (46)
h) □₈ price of drinks in the bar	1 2 3 4 5 6 7 (37)	1 2 3 4 5 6 7 (47)
i) □₉ general appearance of the NMB building	1 2 3 4 5 6 7 (38)	1 2 3 4 5 6 7 (48)
j) □₀ postgraduate student committee	1 2 3 4 5 6 7 (39)	1 2 3 4 5 6 7 (49)

Are you aware of the Postgraduate Student Committee?   Yes □₁   No □₂ (50)

student experience

If you feel there are any questions which are not relevant to you, please tick the 'not applicable' box.

9. STUDENT FINANCES
Please rate the extent to which you are satisfied with the following in relation to <u>your costs,</u> and then rate how important it is <u>to you</u>.

	(51) **Student Services** Not applicable		SATISFACTION Totally Dissatisfied — Neither Nor — Totally Satisfied	IMPORTANCE Not at all Important — Neither Nor — Very Important
a)	☐₁ cost of field trips/visits/placements		1 2 3 4 5 6 7 (52)	1 2 3 4 5 6 7 (58)
b)	☐₂ cost of materials you need for assessments		1 2 3 4 5 6 7 (53)	1 2 3 4 5 6 7 (59)
c)	☐₃ cost of photocopying		1 2 3 4 5 6 7 (54)	1 2 3 4 5 6 7 (60)
d)	☐₄ cost of computer printing		1 2 3 4 5 6 7 (55)	1 2 3 4 5 6 7 (61)
e)	☐₅ cost of childcare		1 2 3 4 5 6 7 (56)	1 2 3 4 5 6 7 (62)
f)	☐₆ value for money of your course		1 2 3 4 5 6 7 (57)	1 2 3 4 5 6 7 (63)

How would you describe your financial situation?

Very Poor		**Neither/Nor**		**Very Good**	
1	2	3	4	5	6	7	(64)

What impact (if any) does your financial situation have upon your academic work?

A very bad impact on my performance		**No impact at all**		**A very good impact on my performance**	
1	2	3	4	5	6	7	(65)

10. YOUR EXPECTATIONS
We would like to know to what extent the University has <u>met your expectations so far.</u>

Please rate this by circling the appropriate number on the scale:

		Definitely Not		Possibly		Definitely Yes
a)	Has your course met your expectations?	1	2	3	4	5	6	7 (66)
b)	Has SHU met your expectations?	1	2	3	4	5	6	7 (67)
c)	Has Sheffield, the City, met your expectations?	1	2	3	4	5	6	7 (68)

11. YOUR RECOMMENDATIONS
We would like to know to what extent you would recommend each of the following to others.

Please rate this by circling the appropriate number on the scale:

		Definitely Not		Possibly		Definitely Yes
a)	Your course	1	2	3	4	5	6	7 (69)
b)	Studying at Sheffield Hallam University	1	2	3	4	5	6	7 (70)
c)	Studying in the City of Sheffield	1	2	3	4	5	6	7 (71)
d)	If you had your time again, would you still choose your course?	1	2	3	4	5	6	7 (72)
e)	If you had your time again, would you still choose SHU as a place to study?	1	2	3	4	5	6	7 (73)

**student
exᴧperience**

CARD 7

12. OVERALL SATISFACTION

Please rate your <u>overall satisfaction</u> with your student experience here at Sheffield Hallam University.

	Totally Dissatisfied			Neither/ Nor			Totally Satisfied	
	1	2	3	4	5	6	7	(6)

13. If you have any further views to express on how Sheffield Hallam University could improve your experience as a student here, please write them below. *It will help us if you indicate the sections to which you are referring, eg. 'student administration'. Please use additional sheets if required.*

_____

_____

_____

_____ (7 - 10)

SECTION 2 *This section contains questions, which will enable us to classify the information you have provided.*

Please tick ONE box only for each question unless otherwise stated.

14. **In which school are you enrolled?** *Students enrolled on <u>Combined Studies Programmes</u> should <u>tick TWO Boxes</u> - the Combined Studies box AND the school where you are currently receiving the most tuition.* (11)

Computing & Management Sciences ☐₁	Health & Social Care ☐₇
Environment and Development ☐₂	Engineering ☐₈
Cultural Studies ☐₃	Leisure & Food Management ☐₉
Education ☐₄	Science and Mathematics ☐₀
Social Science and Law ☐₅	Sheffield Business School ☐ₓ
Business and Finance ☐₆	Combined Studies Programme ☐ᵥ

15. **At which SHU campus are you <u>mainly</u> based?** (12)

Collegiate Crescent campus ☐₁   Psalter Lane campus ☐₂

City campus	Howard Building ☐₃	Harmer Building ☐₈
	Owen Building ☐₄	Surrey Building ☐₉
	Norfolk Building ☐₅	Stoddart Building ☐₀
	Sheaf Building ☐₆	Science Park ☐ₓ
	Northern Media School ☐₇	Eric Mensforth Building ☐ᵥ

16. **What is your age?** (13)

18 ☐₁	19 ☐₂	20 ☐₃	21 ☐₄	22-24 ☐₅
25-34 ☐₆	35-44 ☐₇	45-54 ☐₈	55+ ☐₉	

17. **What is your gender?**   Male ☐₁   Female ☐₂ (14)

student experience

Please tick ONE box only for each question unless otherwise stated.

18. **Do you have any of the following disabilities?** *(You may tick more than one box.)* (15)

Sensory disability (eg. vision, hearing) .... ☐1
Physical disability (eg. mobility related) .... ☐2
Dyslexia .... ☐3
Mental health problems .... ☐4

Unseen disabilities (eg. asthma, diabetes, epilepsy) .... ☐5
Other, not listed above .... ☐6
No, none.. ☐7
I prefer not to answer................................. ☐8

19. **Do you have the main or joint caring responsibilities for any of the following?** *(You may tick more than one box.)* (16)

Pre-school children .... ☐1
School age children .... ☐2
Adult dependents .... ☐3

Elderly dependents .... ☐5
No, none.. ☐6
I prefer not to answer................................. ☐7

20. **How would you describe your ethnic origin?** *(As indicated by the Commission for Racial Equality guidelines.)* (17)

White .... ☐1
Black African .... ☐2
Black Caribbean .... ☐3
Black Other .... ☐4
Black British .... ☐5
Irish .... ☐6

Indian .... ☐7
Pakistani .... ☐8
Bangladeshi .... ☐9
Asian British....................... ☐9
Chinese/Other Asian............... ☐x
Other Ethnic Group .... ☐v

I prefer not to answer .... ☐1   (18)

21. **Is English your first language?**   Yes ☐1   No ☐2   (19)

22. **Are you a UK or an International student?** (20)

UK student .... ☐1   *Continue to next question*
International - EU .... ☐2   *Go to Question 25*
International - Other .... ☐3   *Go to Question 25*

23. **UK STUDENTS ONLY - Did you live in Sheffield before coming to SHU?** (21)

No ☐1 *Continue to next question*   Yes ☐2 *Go to Question 26*

24. **In which region is the nearest major town/city to your home address before coming to SHU?** (22)

North .... ☐1
North West .... ☐2
Yorkshire/Humberside .... ☐3
West Midlands .... ☐4

East Midlands .... ☐5
East Anglia.......................... ☐6
South East .... ☐7
South West .... ☐8

Wales .... ☐9
Scotland .... ☐0
Northern Ireland .... ☐x

Go to Question 26

25. **INTERNATIONAL STUDENTS ONLY - What is your country of origin?** (23-24)

student experience

Please tick ONE box only for each question unless otherwise stated.

26.   What was the highest qualification that you used to gain entry to your current course of study?   (25)

No formal qualification . . . . □₁   Postgraduate Award . . . . □₆

Up to and including A/AS Levels . . . . □₂   Overseas Degree or Equivalent . . . . . . □₇

GNVQ / GSVQ . . . . □₃   Professional Qualification . . . . □₈

NVQ / SVQ . . . . □₄   Other *(please state)* . . . . □₉   _____

HND/HNC/Sub Degree . . . . □₅

27.   Who is paying your course fees? *(You may tick more than one box.)*   (26)

Yourself/partner/parents . . . . □₁   SHU bursary/scholarship . . . . □₄

Your Employer . . . . □₂   External bursary/scholarship . . . . □₅

LEA Funding . . . . □₃   Other *(please specify)* . . . . □₆   _____

28.   Which sources of income do you receive to support your period of study? *(You may tick more than one box.)*   (27)

Student loan . . . . □₁   Sponsorship/employer contribution . . . □₅

Earnings from employment . . . . □₂   Parent/partner support . . . . □₆

Access fund . . . . □₃   State benefits . . . . □₇

Bank/building society loan . . . . □₄   Other *(please state)* . . . . □₈   _____

29.   STUDENTS CURRENTLY LIVING IN HALLS OF RESIDENCE ONLY - Which halls do you live in?

(28)   (29)   (30)

Broomgrove . . . . □₁   Norfolk Park . . . . □₁   Newfield Green . . . . □₁

Marshall . . . . □₂   Truro Court . . . . □₂   Phoenix Court . . . . □₂

Woodville . . . . □₃   Truro Works . . . . □₃   Partnership Houses . . . . □₃

Norfolk Park . . . . □₄   Bramall Lane . . . . □₄   Other . . . . □₄

Ballard Hall . . . . □₅

30.   POSTGRADUATE STUDENTS - Did you study for an Undergraduate Degree at SHU?   Yes □₁   No □₂   (31)

31.   ALL STUDENTS - What is your <u>current</u> employment status?   (32)

Employed 1-5 hours a week on average . . . . □₁   Self employed . . . . □₆

Employed 6-18 hours a week . . . . □₂   Unemployed . . . . □₇

Employed more than 18 hours a week but not full time . □₃   Retired . . . . □₈

Employed full time . . . . □₄   Not employed at all . . . . □₉

Employed during vacation time only . . . . □₅

student
experience

137

Please tick ONE box only for each question unless otherwise stated.

32.   Which of the following best describes your <u>current or most recent</u> occupation?   (33)

Managers and Senior Officials	Managers and senior officials across all business and industry	☐₁
Professional Occupations	Science and Engineering Professionals Lecturers Others including Health, Legal, Business and Finance	☐₂
Associate Professional and Technical Occupations	Science and Engineering Associate Professionals Health Associate Professionals Other Associate Professionals	☐₃
Clerical, Secretarial and Administrative Occupations		☐₄
Skilled Trade Occupations	Skilled Construction Trades Skilled Engineering Trades Other skilled trades	☐₅
Personal Service Occupations	Personal Service Occupations (eg. nursing/catering/travel/childcare)	☐₆
Sales/Customer Service Occupations	Buyers, Brokers and Sales Representatives Other Sales Occupations	☐₇
Process, Plant and Machine Operatives	Drivers and Mobile Machine Operators Industrial Plant and Machine Operatives	☐₈
Elementary Occupations	Mainly low skill manual jobs	☐₉
Not applicable	No current or previous recent employment	☐₀

33.   Which of the following best describes the industry that you <u>currently or most recently</u> worked in?

(34)

Mining and quarrying, supply of electricity, gas and water . ☐₁

Agriculture, hunting, forestry and fishing . . . . ☐₂

Manufacturing industries . . . . ☐₃

Construction . . . . ☐₄

Wholesale and retail trade and repairs . . . . ☐₅

Hotels, restaurants and bars . . . . ☐₆

Transport and storage . . . . ☐₇

Postal and telecommunications . . . . ☐₈

Other community, social and professional activity . . . . . . ☐₉

(35)

Real estate . . . . ☐₁

Renting, research, computer and other business activities. . ☐₂

Banking, finance and insurance, etc. . . . . ☐₃

Public administration and defence. . . . . ☐₄

Education . . . . ☐₅

Health activities . . . . ☐₆

Social work activities . . . . ☐₇

Other. . . . . ☐₈

Not applicable . . . . ☐₉

Thank you very much for taking part in this survey. Now, please return the questionnaire in the pre-paid envelope to:
B2B INTERNATIONAL LTD., BRAMHALL HOUSE, 14 ACK LANE EAST, BRAMHALL, STOCKPORT SK7 2ZX.
When the answers to the questionnaire have been analysed and a report completed, you will be made aware of the results.
Again, we would like to reassure you that ALL the information in this survey is confidential and completely anonymous.

student
eXperience

The watchwords in planning a postal survey are *attention to detail* to ensure that nothing goes wrong. Things to look out for are:

- missing out key questions;
- lack of clarity in the questions;
- undue complications in the questions or the routings;
- spelling or grammatical errors in the questionnaire or cover letter;
- failing to enclose the cover letter, questionnaire or reply-paid envelope;
- failing to give precise instructions to respondents on how to fill in the questionnaire or how to return it;
- insufficient funds in the mailing machine to frank all the letters;
- timing the launch badly such as sending it out during a holiday period or when respondents (in business) are away at an exhibition.

9

Data collection methods

Figure 9.1 shows the breakdown of data collection methods used by larger UK market research companies (which carry out some 16 million interviews per year). Face-to-face interviewing is by far the most important method, responsible for half the value of all the survey work. The next most important method is the telephone but, as yet, this accounts for only a fifth of the value of the interviewing 'cake'. Hall tests, group discussions, self-completion/post, mystery shopping, and depth interviews make up the rest.

In this chapter we examine some of the practical issues involved with each of the seven data collection methods.

PERSONAL INTERVIEWS

The pros and cons of personal interviews

Personal interviews are still the most common means of collecting primary information, for good reasons:

- *Better explanations.* In a personal interview respondents have more time to consider their answers and the interviewer can gain a deeper understanding of the validity of a response. Sometimes interviewers need to show advertisements, logos, headlines or samples and this is plainly suited to personal situations.

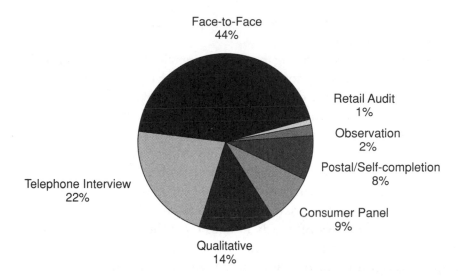

Figure 9.1   *Interviewing methods by value*

- *Depth.* It is easier to maintain the interest of respondents for a longer period of time in personal interviews. Being face-to-face with respondents gives the interviewer more control and refusals to answer questions are less likely than over the telephone. Concern about confidentiality can be more readily satisfied than with an 'anonymous' person at the end of a phone. An interviewer on the doorstep or in the high street can show an identity card.
- *Greater accuracy.* In a personal interview respondents can look up information and products can be examined. If the interview is at a business, files of information can be referred to, or phone calls made to colleagues to confirm a point. The interviewer may be able to make a visual check to ensure that the answers are correct.
- *Product placements.* Product placements can be sent through the post but it is usually better for them to be delivered by hand by the interviewer. Face-to-face contact with respondents permits a more thorough briefing on how to use the product. Pre-test questions can be asked, and arrangements can be made for the follow-up.

Against the advantages of personal interviewing, there are a number of disadvantages:

- *Organization.* Personal interviews are difficult to organize. If the interviews are country-wide, a national field force is required. The subject may be complex and demand a personal briefing, which is expensive to arrange when interviewers are scattered geographically.

Monitoring and controlling personal interviews is more difficult than with telephone interviews. Personal interviews need to have occasional supervision and check-backs by visit or post. For the most part, however, the interviewer is working in isolation and the quality of the work has a considerable dependency on the conscientiousness of the individual.

- *Cost*. The cost of personal consumer interviews varies considerably between those carried out in the street and the home. In-home interviews based on prese-lected addresses are, in turn, more expensive than those to a quota. In general, street interviews cost the same to carry out as telephone interviews. In some cases, street interviews offer advantages over the telephone by allowing show cards and visuals, while at other times the facility to random sample and achieve complete geographical coverage could swing the benefits in favour of telephone interviewing.

- *Time*. In-home interviews are time consuming because of the travel time between respondents (this is not the case, of course, when the interviews are carried out in the street). The prior commitments of the field force and the delays caused by questionnaires being mailed out and returned normally mean that at least a two-week period is necessary for organizing a personal interviewing project. A month is more reasonable. A programme of business-to-business interviews may have less personal interviews than a consumer study but they too take an inordinate time to organize as the researchers struggle to set up interviews in the diaries of busy managers.

Street and in-home interviews

Most face-to-face interviews are carried out in the home or in the street (some are also carried out in airports, in places of work and other places).

Street interviewing is appropriate if the questionnaire is short and simple. Using a short questionnaire, and assuming that the questions are applicable for most of the passers-by, an interviewer can achieve 30 and sometimes more interviews in a day. (Interviewer days are normally six hours.) Because a large number of interviews can be carried out in a day, they are quicker, easier and cheaper than in-home visits.

However, interviewing in the street is not always possible, especially where the questionnaire is long and complicated. It is difficult to show visuals or prompt cards in a street interview. Respondents may be caught without their glasses, the light may be poor, the rain or wind could cause problems and, if the shopper's hands are full, the show cards cannot be held conveniently. Nor is the street the best place to find a good cross-section of the population as many are at their offices or factories while others may keep away form the busy city centre sites where interviewers work.

Because certain groups of the population can escape the net in street interviews, it is usual for street interviews to be carried out against a quota to ensure that all groups are included in the correct proportions. Quota sampling, however, is less rigorous and, as discussed in Chapter 7, does not allow the calculation of sampling error. If it is important to obtain a probability sample of the population, the researchers must use in-home interviews, selecting the sample either randomly from the electoral register or by means of a random walk.

Obtaining cooperation and carrying out interviews with the public

Wherever the interview is carried out, in the street or the home, it is usually with a complete stranger. The interviewer asks this stranger to part with his or her time, views, facts and opinion, usually with no reward. The person may be busy, aggravated by personal problems, or resent the intrusion of his or her privacy. The interviewer has no rights whatsoever to demand cooperation. Everything depends, therefore, on the interviewer's approach.

The first few seconds of contact are critical. Respondents need to feel that they are being asked to take part in a worthwhile project and they are in the hands of an expert. If the interviewer has an identity card or a letter of authority, it should be shown to the respondent as part of the introduction. In most surveys, the interviewers will be given a script of their opening lines. In this they will probably explain that a survey is being carried out (here emphasizing that there is no selling motive involved), which market research company is carrying out the survey, and the length of time the interview is expected to take.

On completion, the interviewer owes the respondent a thank you. Sometimes a card is given to the respondent which explains who carried out the interview and why. In street interviews it is normal practice to ask respondents for their name and address. This is used to check back on a percentage of the interviews (usually 10 per cent) to see that the work has been carried out satisfactorily. Diplomacy and a special explanation may be needed for people reticent about giving their address to a stranger.

Computer aided personal interviewing (CAPI)

Traditionally, responses to questionnaires are recorded on paper questionnaires and mailed back to the agency headquarters for processing. Increasing use is being made of hand-held computers for logging responses. These speed up the interviews as responses are a simple matter of entering a numeric code and routing is automatic. At the end of the day or the work period the completed interviews are despatched electronically by modem to the research agency's computer. Transmission is safer, much quicker and less costly than the post.

There are two major disadvantages of CAPI interviewing: the high cost of equipping the fieldforce and the requirement for the questionnaire to be as structured as possible. CAPI software and interviewer skills (or lack of keyboard skills) have tended to limit the inclusion of open-ended questions in CAPI fieldwork. However, the technology is, in this respect, constantly improving and this limitation is likely to disappear shortly.

TELEPHONE INTERVIEWS

Pros and cons of telephone interviews

The greatest advantages of the telephone against personal interviewing are its speed and low cost. These are most evident in business-to-business market research.

In favourable circumstances, perhaps five to six 20-minute interviews with managers in industry can be completed in a day over the telephone. In the same time only one or two interviews can be achieved face-to-face.

In consumer research the time and cost advantages of telephone interviewing are not quite so clear-cut. If the comparison is between street and telephone interviewing then there is probably little difference in either time or cost – in fact, street interviewing might even be cheaper. However, when compared with in-home interviews, the telephone is both quicker and cheaper since there is no time wasted in travel between interview points.

Concerns about doorstep security also favour the telephone as an interviewing medium. Householders do not have to answer the door to a stranger while interviewers are saved the risk of entering dubious neighbourhoods. Not surprisingly, telephone interviewing is a far more popular data collection method in the United Sttes than in Europe.

Where large-scale telephone interviewing is carried out from a central location (the normal practice of research agencies) supervision of interviewers is much stronger than for the work of outside fieldforces. Supervisors can monitor interviewing as it takes place by listening-in and this is a far more effective method of quality control than recalling respondents after the event (the normal method of validating face-to-face interviews). Arguably, therefore, telephone interviewing offers quality benefits through the reduction of interviewer variability.

We have seen that there are a number of strong arguments in favour of telephone interviews, with particularly important benefits in cost and speed. However, there are sometimes good reasons for not using telephone interviews. Visuals are difficult to use. If something has to be shown, then the telephone is not the right approach. Nor is the telephone suitable when it is necessary to ask respondents to consider a number of predetermined factors in order to test their views. More than five or six factors on a list are difficult to hold in the mind and would normally be shown on a card so that they can be given fair consideration.

Telephone interviewing is, on the whole, better suited to shorter interviews and 10 to 15 minutes is probably the ideal length. In telephone interviews the questions and answers are generally kept short and so the medium is not ideal for depth interviewing; it does not encourage long and discursive responses. Furthermore, the lack of personal contact prohibits the interviewer assessing respondents and obtaining an extra feel for what is behind the reply.

Despite these limitations, the advantages of the telephone in data collection are considerable and the method is likely to continue to make inroads against street and face-to-face interviews. Continuing improvements in telecommunications will also extend applications – eg phone or phone/video group discussions.

Computer aided telephone interviewing (CATI)

In the same way that computers are replacing the clip-board and questionnaire in face-to-face fieldwork, so too they are taking over in telephone interviews. Interviews carried out by telephone can be guided by a questionnaire displayed on the screen of a computer. The interviewer records via the keyboard, entering numbers that correspond with the pre-coded responses displayed on the screen.

CATI interviewing offers considerable advantages:

- The interviewer is left free to concentrate on the interview itself as the routing instructions are taken care of.
- Data is entered directly and the subsequent activity of data entry is eliminated.
- Costs and punching errors are reduced.
- The whole process is speeded up because data is entered as it is obtained.
- At intervals during the survey, the researcher can interrogate the computer to examine the results.
- An analysis of results can be obtained immediately after the last interview has been completed.
- Interviewers can be more closely supervised and monitored. Where the work is done from a central phone unit, supervisors can both listen-in to the interview and watch the responses being inputted in real time.

There are some disadvantages to CATI interviewing. A conventional questionnaire can be knocked up in no time and without the help of someone who knows their way around the technical nuances of a CATI system. Getting a questionnaire set up and running, fault free, on a CATI system takes time. Coping with open-ended responses presents some problems on CATI because, although the systems can accommodate open-ended comments, capturing them requires interviewers to have good typing skills. If a respondent makes changes to an earlier answer when part way through the interview, it is more difficult to return and make alterations than is the case with paper questionnaires. In general, CATI is best suited to structured interviews carried out in large numbers, especially repeated surveys where all the possible answers have been worked out and can be listed as pre-coded responses.

GROUP DISCUSSIONS

The purpose of focus groups has been discussed in Chapter 5. In this chapter we consider some of the practical issues of planning and carrying out groups.

Some critical aspects of planning groups include:

The group composition

The characteristics of the respondents attending the groups have to relate to the aims and objectives of the research. Group composition is generally defined in terms of demographics, attitudes, beliefs or behaviour membership status. Fairly often, a combination of criteria is appropriate.

Deciding the number of groups

Groups typically include only eight to nine respondents and four groups provide only a small sample of around 30 respondents. However, as discussed earlier, groups are not meant to be a quantitative research tool and the limitations of small samples should be accepted.

If groups are to be a 'stand alone' research technique, then four is probably the minimum number to hold. Groups can, however, be used at the 'exploratory' stage of the research; an aid, for example, to designing an effective questionnaire in a later quantitative stage. In this situation two or even one group may be adequate.

On the whole, groups work best when the members are relatively homogeneous. For example, in a consumer research project, the intention may be to cover a spectrum of social classes and a wide range of ages as well as both sexes. In this case it is probably best to limit each group to a fairly narrow range, eg one group of lower income males aged 25–45; one of older, higher income men, etc. If this principle is followed it has obvious implications for the number of groups held (assuming two income/status bands, two age ranges and both sexes, the minimum number of groups to cover all relevant respondents is eight).

The principle of homogeneous groups is not immutable and there may be particular reasons to aim for a mix of respondents if an element of conflicting opinion would help flush out the contrasting views.

Topic planning

The moderator or group leader will require a 'script' to guide the discussion. This checklist should include:

- Notes on how the subject is to be introduced.
- The subjects to be covered during the group. These will probably be listed as topics and grouped in some sort of sequence.
- Notes to remind the group leader when to show visual aids, etc.
- Notes on when respondents are to do particular things – complete mini-questionnaires, write something down, draw pictures, etc.

Questions in a group discussion guide are not cast in stone. It is normal practice for the group moderator to formulate questions on the spot to suit the circumstances.

It is worth mentioning at this point that formal questionnaires may be used as part of a group. Group members may, for example, fill in a self-completion questionnaire before, during or after the group meeting. The purpose of this may be to obtain simple, factual information about respondents and their behaviour. It could also provide an uncontaminated view which can help the researcher to interpret the responses of the actual discussion. An alternative to paper questionnaires is to use computer technology – see Sweeney *et al* (1997) – also referred to in Chapter 5.

The venue

Within reason, a group can be held more or less anywhere. However, a well-chosen venue will help the group go well and may affect attendance.

Consumer groups used to be held in private homes. Today focus groups are held in specialist viewing centres. These venues are often houses which have been converted for the purpose and are equipped with video cameras, audio equipment, and one way mirrors which allow the research sponsor or other members of the research team to view without disturbing the proceedings.

Time and dates

Generally, groups are held in the evening, from 7.00 pm onwards. Other times of the day, however, can be acceptable for those who do not work, while lunchtime or early evening is normal for business-to-business groups.

Recruiting groups

The aim of group recruitment is very simple: *to have the right number of qualified respondents attend at the right time.* Who is qualified is determined by the group composition criteria and obviously recruitment cannot start until this is settled. There is, however, another 'qualification' issue which should be mentioned; this is the problem of 'professional' group respondents – respondents who repeatedly attend groups. This problem can arise when a recruiter is tempted to invite respondents who have attended groups recently. This should be overcome by stipulating that respondents should not have attended a group in the last six or 12 months, or whatever is thought reasonable. There is also the problem of respondents being other than they claim – eg they are not frequent purchasers of a particular product – and sometimes these problems are the result of poor or even dishonest work by the recruiter. To minimize such undesirable effects, quality control is essential, including re-checking respondents' qualifications for inclusion at the start of the group.

In group recruitment it is necessary to contact and screen more potential respondents than will actually attend. Some people who are approached will not qualify for attendance while others will be unavailable or unwilling. The ratio of contacts to attendees varies according to the type of respondent, the subject of the group etc. Often it is at least 5:1.

For the purposes of recruiting a group, a questionnaire is required so that the interviewers searching for appropriate respondents can ask and record appropriate screening questions. Typically, screening questionnaires determine whether respondents are eligible by finding out if they purchase certain products, are a lapsed consumer or whatever is relevant to the subject in hand. Demographic data on respondents would also be collected at this stage. Recruitment questionnaires are also essential for quality control purposes – eg checking respondent qualifications – as mentioned above.

A general principle in group recruitment is to fear the worst and assume that every respondent will not turn up on the night. Consumer attendees are usually reliable and if nine are recruited then it is almost certain that eight or nine will turn up. In business-to-business groups the situation is rather different and there is a need to over-recruit; 12 to 14 firm promises will generate around eight or nine respondents on the night. At worst, it is usually possible to fit a couple of extra respondents into the meeting rather than send them away disgruntled after they have gone to some trouble to get there.

Consumer group recruitment is generally done on a house-to-house basis or on the phone, the latter being especially relevant when there is a list of individuals who specifically need inviting and for business-to-business respondents. Occasionally, the recruitment takes place in the street. For 'difficult' groups where the relevant criteria approach the 'needle in a haystack', informal referrals may be used – one respondent suggests another who fits the bill.

Recruitment is helped by an incentive and around £20 to £30 per head is the current rate.

How to lead groups

The aim of the group leader is to create the right climate for getting the respondents to open up. A short, light-hearted welcome and introduction will start to lower the barriers. Involvement is encouraged from the beginning by asking people to introduce themselves.

The group is now primed and ready. The moderator's own attitudes will mould, manoeuvre and lead the group. However, *the group is not an ego trip for its leader*. On the transcript, the moderator's input should be only one tenth, possibly one twentieth, of the total words. The moderator also must be wary of projecting views and attitudes onto the group. Undoubtedly, the moderator has some opinions on the subject but these must be kept hidden. Any obvious bias will either produce a group that is in agreement or one that has a strong anti-reaction. It is also desirable that the moderator makes this impartiality clear. If, for example, the subject of the group is a new concept, it should be emphasized that both praise and criticism are welcome as long as the respondents honestly express their own beliefs.

In leading the group and probing for answers, the moderator may use the enabling techniques discussed in Chapter 5.

HALL TESTS AND CLINICS

In hall tests, respondents are brought to a 'hall' or local room which has been rented for the day, and asked to view or taste products. The hall is generally close to a busy shopping precinct so that the recruitment and interviewing takes place at the same time. The term 'hall test' is largely confined to applications in consumer market research and 'clinics' for the industrial or business-to-business field. The two terms are, however, often used loosely and interchangeably.

Choice of a suitable venue is a vital aspect of planning a hall test. The venue must be located suitably for respondent recruitment and, in the main, the recruitment of respondents for a hall test is invariably off a busy shopping street. Apart from perhaps a cup of tea and a biscuit, incentives are not usually required for street-recruited respondents.

The room should be easily accessible from the street so that respondents do not have to negotiate too many stairs, not to mention the research staff when setting up. With some products, some preparations may be required such as dispensing drinks, cutting up things, diluting, or perhaps heating up. A kitchen facility may therefore be needed as part of presenting the product and increasingly there is a need to take account of hygiene regulations. Even if food and drink are not the subject of study, refreshments may be required for respondents and research staff.

The room should be big enough for the anticipated number of respondents and research staff. A typical arrangement is for an interviewer to bring a respondent into the hall, show product samples and administer an interview. There should be sufficient space to do this without getting in the way of other interviewers and respondents. Ideally, respondents should not be able to overhear other respondents being interviewed elsewhere in the room and screens may help in this regard.

Needless to say, the products to be tested also must be arranged in advance and available on the day. A new product may be specially prepared at the factory and the researcher's role is limited to ensuring that it is delivered on time. Any established products are brought in for the test.

Adequate staffing is required at the hall for the recruitment, interviewing and support duties which include preparing test products, clearing up between respondents, preparing refreshments, etc. If it is assumed that each test will take around 10 to 15 minutes and that recruiters also act as in-hall interviewers, three respondents per hour per interviewer should be achievable – say 20 interviews a day per interviewer. A team of five or six interviewers, with some additional helpers in the hall, could therefore process around 100 respondents per day, though this should be considered good going. Involving more interviewers would not necessarily improve the numbers to any great extent as diminishing returns will set in. For example, there may be problems in having too many interviewers attempting recruitment at once outside the hall. It may be better instead to have a smaller team and to run the hall test over two days.

To meet the needs of just one project, hall tests might have to be carried out in several towns to achieve an overall sample of, say, 500 or more. If only one town is used, there is a danger of reflecting local tastes in the results. In some product fields strong local or regional tastes could lead to a misleading national extrapolation.

POSTAL AND SELF-COMPLETION SURVEYS

Chapter 8 discusses the principles of designing self-completion and postal questionnaires. Here we look at the factors which influence postal response rates and offer tips for carrying out a survey of this kind.

Factors influencing the response of postal surveys

The factor that influences the response rate of a postal survey more than anything else is the interest that respondents have in the subject. A postal survey of customers is likely to achieve a higher response than one of non-customers because there is an interest in and a relationship between customers and the sponsor of the study.

Response rates of 30 per cent and higher from a single mailing are quite common when the subject is about a new car or on behalf of a company with some apparent authority such as British Gas or one of the water companies. In contrast, respondents receiving a questionnaire through the post enquiring about the type of pen they use would most probably yield a low response (less than 5 per cent is likely), because the subject is not compelling.

This fundamental point means that researchers should avoid using postal surveys except when respondents are highly motivated to answer.

Postal surveys depend on suitable databases containing the correct names and addresses of respondents. If lists are out-of-date, contain inaccuracies in spelling of the names and addresses, or are made up of unsuitable respondents, the questionnaires will fall on stony ground and the response rates will be low. Returned and unopened envelopes will indicate that there are problems with the mailing list and could indicate the need for a check-back to find out the true reply rate among valid respondents. While check-backs are useful, they substantially add to the cost and complexity of the study.

The shorter the questionnaire, the more likely it will be completed and returned. Forty questions carefully laid out on two sides of A3 (folded to make four pages of A4) can look less than 20 questions spread over six single pages. However, the number of questions does not influence responses as much as the interest factor and there are many examples of questionnaires the size of booklets obtaining high response rates.

Respondents want to feel that their efforts in completing the questionnaire are valued. It is important, therefore, that the cover letter gives purpose to the study and convinces recipients that their replies really matter. Legitimacy influences response rates in all types of surveys and it is especially important in postal studies. If possible a benefit should be mentioned such as the promise of better products, improved service or a gift.

Postal surveys which offer anonymity have a higher response than those where respondents must identify themselves. Much depends on the circumstances. In many business-to-business surveys respondents may be happy to be identified as long as they are confident that the research is bona fide and not a surreptitious attempt at selling.

Response rates can be boosted by a second mailing. If the first mailing yields a 25 per cent response, a second one could draw a further 10–15 per cent. The researcher needs, therefore, to consider whether to send a second mailing to the non-respondents and accept the fall-off in response rate or to draw up an extension to the first sample and achieve a 25 per cent response from a fresh list.

Much depends on the importance of winning a high overall response rate. If a high rate from the given sample is critical, then a second mailing is justified and should take place about two weeks after the first. Of course, time could be a prohibiting factor as the second mailing, together with the waiting time for the responses to come in, will add at least a further four weeks to the survey. It is preferable, though not essential, that the second mailing misses out those who have returned a questionnaire already. Eliminating the initial replies requires respondents to have identified themselves. Also, it is laborious removing respondents from the list if there are hundreds of names and addresses on the sample frame.

There are times of the year when a mailing list will yield a poor response. The August holiday month and Christmas are obvious periods to avoid. It is worth trying to avoid any day of the week when people may be extra busy or distracted. On these grounds Monday is a bad day as people face a mountain of work for the week ahead. Friday could also be a poor day for, if the questionnaire is not completed immediately, it could be forgotten over the weekend.

Table 9.1 summarizes a number of the key tasks that require carrying out in the planning of a postal survey and some of the pitfalls of which to be aware.

INTERNET RESEARCH

A change since publication of the first edition of this book is the use of the Internet for data collection. Within only three years this approach has moved from the very experimental to become nearly a standard technique – see Dodd (1998) and Perrot (1998). An indicator of the future importance of research is that companies supplying special research software (discussed in Chapter 12) are now offering modules for the design and analysis of net-based surveys.

The Internet can be used in several ways for data collection. The most common is respondent self-administered questionnaires. These can be thought of as an elec-

Table 9.1 *Summary of key tasks in planning a postal survey*

Key tasks	Possible pitfalls
Order the list of respondents	Can it be obtained on disk?
Book help for typing, folding, inserting and franking	Work out number of people required by estimating time to do each task
Obtain quotes from printers for questionnaire, cover letter and reply-paid envelopes	Check quality of paper Check on turn around time
Design questionnaire and cover letter	Obtain approval of client
Test questionnaire by watching half a dozen colleagues complete it	Do they understand the questions, do they follow instructions?
Order stationery and printed material – outward envelopes, letterhead, reply-paid envelopes, questionnaire	Check licence number for reply paid envelope is up to date Check that envelopes are of the right size for holding the return questionnaires and assembly of out-bound pieces
Arrange for the franking machine to be filled	Note that the Post Office offers a franking service for large quantities of mail
Brief staff who will be helping with typing and stuffing envelopes	Arrange for checking a sample of each person's work to see it is being done correctly
Advise Post Office if there are quantities of over 1,000	You may need to open an account with the Post Office
Mail	Try to plan for the questionnaire to be received on Tuesday (Monday is busy after the weekend and the rest of the week is available for filling it in)
Brief staff who deal with incoming mail on requirements for opening (or not opening) the returned questionnaires	Is there a necessity to check the franked return questionnaire to determine the location of the respondent?
Track numbers of responses each day to determine when to close the survey	Consider data processing after two weeks or re-mailing with a reminder

tronic version of mailed questionnaires but with the option of including many features that are not possible with traditional postal surveys. Illustrations can be added at any point – even in video form – sound can be used and full (and complex) question routing is possible and allows the questions put to be dependent on earlier responses (eg in conjoint analysis work). The 'questionnaire' does not even need to look anything like a traditional paper one (as is the case with CATI and CAPI questionnaires). Delivery of questionnaires can be via e-mail or Web site. In the former cases the questionnaires are sent as attachments to a selected list of e-mail addresses and responses are requested. In the Web site approach the questionnaire is linked to a site and visitors are invited to complete it.

The scope for imaginatively exploiting the potential of data collection is, therefore, considerable and exciting, but what of the problems? Despite all the gee-whizzery these are as much as are found in other forms of data collection. Firstly and most obviously, research is only possible amongst those connected to the Internet and as yet users are still a minority of the population. However, this limitation will tend to decline as penetration grows (as it did with telephones) and providing that it is recognized that the sampling universe boundary is users, this problem does not itself lessen the validity of the technique. Rather more seriously, however, is the problem of self-selection. Just as only a proportion of postal survey recipients choose to respond to a traditional mailed questionnaire, so only some recipients will reply. Because of its novelty, response rates may actually be higher than with postal surveys but there is still the problem that those who respond may well be different to those (invariably the majority) who do not. With the e-mail approach there are also some additional problems of lack of any real sample frames. With Web site questionnaires, the effective sample is limited to those who visit the site in the first place and this is uncontrolled and haphazard.

It is difficult to see how some of the above problems can ever be wholly avoided. However, this is not a reason for ignoring the Internet as a data collection tool. In some applications the advantages will outweigh any problems and, furthermore, the same sort of problems are found with other methods – eg all techniques involve some non-response bias. What is important is that limitations are recognized and made clear to research users and not disguised by the wonders of new technology. E-based surveys are ideal for carrying out employee research in a single company where all staff have access to e-mail, e-mail addresses are freely available and respondents have a strong incentive to reply. The DIY researcher will find inexpensive software and helpful tips on e-based survey on www. perseus.com.

Apart from self-completion surveys, data collection includes on-line focus groups and various sorts of panels. In the former case, the group interacts in the equivalent of Net 'chat sessions' with the researcher acting as virtual moderator. Because respondents are not face-to-face, it is claimed that the 'discussion' can reveal more than the traditional face-to-face group. However, it can also be argued that respondents can also play 'false' roles and strike extreme attitudes without this being transparent (possible also in a traditional group but much easier to detect). In the case of panels, members agree to participate regularly to research through responding to questionnaires, reporting data, etc. In both online groups and panels the design potential of the Net can be used in many different ways. Recruitment to groups and panels can be via the Internet itself or by traditional means but obviously participants need access to the Net (ie have a computer and software) and the ability to communicate easily in this way.

MYSTERY SHOPPING

A relatively new and rapidly growing sector of the market research industry is mystery shopping. Mystery shopping sits partly in the wings of the market research process as it is concerned more with testing sales methods in commercial establishments than measuring or explaining things through survey methods. There is also a fear that the integrity of research could be compromised by market research fieldworkers purporting to be someone who they are not in their pretence as shoppers. However, there is a real role to play for mystery shopping as it is part of the whole consumer satisfaction measurement process. Sometimes it is only possible to find out to what extent a company accomplishes real customer satisfaction by testing the system with a supposed enquiry or purchase.

Mystery shopping has many features in common with the fieldwork methods of personal and telephone interviewing which have been discussed earlier in this chapter. Sometimes the mystery shoppers observe and at other times they purport to be making a real enquiry. There are two principal differences from conventional market research interviewing. Firstly, the interviewers who mystery shop take on the mantle of buyers or enquirers and seek to examine the efficiency of the sales process. Secondly, they complete a questionnaire after and not during the event (except when the shopping is over the phone) and this introduces potential problems of accuracy through forgetfulness. See Morrison et al (1997).

Typically mystery shopping is used to test:

- the speed with which phones are answered;
- the length of time it takes to get through to someone who can help a sales enquiry;
- the courtesy of the sales assistants;

- the knowledge and skills of the sales assistants;
- the quality of the product (as in restaurants);
- the total time taken to 'process' the customer in the shop/showroom/restaurant;
- the efficiency of the sales team in following up enquiries.

There are occasions when it is difficult for people who are not genuine buyers to achieve credibility as mystery shoppers. With certain products and services the would-be buyer is assumed to have certain credentials. For example, it would not be believable for a buyer of a heavy truck to place an enquiry if he or she did not have a business address and patently lacked knowledge on how to specify a vehicle.

10

Product testing

There is no excuse nowadays for the launch of a banking service which no one wants, a car in which the controls are out of reach or a disgusting tasting chocolate drink. And yet failures are widespread. In fact it is often stated that only one in ten new products make it to market; the rest are screened out by some sort of early filtering process. And despite this fall out, about 40 per cent of new products launched, actually fail (Chay, 1989). Surely market research, with all the sophistication it has developed over the past 50 years, can predict more closely what will and will not sell?

Nothing in life is certain and market research makes no claim to be a crystal ball with all the answers. However, it does provide a logical structure and analytical framework which, if followed, will be an important supplement to managers' judgement. We are back to the principal role of market research which is to reduce business risk. Would any sensible person launch a new product without first finding out what people think of it? Many still do.

In this chapter we focus on product research, with two key themes; first we examine what can and cannot be achieved and then move on to look at methods that have been shown to be effective.

WHAT CAN BE ACHIEVED BY PRODUCT RESEARCH?

Generating ideas

In Chapter 2 we introduced the concept of the product life cycle which maintains that it is only a matter of time before all products atrophy and die. Finding new products to replace those which are in decline is essential to the continuance of businesses. For many companies, finding a new product is serendipity. By chance an idea is mentioned by a customer or arises like some spontaneous combustion from internal suggestions. The idea may be a good one, but its appearance may not be at an opportune time if the company faces a lack of development capital or an existing product is still selling well.

Market research brings a more planned approach to idea generation. A simple word search for the number of times embryonic ideas are mentioned in the press may, over time, indicate that there is a trend worth exploring further.

Qualitative market researchers are skilled at getting people to come up with ideas and these talents can be employed to draw out new product suggestions from both internal staff or customers. The purpose of this idea generation is not to arrive at the definitive new product recommendation but to originate as many concepts as possible for further consideration. Whether or not the ideas appear crazy at this juncture is less important than working up as long a list as possible which can be refined later.

Researchers also can help with the refining process. They can use desk research to pass the ideas through a 'viability' screen, making sure that the market size is big enough, that there is growth potential in the market, that the market is not dominated by some monolithic competitor and that price levels allow an acceptable profit margin. As much as anything, the researchers are looking for any good reasons why the idea should be abandoned at this early stage. They are also searching for opportunities – gaps in the market which may become apparent from research which shows that existing products do not match up to their ideal.

Determining taste and design preferences

Before a product (or service) is conceived, the designers must understand what needs satisfying. Through conventional questioning of consumers, market researchers can identify the base features that should be included in a product in order to interest the greatest number of consumers. They can also go beyond the 'givens' and show what additional features would delight consumers and so lift the new product above its competitors by true differentiation.

Qualitative and quantitative researchers can play their part in determining the design features of a new product but the head counters are winning the day. Managers want to know what effect the inclusion of a certain feature will have on demand. Will an automatic inking device on a new franking machine sell more machines and if so how many and at what price? Will a car with an air bag pull many more customers than one without? At what premium can the new gizmo be sold? These questions can be answered by 'trade-off models' which we discuss in more detail later in this chapter.

Determining taste preferences in food, fragrances and drink is not the same as in products which have more identifiable features such as automatic inking devices and air bags. Features of food, fragrances or drink are intermingled so that it is more difficult for consumers to comment on specific components of the taste, texture or smell. Distinguishing these differences and recording how they are perceived is an important task of 'sensory evaluation'. Sensory evaluation is concerned with the accurate description of the taste or smell of a product rather than any evaluation of whether it is nice or not, or whether it will sell or not.

Most people have difficulty in describing exactly what they think of the taste, texture or smell of a product. They may be able to say if they like it or not, indeed how likely they are to buy it; but they may have some difficulty in articulating in exactly what way it pleases or displeases. If they cannot do this then it means that average consumers may not be able to suggest how new food, drinks or fragrances can be modified appropriately.

To overcome this problem, sensory evaluation uses panels of trained people who are taught to recognize the elements of products they are testing. Sensory perceptions are more stable than likings for a product which means that the specially trained panels of people who undertake product tasting can be quite small – 10 to 30 in size is quite normal. This is good news as training panels of people with sensory skills is expensive.

Sometimes, however, image perceptions are more important in influencing the acceptance of a product than taste. Here a larger sample is required to take account of the likely range of opinion. This takes us away from the small and specially trained sensory evaluation panels to surveys of the general public and sample sizes of 200 (or more if demographic or user groups need to be explored separately – see Chapter 7 on sampling).

When sampling among the general public, the researcher must decide if the new product should be tested on its own (a monadic test) or in a comparative way (diadic tests or a paired comparison test of two products; triadic tests compare three products at once). It very much depends on what is being tested and why. A novel product is likely to stand alone and merit monadic testing. A new cola product which is aimed to take on the market leader would be tested against it in a paired comparison. New products are usually tested blind to determine the preferences without the effect of branding, though in further questioning or tests the brand may be named so as to bring the situation closer to reality.

Determining acceptable price levels

The price of a new product is likely to have as much effect on its success as its design. The initial price positioning of the product is critical to long-term pricing strategy as the introductory level creates an expectation which is very hard to change. In its most primitive form, market researchers can test reactions to price by showing consumers random price cards and asking (on some sort of scale) how likely or unlikely they would be to buy the new product. The result is likely to be a classic demand curve which is a concept fundamental to all price theory (Figure 10.1).

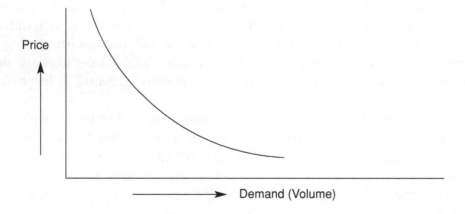

Figure 10.1 *Classic price – demand curve*

As with all theory, the practice can be somewhat different. Research (Eassie, 1979) has shown that there are price points after which demand can fall off dramatically. This is illustrated in Figure 10.2 where we see that 25 pence was the turning-point for many consumers in determining their likelihood of buying a new product.

Price tests of this type are useful to managers as they provide a simple understanding of price/volume relationships. They are, however, based on one product without reference to other options or the wider competitive environment. To this extent it is monadic. More sophisticated models, such as 'conjoint analysis', attempt to place the new product among alternatives and this is discussed later in this chapter.

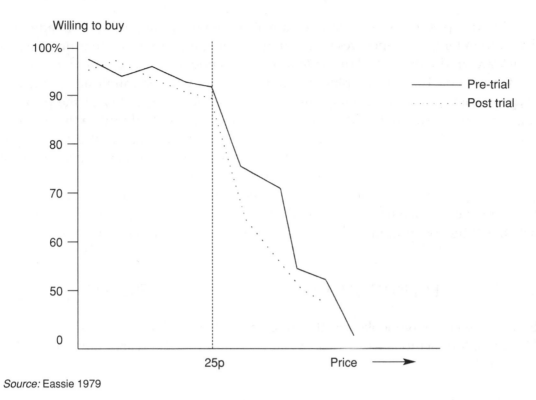

Figure 10.2 *Eassie's buy – response, pre and post-trial*

PACKAGING RESEARCH

An integral part of a new product is its packaging. Indeed, much product research is old wine in new bottles and it is the packaging itself which is the principal feature of the new product. Packaging has both functional as well as aesthetic appeal and both aspects can be tested. In the examination of the function of the pack, observation can play an important role. Respondents can be asked to open packets of biscuits, tear milk cartons or unscrew bottles. Difficulties can be observed and comments recorded. The testing of new packs is important in the medical field where closures are obliged to be child resistant and yet acceptable to old and arthritic people.

Beyond the function of the pack, its surface design plays a vital part in determining acceptability. The pack is likely to include a large number of variables: colours, typestyles and illustrations. People's attitudes to the visual appearance can be tested on techistocopes (or 'T' scopes) which are electronic instruments providing controlled exposure to the pack (they are also used for testing reaction to adverts). The respondent sees exposures which start by being too rapid for identification and which are gradually slowed until identification is possible. The length of time taken to identify a pack and its graphics is a test of its ability to communicate. Using a 'T' scope, measures can be taken of the effectiveness of the legibility of the pack, its impact on the shelf and brand recognition. Each respondent's ability on the 'T' scope is determined before he or she begins the test and the results are applied as weights against the individual's answers. Using these tight controls it is possible to obtain valid results with sample sizes of only 30 respondents.

The design of the pack should not be looked at in isolation. The acceptability of an unbranded pack for a new chocolate drink would change markedly by repeating the test, this time incorporating a well known brand such as Cadbury or Mars.

TECHNIQUES USED IN PRODUCT TESTING

Earlier chapters have looked at the different tools used by the market researcher. Nearly all the methods have some application in product research (summarized in Table 10.1).

Table 10.1 *Market research methods and their application in product research*

Method	Application
Observation	Ways in which providers are used The effectiveness of the design of new packs
Desk research	Word counts to indicate trends Statistical data on trends Screening data for filtering new product ideas
Group discussions	Ideas for new products Testing new product concepts
Hall tests	Testing taste and appearance of new consumer products 'T' scope tests Sensory evaluation
Clinics	Testing attitudes to new cars or industrial products
Home placements	Testing attitudes to new products in a working environment

Home placements, the last of the methods listed in Table 10.1, requires a fuller description as it has not been covered elsewhere in this book. Testing a new product in a hall or clinic is no substitute for a test in the home. Attitudes to products in the artificial environment of a hall can lead to perfunctory remarks. Wallpaper or carpets that receive most votes may not be bought when the practicalities of wear and tear are not taken into consideration. Foods that are tested on the end of a spoon may not receive the same ratings when they are eaten in larger quantities over a few weeks. Researchers need to replicate real use as much as possible and almost certainly this demands getting products into the home.

Nor are all products appropriate for testing in halls. Personal hygiene products such as soaps, shampoos and deodorants need to be placed in the home. Products which have to be tested over a period of time (such as a plant fertilizer) or those which require a complex test of some time (such as an adhesive) must similarly be tested in the home.

The principles of sampling which were discussed in Chapter 7 will be used to determine the numbers of households into which the product will be placed. Cost and time may be the final arbiters but it is likely that somewhere between 300 and 500 (or more) interviews will be required to obtain a robust answer. Almost certainly there will be a quota imposition on the sample to ensure that people are chosen for the test who are target buyers either because of their gender, age, income group, family composition, disposition to certain products, etc. As we have emphasized repeatedly, the cost of the research is not just a function of the size of the sample but also the difficulty of finding it. As a matter of note, some people are deliberately excluded from tests, perhaps because they work in the food industry or are involved in market research or advertising. These could be routes back to competitors and provide an untimely leak as to what is being tested.

Another decision to make prior to the placement is what exactly will be tested – one product in isolation or a number of products. Clearly, the larger the number of products for test, the more complicated it will be for respondents in terms of the instructions they must follow, rotating their consumption of each product and answering the appropriate questions.

When foodstuffs are involved, great care is required to ensure they arrive at each home in as perfect a condition as possible. The freshness, physical size or weight of the products may preclude delivery by the fieldforce of interviewers in which case special couriers are required. Delivering products into the field is sure to be expensive, especially if the homes are scattered around neighbourhoods and across the country.

In most product placements an interviewer calls to recruit the respondent and explain what is required in the test – the numbering of the products, the product rotations, when to sample them, when and how to complete the questionnaire (during the period of the test the views of respondents are usually captured on self-completion questionnaires). Sometimes it is necessary for the interviewer to call at the end of the test, perhaps to run through a debriefing questionnaire or to pick up the redundant sample. The logistics of the operation are manifestly complex and require great attention to detail if problems are to be avoided.

Face-to-face omnibuses can be used to drop off products to relevant respondents for product testing. A self-completion questionnaire or telephone follow up may be used to test reactions. However, it should be noted that not all omnibuses will place new products and those that do will want them to be small, light and easy to carry.

The questionnaires which accompany a product test will, of course, be designed to cover points specific to the subject. Typically, they will comprise a recruitment questionnaire, a self-administered questionnaire, and possibly one which captures views at the end of the test. These could cover:

- Current behaviour of the respondent:
  - purchase experience of the products;
  - demographics (sex, age, social class, income, family composition, etc);
  - attitudes to products and brands.
- Detailed evaluation of the products:
  - likes and dislikes of products;
  - preference for products;
  - reasons for likes, dislikes and preferences;
  - likelihood of buying the product.
- Post-test debrief:
  - personal views on the products not captured in the self-completion questionnaire.

METHODS OF QUESTIONING

In group discussions and depth interviews, open-ended questioning and enabling techniques are used to flush out views on products. Where quantitative methods are used, closed questioning is more common though there is still a role for free responses. Quantitative research of this kind can establish preferences on the basis of today's values. It can state which are the best of the products that have been tested. It can show the strengths and weaknesses of products and individual features of both the product and its pack and it can give guidance on the image, advertising and marketing strategy. But just because a respondent has said that he or she likes a product in the home or in a hall does not mean he or she is likely to buy it.

Much work has been carried out by researchers to try and determine the types of question that are most likely to predict market success. We now examine some of these.

A frequent approach is to use some sort of scale to estimate the demand for products. A scale developed by Juster (1966) has been found to be effective and covers 11 points of purchase probability. An introduction to the Juster scale may be as follows:

> We would like to know what the chances are of you buying this product during the next four weeks. The answers you might give are provided below and are arranged on a scale, a bit like a thermometer. If you are certain, or practically certain that you will purchase the product then you would choose the answer '10'. If you think there is no chance, or almost no chance of purchasing, the best answer would be '0'. If you are uncertain about the chances, choose another answer as close to '0' or '10' as you think it should be.

10 – Certain, practically certain (99 in 100)
 9 – Almost sure (9 in 10)
 8 – Very probable (8 in 10)
 7 – Probable (7 in 10)
 6 – Good possibility (6 in 10)
 5 – Fairly good possibility (5 in 10)
 4 – Fair possibility (4 in 10)
 3 – Some possibility (3 in 10)
 2 – Slight possibility (2 in 10)
 1 – Very slight possibility (1 in 10)
 0 – No chance, almost no chance (less than 1 in 10)

The scale is more discriminating than a Likert five point scale and therefore has a greater chance of forcing a more considered answer.

There are occasions when the answer from this type of scalar questioning is not enough. It may indicate quite accurately the likelihood of buying a product, but it will not predict which product out of a range of options would be chosen. Nor will it put a price on each of the features of a new product and show the likely up-take of each version of the product at the different prices. Answers to these types of questions are obtained from trade-off models.

One problem with product research is getting the respondent to think of the subject both in its separate attributes and as a whole – after all, products are bought as a whole and not as a bundle of attributes. Asking how likely someone is to buy a car just because it has a sunroof is not entirely reasonable as the car will have many other features as well which could confuse the answer. The sunroof must be considered along with all the other features that make up the product. The concept needs to be addressed in the round. When an attempt is made to have respondents state their preference for different features in the car (air bag, sunroof, leather seats etc) rating scales may indicate very little discrimination; that is, all the scores could tend to be the same. There is also a chance that some attributes may be singled out because they are considered 'socially' important. Safety is an issue which scores well in isolation but in actuality it has a much less important impact on the motivation to buy a car. Catalysers and environmental issues are rated similarly.

Researchers have tried to overcome the problem of looking at factors in isolation by grouping them into concepts, the sort that may be relevant to real-life situations. Using multivariate analysis, made easy by special computer programs, this data produces an indirect measure of customer preferences. Examining and processing data in such a way that the different experimental conditions can be separated and quantified systematically is known as 'conjoint analysis'.

Imagine that we have to determine the design of a new envelope and there are three different attributes each with two variations. That is:

Method of sealing	Address facility	Colour
Self-seal	Window	White
Glue	No window	Brown

We can devise eight different types of envelope concept from these variations, namely:

Concept	Method of sealing	Address facility	Colour
1	Self-seal	Window	White
2	Self-seal	Window	Brown
3	Self-seal	No window	White
4	Self-seal	No window	Brown
5	Glue	Window	White
6	Glue	Window	Brown
7	Glue	No window	White
8	Glue	No window	Brown

Each of these concepts can then be presented to respondents who are asked to classify them into piles, correspondent to 'very interesting' through to 'not particularly interesting'. Having done this, they are asked to rank the concepts in each pile to show which is most appealing and least appealing.

> I would like you to look through these cards on which you will see different styles of envelope. Place the cards into three piles which illustrate whether you think that for your company the envelopes would be:
>
> Interesting
> Maybe interesting
> Not interesting at all.
>
> Now would you take each pile in turn and sort them into an order so that the card on the top is the envelope style you think is best for your company and that on the bottom is the one you think is worst.

The conjoint analysis works to separate statistically the effects of the different variables (method of sealing, address facility and colour) and estimates the contribution of each, together with the way that these variables interact with each other. This type of questioning can work with products which have a relatively small number of variables but if there are too many it can lead to an impossibly large number of hypothetical designs to test – all combinations being known as a 'full design'. Twenty-five to 30 concepts is about the maximum that should be attempted.

Conjoint analysis is just one type of trade-off models. Another which finds common use among researches and can be used in product development is SIMALTO. SIMALTO is an acronym for 'simultaneous multi-attributes levels trade-off'. The technique measures people's perceptions of the service and product attributes they receive and compares it to their expectations. It then goes one stage further by allowing people to prioritize the aspects of the service they would like to improve by providing a trade-off element.

The technique does not just gather information on the aspect of service but also indicates the level of performance that should be provided. It shows which groups of attributes are essential and desirable in a product or service and what price each would command.

Using this data SIMALTO allows researchers to identify the nature of improvements that should be made (eg communication issues or improvements to processes) and the emphasis that should be put on those improvements (eg priority, secondary or maintenance).

SIMALTO works by asking respondents to say which level of attribute they receive at the present and what would be their ideal. Respondents are then asked to spend points to indicate where they would like improvements to take place, given that there are only so many points to spend and some trading-off will be necessary. An example of a SIMALTO questionnaire that was used in improving a company's service levels is shown in Figure 10.3. Questioning determined people's ideal level of service and that which they receive from their current supplier. In a separate question not shown here, they were asked how much more they would pay for the improved service levels.

SIMALTO interviewing also can be used in customer satisfaction research to determine how far adrift is the reality of service or product attributes from what people want.

LIMITATIONS OF PRODUCT DEVELOPMENT RESEARCH

Despite the development of trade-off models and the wide body of experience that the market research industry has built up in product research, there are some limitations.

It is sometimes difficult if not impossible for respondents to give a considered view on whether or not they will buy a product or service in the future when they just do not know enough to answer the question. The example quoted in Chapter 2 of the underestimation of demand for the novel Xerox process illustrates the problem of assessing an unknown quantity. Equally, stated intentions to buy a new confectionery bar may come to naught if the product does not obtain widespread distribution. A chocolate bar may not be something that the 'likely buyer' will travel far to find. And can we really say with any exactitude our likelihood of visiting a cinema to see a film due for release in a month or so? Unseasonably hot weather may keep us in the garden or, at the time, there may be better alternatives for the evening's entertainment or worse, pressures at work may chain us to the desk. Predicting future actions is hazardous.

Models of buying behaviour on products also assume that the competition will remain as it is at present: this is most unlikely. If a competitor finds its sales under attack, it is sure to fight back with aggressive promotion and pricing, and perhaps countering eventually with its own new product development. News of a test market is a region could even prompt the competition to flood the area with salespeople, advertising and special offers to spoil the trial. The research may suggest a trial take-up rate which can never be achieved in reality.

There is also another chance that product research will result in findings which lead to self-fulfilment. If in a test a certain product is selected as the most preferred and a prediction is made as to its market share, the wise client who has

	Service Attributes	Levels				
[ ]	Telephone answering	Usually engaged	Rings, but often unanswered	Answered within 7–10 rings	Answered within 4–6 rings	Answered within 3 rings
[ ]	Attitude of telephone staff	Treat me like a nuisance	Treat me with indifference	Treat me with politeness and courtesy	Treat me like a valued customer	
[ ]	Staff knowledge on the telephone	Can't answer simple queries	Can answer simple queries but pass complicated ones to someone else	Can answer most queries	Can answer all queries	
[ ]	Attitude of office staff	Treat me like a nuisance	Treat me with indifference	Treat me with politeness and courtesy	Treat me like a valued customer	
[ ]	Ease of understanding the deal	It is almost always impossible to understand	It is usually hard to understand	It is usually quite easy to understand	It is always very easy to understand	
[ ]	Availability of literature	You can never get hold of the literature you want	You can get hold of some of the literature you want, but not all	You can get hold of all of the literature you want		
[ ]	Warnings of delays in delivery	They don't warn you at all	They tell you, but not until you have been waiting ages	They warn you in advance but do no provide regular updates	They warn you in advance and give regular updates	
[ ]	Explanation of delays	They never give a proper explanation	They rarely give a proper explanation	They sometimes give a proper explanation	They always give a proper explanation	

Figure 10.3 *SIMALTO questionnaire*

commissioned and believes in the research will tool up to meet this level of demand. His or her ultimate sales will then equal those of the market research target. Conviction in the success of market research tests could now spiral upwards as the client congratulates the researchers on their correct prediction and the researchers use the results as evidence of the integrity of the model to win more commissions which lead to more self-fulfilling prophecies.

With some products it is simply not easy to test reactions in an artificial environment. Attitudes to shapes or cars change as they are seen on the road. Familiarization may improve (or worsen) attitudes to design. Car manufacturers are aware of this and attempt to account for it by recruiting groups of people who are prepared to return a number of times over weeks or months to view a new model and check their ratings. This is certainly an advance on a one-off rating at a clinic but it is no substitute for seeing the cars in volume in the daily round.

Around 20 years ago I carried out a beer test in halls around the country in which beer drinkers were recruited off the street. Besides learning that winos can spread the word about free beer in just three picoseconds, I also found out that the sweeter and gassier the beer, the more likely it is to test well when set alongside other beers and drunk in small quantities. However, sweet and gassy beers are the last thing a drinker wants who is downing more than a few pints a night. Nowadays beer testing attempts to get closer to reality and tests are held in clubs and pubs where drinkers can condition their palate over days or weeks.

A final concern about the use of market research in product testing is that there is a tendency for results to lead towards mediocrity. The best products may well fail in a product test. Imagine a clinic which featured the Volkswagen Beetle or concept research which tested a hi-fi set you could hang around your head. Research works well when people can understand products. When products are beyond their ken they are likely to vote them down. People like what they know and love – by definition products that occupy the middle ground and that have been taken to the bosom of the mass market. No wonder the world is becoming full of products that look very much the same. Market researchers have a responsibility to look beyond the obvious, to see through the expected response and to pick up the minor trends. And like all trends, they begin as a very thin part of a large wedge. Quantitative research in product development has its place but qualitative techniques in the hands of skilled practitioners may well be the best means of identifying the really big opportunities.

11

Customer satisfaction surveys

WHY CUSTOMER SATISFACTION IS SO IMPORTANT

It seems self-evident that companies should try to satisfy their customers. Satisfied customers usually return and buy more, they tell other people about their experiences, and they may well pay a premium for the privilege of doing business with a supplier they trust. Statistics are bandied around that suggest that the cost of keeping a customer is only one-tenth of winning a new one. Therefore, when we win a customer, we should hang on to them.

Why is it that we can think of more examples of companies failing to satisfy us than we can of occasions when we have been satisfied? There could be a number of reasons. When we buy a product or service, we expect it to be right. We don't jump up and down with glee saying 'Isn't it wonderful, it actually worked'. That is what we paid our money for. Add to this our world of ever-exacting standards. We now have products available to us that would have astounded our great-grandparents and yet we quickly become used to them. The bar is getting higher and higher. At the same time our lives are ever more complicated with higher stress levels. Delighting customers and achieving high customer satisfaction scores in this environment is ever more difficult. And even if your customers are completely satisfied with your product or service, many of them could leave you and start doing business with your competition.

A market trader has a continuous finger on the pulse of customer satisfaction.

Direct contact with customers indicates whether what he or she is doing right or where he or she is going wrong. Such informal feedback is valuable in any company but hard to formalize and control in anything much larger than a corner shop. For this reason surveys are necessary to measure and track customer satisfaction.

Developing a customer-satisfaction programme is not just about carrying out a survey. Surveys provide the reading that shows where attention is required, but in many respects this is the easy part. Very often major long-lasting improvements need a fundamental transformation in the company, probably involving the training of the staff, possibly involving cultural change. The result should be financially beneficial with less customer churn, higher market shares, premium prices, stronger brands and reputation, and happier staff. However, there is a price to pay for these improvements. Costs will be incurred in the market research survey. Time will be spent working out an action plan. Training may well be required to improve the customer service. The implications of customer satisfaction surveys go far beyond the survey itself and will be successful only if fully supported by the echelons of senior management.

There are six parts to any customer satisfaction programme:

1. Who should be interviewed?
2. What should be measured?
3. How should the interview be carried out?
4. How should satisfaction be measured?
5. What do the measurements mean?
6. How are customer satisfaction surveys used to greatest effect?

WHO SHOULD BE INTERVIEWED?

Some products and services are chosen and consumed by individuals with little influence from others. The choice of a brand of cigarettes is very personal and it is clear who should be interviewed to find out satisfaction with those cigarettes. But who should we interview to determine the satisfaction with breakfast cereal? Is it the person that buys the cereal (usually a parent) or the person who consumes it (often a child)? And what of a complicated buying decision in a business-to-business situation. Who should be interviewed in a customer satisfaction survey for a truck manufacturer – the driver, the transport manager, the general management of the company? In other business-to-business markets there may well be influences on the buying decision from engineering, production, purchasing, quality assurance, and research and development. Because each department evaluates suppliers differently, the customer satisfaction programme will need to cover the multiple views.

The adage in market research that we turn to again and again is the need to ask the right question of the right person. Finding that person in customer satisfaction research may require a compromise with a focus on one person, the key decision maker – perhaps the transport manager in the example of the trucks. If money and time permit, different people could be interviewed and this may involve different interviewing methods and different questions.

The traditional first-in-line customer is an obvious candidate for measuring customer satisfaction. But what about other people in the channel to market? If the products are sold through intermediaries, we are even further from our customers. A good customer satisfaction programme will include at least the most important of these types of channel customers, perhaps the wholesalers as well as the final consumers.

One of the greatest headaches in the organization of a business-to-business customer satisfaction survey is the compilation of the sample frame – the list from which the sample of respondents is selected. Building an accurate, up-to-date list of customers with telephone numbers and contact details is nearly always a challenge. The list held by the accounts department may not have the contact details of the people making the purchasing decision. Large businesses may have regionally autonomous units and there may be some fiefdom that says it doesn't want its customers pestered by market researchers. The sales teams' Christmas card lists may well be the best lists of all, but they are kept close to the chest of each salesperson and are not held on a central server. Building a good sample frame nearly always takes longer than was planned, but it is the foundation of a good customer satisfaction survey.

Customer satisfaction surveys are often just that – surveys of customers without consideration of the views of lost or potential customers. Lapsed customers may have stories to tell about service issues, while potential customers are a good source of benchmark data on the competition. If a survey is to embrace non-customers, the compilation of the sample frame is even more difficult. The quality of these sample frames influences the results more than any other factor, since they are usually outside the researchers' control. The questionnaire design and interpretation are within the control of the researchers and these are subjects where they have considerable experience.

WHAT SHOULD BE MEASURED?

In customer satisfaction research we seek the views of respondents on a variety of issues that will show how the company is performing and how it can improve. This understanding is obtained at a high level ('How satisfied are you with ABC Ltd overall?') and at a very specific level ('How satisfied are you with the clarity of invoices?').

High-level issues are included in most customer satisfaction surveys and they could be captured by questions such as:

- What is your overall satisfaction with ABC Ltd?
- How likely or unlikely are you to buy from ABC Ltd again?
- How likely or unlikely would you be to recommend ABC Ltd to a friend or colleague?

It is at the more specific level of questioning that things become more difficult. Some issues are of obvious importance and every supplier is expected to perform to a minimum acceptable level on them. These are the hygiene factors. If a company fails on any of these issues, it would quickly lose market share or go out of business. An airline must offer safety but the level of in-flight service is a variable. These variables such as in-flight service are often the issues that differentiate companies and create the satisfaction or dissatisfaction.

Working out what questions to ask at a detailed level means seeing the world from the customers' points of view. What do they consider important? These factors or attributes will differ from company to company and there could be a long list. They could include the following:

- About the product:
    - quality of the product;
    - length of life of the product;
    - design of the product;
    - consistency of product quality;
    - processability of the product;
    - range of products.
- About delivery:
    - delivery on time;
    - speed of delivery.
- About staff and service:
    - courtesy from sales staff;
    - representative's availability;
    - representative's knowledge;
    - reliability of returning calls;
    - friendliness of the sales staff;

- – complaint resolution;
- – responsiveness to enquiries;
- – after-sales service;
- – technical service.
- About the company:
  - – reputation of the company;
  - – ease of doing business;
  - – invoice clarity;
  - – invoices on time.
- About price:
  - – market price;
  - – total cost of use;
  - – value for money.

The list is not exhaustive by any means. There is no mention of environmental issues, sales literature, frequency of representatives' calls or packaging. Even though the attributes are deemed specific, it is not entirely clear what is meant by 'product quality' or 'ease of doing business'. Cryptic labels that summarize specific issues have to be carefully chosen, for otherwise it will be impossible to interpret the results.

Customer-facing staff in the research-sponsoring organization will be able to help at the early stage of working out which attributes to measure. They understand the issues, they know the terminology and they will welcome being consulted. Internal focus groups with the sales staff will prove highly instructive. This internally generated information may be biased, but it will raise most of the general customer issues and is readily available at little cost.

It is wise to cross-check the internal views with a small number of in-depth interviews with customers. Half a dozen may be all that is required.

When all this work has been completed a list of attributes can be selected for rating. Figure 11.1 shows how they are incorporated into a questionnaire.

HOW SHOULD THE INTERVIEW BE CARRIED OUT?

There are some obvious indicators of customer satisfaction beyond survey data. Sales volumes are a great acid test, but they can rise and fall for reasons other than customer satisfaction. Customer complaints say something, but they may reflect the views of a vociferous few. Unsolicited letters of thanks and anecdotal feedback via the salesforce are other indicators. These are all worthwhile indicators of customer satisfaction but on their own they are not enough. They are too haphazard and

VOLVO

FL10
INTERCOOLER

9. And, how satisfied are you with our ability to service vehicles at a time which is suitable to you?

	completely dissatisfied	fairly dissatisfied	fairly satisfied	very satisfied	completely satisfied	
	⌐	⌐	⌐	⌐	⌐	(25)

If we are unable to service vehicles within our standard opening times please give details of acceptable alternatives.

_____

_____

10. How satisfied are you with the following aspects of our service support?

	completely dissatisfied	fairly dissatisfied	fairly satisfied	very satisfied	completely satisfied	
Workshop flexibility	⌐	⌐	⌐	⌐	⌐	(26)
Quality of service/repair work	⌐	⌐	⌐	⌐	⌐	(27)
Value for money	⌐	⌐	⌐	⌐	⌐	(28)
Emergency repair/breakdown services	⌐	⌐	⌐	⌐	⌐	(29)

11. And, how satisfied are you with the following aspects?

	completely dissatisfied	fairly dissatisfied	fairly satisfied	very satisfied	completely satisfied	
Handling warranty work	⌐	⌐	⌐	⌐	⌐	(30)
Providing estimates or quotations	⌐	⌐	⌐	⌐	⌐	(31)
Specifying when the vehicle will be ready	⌐	⌐	⌐	⌐	⌐	(32)
Completing all work first time	⌐	⌐	⌐	⌐	⌐	(33)
Completing work correctly	⌐	⌐	⌐	⌐	⌐	(34)
Completing work when promised	⌐	⌐	⌐	⌐	⌐	(35)
Informing you of additional work and cost	⌐	⌐	⌐	⌐	⌐	(36)
Returning vehicles in good condition	⌐	⌐	⌐	⌐	⌐	(37)

Figure 11.1 Sample page from Volvo questionnaire

Table 11.1 *Advantages, disadvantages and typical applications of different methods of data collection*

Tool	Advantages	Disadvantages	Typical applications
Postal surveys (or e-research)	● Easy for a DIY researcher to administer ● Low cost ● Respondents can complete in a time to suit them ● Easy to complete scalar questions ● Visual explanations can be provided	● Low response rates ● Poor response to open-ended questions ● Misunderstanding of questions cannot be rectified by an interviewer ● Attracts response from complainers or the very satisfied	● Where there is a strong relationship with the subject (eg new car and new home buyer surveys) ● Where there is a strong relationship with the company (key supplier surveys, employee attitude surveys) ● Where people feel obliged to fill it in (eg utilities research)
Face-to-face interviews	● Ability to build rapport and hold the respondent longer ● Queries can be answered ● Show cards can be used ● Good response to open-ended questions ● Can ask respondent to self-complete tedious scalar response	● Expensive for a geographically dispersed population ● Takes longer to carry out the fieldwork because of the logistics	● For key customers ● Where customers are tightly grouped geographically ● Where the subject is complicated or lengthy
Telephone interviews	● Low cost ● High control of interviewer standards ● High control of sample ● Easy to ask for ratings using simple scales ● Quick turnaround of fieldwork	● Tedious for respondents when there are dozens of attributes to rate ● Some consumers are hard to access by phone ● Cannot show explanatory visuals	● Used widely in all types of business-to-business surveys

provide cameos of understanding rather than the big picture. In-depth interviews and focus groups could prove useful insights into customer satisfaction and be yet another barometer of performance. However, they do not provide benchmark data. They do not allow the comparison of one issue with another or the tracking of changes over time. For this, a quantitative survey is required.

The tool kit for measuring customer satisfaction boils down to three options, each with its advantages and disadvantages (see Table 11.1). The tools are not mutually exclusive and a self-completion element could be used in a face-to-face interview. So too a postal questionnaire could be preceded by a telephone interview that is used to collect data and seek cooperation for the self-completion element.

When planning the fieldwork there is likely to be a debate as to whether the interview should be carried out without disclosing the identify of the sponsor. If the questions in the survey are about a particular company or product (as in the Volvo Trucks example), it is obvious that the identity has to be disclosed. When the survey is carried out by phone or face to face, cooperation is helped if an advance letter is sent out explaining the purpose of the research. Logistically this may not be possible, in which case the explanation for the survey would be built into the introductory script of the interviewer.

If the survey covers a number of competing brands, disclosure of the research sponsor will bias the response. If the interview is carried out anonymously, without disclosing the sponsor, bias will result through a considerably reduced strike rate or guarded responses. The interviewer, explaining at the outset of the interview that the sponsor will be disclosed at the end of the interview, usually overcomes this.

HOW SHOULD SATISFACTION BE MEASURED?

Customers express their satisfaction in many ways. When they are satisfied, they mostly say nothing but return again and again to buy or use more. When asked how they feel about a company or its products in open-ended questioning they respond with anecdotes and may use terminology such as delighted, extremely satisfied, very dissatisfied, etc. Collecting the motley variety of adjectives together from open-ended responses would be problematical in a large survey. To overcome this problem market researchers ask people to describe a company using verbal or numeric scales with words that measure attitudes.

People are used to the concept of rating things with numerical scores and these can work well in surveys. Once the respondents have been given the anchors of the scale, they can readily give a number to express their level of satisfaction. Typically, scales of 5, 7 or 10 are used, where the lowest figure indicates extreme dissatisfaction and the highest shows extreme satisfaction. The stem of the scale is usually quite short, since a scale of up to 100 would prove too demanding for rating the dozens of specific issues that are often on the questionnaire (more about this in Chapter 8, Questionnaire design).

Measuring satisfaction is only half the story. It is also necessary to determine customers' expectations or the importance they attach to the different attributes, otherwise resources could be spent raising satisfaction levels of things that do not matter. The measurement of expectations or importance is more difficult than the measurement of satisfaction. Many people do not know or cannot admit, even to themselves, what is important. Can I believe someone who says they bought a Porsche for its 'engineering excellence'? Consumers do not spend their time rationalizing why they do things, their views change and they may not be able easily to communicate or admit to the complex issues in the buying argument.

The same interval scales of words or numbers are often used to measure importance (5, 7 or 10 being very important and 1 being not at all important). However, most of the issues being researched are of some importance for otherwise they would not be considered in the study. As a result, the mean scores on importance may show little differentiation between the vital issues such as product quality, price and delivery and the 'nice to have' factors such as knowledgeable representatives and long opening hours. Ranking can indicate the importance of a small list of up to six or seven factors, but respondents struggle to place things in rank order once the first four or five are out of the way. It would not work for determining the importance of 30 attributes.

As a check against factors that are given a 'stated importance' score, researchers can statistically calculate (or 'derive') the importance of the same issues. Derived importance is calculated by correlating the satisfaction levels of each attribute with the overall level of satisfaction. Where there is a high link or correlation with an attribute, it can be inferred that the attribute is driving customer satisfaction. Deriving the importance of attributes can show the greater influence of softer issues such as the friendliness of the staff or the power of the brand – things that people somehow cannot rationalize or admit to in a 'stated' question.

WHAT DO THE MEASUREMENTS MEAN?

The scores that are achieved in customer satisfaction surveys are used to create a customer satisfaction index or CSI. There is no single definition of what comprises a customer satisfaction index. Some use only the rating given to overall performance. Some use an average of the two key measurements: overall performance and the intention to re-buy (an indication of loyalty). Yet others may bring together a wider basket of issues to form a CSI.

The average or mean score of satisfaction given to each attribute provides a league table of strengths and weaknesses. As a guide, the following interpretation can be made of scores from many different customer satisfaction surveys:

Mean score of over 8 out of 10   – Market leader, excellent supplier

Mean score of 7 to 8 out of 10   – Adequate but needs attention

Mean score of below 7 out of 10   – Serious cause for concern; the company will almost certainly be losing market share (except for the score given to price – here a high satisfaction score may mean that the company is selling the product too cheaply)

Someone once told me that the halfway point in a marathon is 22 miles. Given the fact that a marathon is 26.2 miles it seemed that their maths was awry. Their point was that it requires as much energy to run the last 4.2 miles as it does the first 22. The same principle holds in the marathon race of customer satisfaction. The halfway point is not a mean score of 5 out of 10, but 8 out of 10. Improving the mean score beyond 8 takes as much energy as it does to get to 8 and incremental points of improvement are hard to achieve.

Other researchers prefer to concentrate on the 'top box' responses, those scores of 4 or 5 out of 5 – the excellent or very good ratings. It is argued that these are the scores that are required to create genuine satisfaction and loyalty. In their book *The Service Profit Chain*, Heskett, Sasser and Schlesinger argue that a rating of 9 or 10 out of 10 is required on most of the key issues that drive the buying decision. If suppliers fail to achieve such high ratings, customers show indifference and will shop elsewhere. Capricious consumers are at risk of being wooed by competitors, readily switching suppliers in the search for higher standards. The concept of the zone of loyalty, zone of indifference and zone of defection as suggested by the three Harvard professors is illustrated in Figure 11.2.

This raises the interesting question of what is achievable and how far can we go in the pursuit of customer satisfaction. Abraham Lincoln's quote about fooling people could be usefully modified for customer satisfaction research to read 'You can satisfy all the people some of the time, and some of the people all the time, but you cannot satisfy all the people all the time'. As marketers, we know that we must segment our customer base. It is no good trying to satisfy everyone, as we do not aim our products at everyone. What matters is that we achieve high scores of satisfaction in those segments in which we play. Obtaining scores of 9 or 10 from around

After Heskett, J, Sasser, W E and Schlesinger, L A (1997), *The Service Profit Chain*, Free Press, New York.

Figure 11.2 *Customer satisfaction and the effect on customer loyalty*

a half to two-thirds of targeted customers on issues that are important to them should be the aim. Plotting the customer satisfaction scores against the importance score will show where the strengths and weaknesses lie.

HOW ARE CUSTOMER SATISFACTION SURVEYS USED TO GREATEST EFFECT?

No company can truly satisfy its customers unless top management is fully behind the programme. This does not just mean that they endorse the idea of customer satisfaction studies but that they are genuinely customer orientated.

Northwest Airlines, the scheduled airline based in Minneapolis/St Paul, makes an interesting case study. It has an excellent Web site and a sophisticated telephone sales centre, a senior executive responsible for customer service, a well-thought-out frequent flyer programme, and 12 customer service commitments signed by Richard Anderson, its chief executive. It also appears to be carrying planeloads of disgruntled passengers. The American Customer Satisfaction Index (ACSI), based on interviews with a random sample of 65,000 consumers, gave Northwest a score of 56 out of a possible 100. Of the 160 named corporations for which data are collected, only Pacific Gas & Electricity, the power utility that failed to keep the lights on in California, scored lower.

So what is Northwest doing wrong? A decision to remove children's meals from in-flight menus will not have helped its case. It is salutary to look at what rivals such as Continental Airlines have been doing right.

Continental was the success story of the 1990s in the US airline industry and, according to the ACSI, the only scheduled carrier to maintain customer satisfaction throughout the decade. Among the unconventional management methods introduced by Gordon Bethune, chairman and chief executive since 1994, is a $65 cash bonus paid to employees each month if Continental is among the most punctual carriers. It makes sense to reward, in Pavlovian fashion, immediately after the event and not six or 12 months down the line when the effect will have been forgotten.

Two companies, both ostensibly committed to customer satisfaction, but one markedly outperforming the other. The customer satisfaction scores are only part of the story.

A customer satisfaction index is a snapshot at a point of time. People's views change continuously and the performance of companies in delivering customer satisfaction also changes. Measuring satisfaction must be a continuous process. Tracking surveys provide benchmarks of one's own company's performance and if competitor suppliers are also being measured, there will be measurements of relative performance. This places a considerable onus on the researcher to design a survey that will accurately show real differences between one survey and another. The questionnaire needs to be consistent, so there is no dispute about answers differing because of changes to questions. The sample of each survey must be large enough to provide a reliable base and the selection of the sample must mirror earlier surveys so like is being compared with like.

Benchmarking in customer satisfaction can go beyond comparisons with direct competitors. Some firms have taken this type of benchmarking a step further. Instead of just developing a benchmark on competitors, they identify the best firm in any industry at a particular activity. L.L. Bean may be benchmarked for telephone order processing or customer service. American Express may be benchmarked for billing and payment transactions.

There has been considerable research into the links between customer satisfaction and employee satisfaction – Kaplan and Norton (1996), Heskett, Sasser and Schlesinger (1997), McCarthy (1997). The argument is a very obvious one. Happy employees work harder and try harder and so create satisfied customers. A coordinated customer satisfaction programme should consider linking with an employee attitude survey. The employee attitude survey could also be used to check out how well staff believe they are satisfying customers, as there could be a dangerous gap between internal perceptions of performance and those of customers.

Developing an action plan that rectifies weaknesses and builds on the strengths

The purpose of customer satisfaction research is to improve customer satisfaction, and yet so often surveys sit collecting dust. Worse than that, customers have generously given their time to assist in the survey believing that some positive action will take place. Their expectations will have been raised. The process of collecting the data seems easier than taking action to improve satisfaction levels.

In any customer satisfaction survey there will be quick fixes – actions that can be taken today or tomorrow that will have immediate effect. These could be quite specific, such as a newsletter, changes to invoicing, or a hotline for technical information. In the longer term, cultural changes may well be required to improve customer satisfaction, and that is more difficult.

A five-step process can be used to make these longer-term improvements.

Step 1: Spot the gap
- Look at the customer satisfaction data to see where there are low absolute scores and low scores relative to the competition.
- Pay particular attention to those issues that are important to customers (use XY graphs as in Figure 11.3 to show this).
- Assume that the scores are correct unless there is irrefutable evidence to the contrary – and remember, perceptions are reality.

Step 2: Challenge and redefine the segmentation
- How do satisfaction scores vary across different types of customer?
- Are segments correctly defined in the light of the customer satisfaction findings?
- How could a change in segmentation direct the offer more effectively and so achieve higher levels of satisfaction?

Step 3: Challenge and redefine the customer value propositions
- Are customer satisfaction scores low because the customer value proposition (CVP) is not being communicated effectively to the market?
- Are customer satisfaction scores low because the CVP is not being effectively implemented?
- Is the CVP right for the segment? How could a change in CVP achieve a higher customer satisfaction index (CSI)?

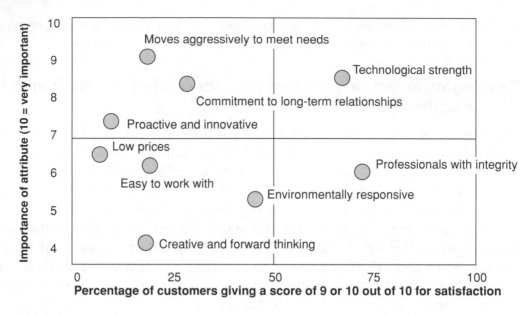

Figure 11.3 *XY graph to show where customer satisfaction needs to improve*

Step 4: Create an action plan
● Describe the problem.
● Think through the issues that need to be addressed and list them.
● Identify the root cause of the problem.
● Identify any barriers that could stop the improvement taking place.
● Set measurable targets.
● Allocate resources (usually money and people).
● Assign people and timescales to the tasks.

Step 5: Measure and review
● How has the CSI moved?
● Is the movement significant/real?
● Has the action recommended in the plan taken place? Has it been enough? Has it had enough time to work?
● Revisit the steps – spot the gap, challenge the segmentation and CVP, take more action.

Many of the issues that affect customer satisfaction span functional boundaries, so organizations must establish cross-functional teams to develop and implement action plans. One of the best ways of achieving this involvement by different groups of employees is to involve them in the whole process.

When the survey results are available, they should be shared with the same groups that were involved right at the beginning. Workshops are an excellent environment for analyzing the survey findings and driving through action planning. These are occasions when the survey data can be made user friendly and explained so that it is moved from something that has been collected and owned by the researcher to something that is believed in and found useful by the people that will have to implement the changes.

As with all good action planning, the workshops should deliver mutually agreed and achievable goals, assigned to people who can make things happen, with dates for achievements and rewards for success. Training may well be required to ensure that employees know how to handle customer service issues and understand which tools to use in various situations. Finally, there should be a constant review of the process as improving customer satisfaction is a race that never ends.

12

Data analysis

Previous chapters have discussed how to collect data through interviews or other sorts of fieldwork. The end result of fieldwork is completed questionnaires. Except in the case of overview interviews or small scale qualitative research, individual questionnaires are of little value or interest. What is required is to generalize from the aggregated data of either the whole sample or of some grouping of respondents out of the whole sample (a subsample). Data analysis is the process of aggregating the individual responses or 'raw' data and is the subject of this chapter. Aspects of data analysis discussed include: the type of data output sought in the simple analysis of 'closed' questions; the treatment of 'open-ended' responses and the more sophisticated tools of multivariate analysis. We also show how the process of data analysis is practically carried out. Finally, the analysis of qualitative research is mentioned.

SIMPLE QUANTITATIVE DATA ANALYSIS – CLOSED QUESTIONS

Simple data analysis is best discussed back to front; the output which is sought before considering how the work can be practically done. To illustrate typical data analysis output we can take as an example research involving 200 interviews using a questionnaire that included the following closed question:

Q5   How likely are you to buy the appliance in the next two years?
      Would you say you are... READ SCALE. ONE RESPONSE ONLY

Very likely   ☐
Fairly likely   ☐
Neither likely nor unlikely   ☐
Fairly unlikely   ☐
Very unlikely   ☐

The responses from all 200 interviews can be presented simply as the number giving each response – very likely = 40, fairly likely = 30, etc. However, it is better to set out the results in a more formal manner such as Table 12.1. This gives the responses as percentages rather than numbers but the total number of responses on which the percentages are based – the base or sample size – is also shown. The inclusion of the base in a table is essential in presenting survey data since, as discussed in Chapter 7, the accuracy of a sample is determined by its size and anyone using the data in the table needs this information in order to make a judgement on their reliability. Another point to note about Table 12.1 is that it is adequately labelled and self-explanatory with a clear title and a definition of which respondents are included; in this case the whole sample – all respondents.

Table 12.1   _Likelihood of buying appliance in the next two years (all respondents)_

Likelihood of buying	%
Very likely	25
Fairly likely	40
Neither likely/unlikely	14
Fairly unlikely	18
Very unlikely	3
Total	**100**
Base	200

Possibly, however, it may be useful to present data for just part of the sample, for example for those respondents who already own the appliance and show their likelihood of purchase. Often questionnaires include questions that only apply to certain respondents – depending on their responses to earlier questions. The term for this is filtering and in the example in Table 12.2 the filter used is existing owners.

   In nearly all quantitive market research, however, comparisons between different groups of respondents are required. This is achieved by cross-analysis. Table 12.3 is

Table 12.2 *Likelihood of buying appliance in the next two years (existing owners of the appliance)*

Likelihood of buying	%
Very likely	40
Fairly likely	0
Neither likely/unlikely	25
Fairly unlikely	30
Very unlikely	5
Total	**100**
Base	100

a simple example of this and compares the likelihood of purchase between owners and non-owners of the appliance together with the breakdown for the whole sample: the data for all respondents (total), owners and non-owners are shown as separate columns. Two points to note are that the figures in the 'owners' column are the same as in Table 12.2 (which by filtering showed responses just for non-owners) and that a base – the number of relevant respondents – is shown for each column. The inclusion of a base for each column is very important in order to judge the reliability of making comparisons between subgroups of the sample – in this case the two subgroups of owners and non-owners each have bases of 100 and at this sample size the range of sampling error is high; it may be appropriate to use a formal significance test (ie as discussed in Chapter 7).

In Table 12.3 the cross-analysis was very simple. It can be far more complex – the likelihood of buying, for example could be compared (cross-analyzed) for different demographic groupings such as age, sex, income group, etc. This sort of analysis is almost standard in most consumer market research – Figure 12.1 provides an

Table 12.3 *Likelihood of buying appliance in the next two years by existing ownership of the appliance (all respondents)*

Likelihood of buying	Total %	Owners %	Non-owners %
Very likely	25	40	10
Fairly likely	40	0	80
Neither likely/unlikely	15	25	5
Fairly unlikely	18	30	5
Very unlikely	3	5	0
Total	**100**	**100**	**100**
Base	200	100	100

	Total	Sex		Age			SEG		Customer type		Frequency of visit		Usually buy from		Income	
		Male	Female	18–34	35–54	55+	ABC1	C2DE	Buyer	Browser	1st time/ rarely	Occ/Reg	Dept store	Other shop	<20k	20k
Base	491	90	401	192	206	91	226	265	171	320	177	314	103	314	187	88
Very important (5.0)	362 74%	68 76%	294 73%	139 72%	149 72%	73 80%	167 74%	195 74%	130 76%	232 73%	141 80%	221 70%	74 72%	233 74%	139 74%	63 72%
Fairly important (4.0)	114 23%	19 21%	95 24%	50 26%	50 24%	13 14%	53 23%	61 23%	37 22%	77 24%	32 18%	82 26%	25 24%	73 23%	44 24%	22 25%
Neither/nor (3.0)	9 2%	2 2%	7 2%	2 1%	5 2%	2 2%	4 2%	5 2%	3 2%	6 2%	4 2%	5 2%	3 3%	4 1%	1 1%	3 3%
Fairly unimportant (2.0)	4 1%	0 0%	4 1%	1 1%	1 *%	2 2%	1 *%	3 1%	1 1%	3 1%	0 0%	4 1%	0 0%	3 1%	2 1%	0 0%
Very unimportant (1.0)	2 *%	1 1%	1 *%	0 0%	1 *%	1 1%	1 *%	1 *%	0 0%	2 1%	0 0%	2 1%	1 1%	1 *%	1 1%	0 0%
DK/WS	0 0%	0 0%	0 0%	0 0%	0 0%	0 0%	0 0%	0 0%	0 0%	0 0%	0 0%	0 0%	0 0%	0 0%	0 0%	0 0%

Figure 12.1 *Specimen cross-analysis table*

example. Cross-analysis in fact can be by any other question included in the questionnaire although by the same token it is too late at this stage to seek an analysis by a variable or possible question that was not asked. The moral is that planning data analysis needs to start when the questionnaire is designed.

The question we have used is a *scalar* question and a common way of presenting the responses from this type of question is by *mean scores* as shown in Table 12.4. Each score (shown for each column) is a weighted average of the numerical values assigned to the pre-coded responses (+2 for 'very likely', +1 for 'fairly likely', etc) and the numbers of respondents giving each response.* The resulting mean score in the example indicates the average likelihood of purchase for the whole sample and for the subsamples of both owners and non-owners; comparisons are easier to make with only one figure per column to look at rather than the whole distribution of responses to the scale. In the table non-owners appear more likely to buy than owners – a mean score of +0.95 to +0.40.

Table 12.4 *Likelihood of buying appliance in the next two years by existing owners of the appliance (all respondents)*

Likelihood of buying	Total	Owners	Non-owners
	%	%	%
Very likely (+2)	25	40	10
Fairly likely (+1)	40	0	80
Neither likely/unlikely (0)	14	25	5
Fairly unlikely (–1)	18	30	5
Very unlikely (–2)	3	5	0
Total	**100**	**100**	**100**
Mean score	+0.66	+0.40	+0.95
Standard deviation	1.14	1.39	0.59
Standard error	0.08	0.14	0.06
Base	200	100	100

Mean scores can be calculated with a pocket calculator but if more than a few are required the work is tedious. Where the data analysis is carried out by specialized data analysis computer software, however, mean scores can be produced

* In the example the total mean score is calculated as $(2 \times 25 + 1 \times 40) - (1 \times 18 + 1 \times 3)/100$. The 'neither likely nor unlikely' response has been given a zero value.

automatically. Interpreting scalar data just from mean scores does, though, have some dangers and the (contrived) example in Table 12.4 illustrates this. Comparison of mean scores of owners and non-owners suggests that it is non-owners who are most likely to buy the appliance. However, if we look at the distribution of responses we see that among owners 40 per cent are very likely to buy compared to only 10 per cent of non-owners and the higher mean score among non-owners is because, compared to owners, far fewer gave a fairly/very unlikely response. Which of these two ways of interpreting the data will give a better indication of future purchase intentions? Whatever the answer, it is clear that interpretation based on mean scores alone has limitations and at the most should be regarded as no more than a sometimes useful way of summarizing data.

Mean scores are just a form of averages – a way of describing a distribution with a single measure of _location_. In interpreting data, however, it is also important to consider its _dispersion_ around the average (or other measure of location). The standard deviation is the most commonly used such measure and is an intermediate step to calculating dispersion in the population from which the sample was drawn – ie standard error which in turn can be used to estimate sampling error or compare two measures (eg from different subsamples) for statistical significance. Table 12.4 includes both standard deviation and standard error and a note at the end of the chapter shows how these can be calculated. Again, specialized data analysis can produce these measures automatically and the researcher can concentrate on their interpretation rather than having to calculate them tediously.

Drawing inferences from a sample to a population requires that the sample is representative – it mirrors the population in at least important characteristics. However, often the achieved sample is not representative and over- or under-represents population groups. Sometimes this may be by design so that adequate numbers of respondents of each important group are included (to allow for statistically meaningful comparisons). Table 12.5 shows the responses from another question in the appliance survey – whether the appliance is owned – and provides a cross-analysis by household tenure (owner-occupies and tenants). It will be seen that in the sample owner-occupiers and tenants each accounted for 50 per cent of the sample (sample percentage across). However, among the population sampled it is known (from other resources) that in fact only 25 per cent are tenants and this group is, therefore, over-represented in the sample (and owner-occupiers under-represented). Possibly this was by design to provide an adequate number of both – 100 of each group (with a representative sample of 200 there would be only 50 tenants). Because of the make-up of the sample, the total 'unweighted' column will not, therefore, be a reliable indication of appliance ownership among the whole population. A solution is to calculate a 'weighted' total column. This is the result of

Table 12.5 *Ownership of the appliance by home tenure: weighted totals (all respondents)*

Own appliance	Total		Owner-occupiers %	Tenants %
	Unweighted	Weighted		
Yes	43	51	60	25
No	57	49	40	75
Total	**100**	**100**	**100**	**100**
Base	200	200	100	100
Sample (% across)		100	50	50
Population (% across)		100	75	25
Weighting factor			1.5	0.5

multiplying the responses among owner-occupiers by a weighting factor* and adding this to the responses from tenants multiplied by another weighting factor and then re-percentaging the combined values to give the weighted column.

In the example weighting was a simple calculation based on only one variable – household tenure. However, in practice, the sample may differ from the population in a number of important aspects (eg age and sex as well as tenure) and several variables may need to be used in weighting to replicate a representative sample. This is beyond any simple calculation but market research data processing software is capable of doing this as required once the population breakdown is inputted.

SIMPLE QUANTITATIVE DATA ANALYSIS – OPEN-ENDED QUESTIONS

To this point we have considered the analysis of only pre-coded questions. However, questionnaires often include open-ended questions of the type shown below. In principle each response to such a question is unique. The responses given by just nine respondents are shown below the question.

> Q8 Why would you not consider buying the appliance in the next two years? DO NOT PROMPT. RECORD VERBATIM.

---

* The weighting factor is calculated by dividing the percentage of the population who are owner-occupiers by the percentage among the sample: 75/50 = 1.5. For tenants the corresponding calculation is 25/50 = 0.5.

Respondent	Response
1	Too big to go in my kitchen
2	I cannot afford to buy one
3	They look so ugly
4	I don't like the colours and they cost me too much
5	I hear they are unreliable
6	With only two of us at home we have no need of one
7	I expect the prices will come down. I will wait until then
8	I think they are complicated to use
9	I don't know really

With only nine responses it is easy to read through them all and make some generalizations (or not). However, with say 100 respondents each giving their own reasons for non-purchase it is much harder or impossible to see any common pattern. What we need to do is to arrange the individual responses into similar groups. This is illustrated below.

Code	Response group	Respondents included
1	Design of the appliance	1,3,4,8
2	Cost factors	2,4,7
3	Unreliability	5
4	Have no need	6
5	Don't know	9

Each response group is designated a code – it is these codes which are inputted in computer processing of the data. The process of categorizing individual response to open-ended questions is called coding and the list of codes and each corresponding response group is a code frame. As can be seen in the example, an individual respondent (4) may give a response which falls in two groups. Grouping individual responses in this way involves a certain judgement – in the example four responses have been grouped as 'design of the appliance'. However, one mentioned size, one appearance (ugly), one colours and one difficulty of use. It may be more useful to group these in different ways (eg 'design – aesthetics' and 'design – function'). There is no absolutely right or wrong approach; it all depends on what the information is to be used for and producing the most appropriate coding frame requires skill and a thorough understanding of the objectives of the research.

The result of this type of coding can be presented in a way such as in Table 12.6. In this case Table 12.6 shows the responses from 70 respondents (ie those not intending to buy). Note that the columns do not total 100 per cent; this is because of

Table 12.6 *Reasons for not considering buying the appliance (those not considering)*

Reason	%
Design of appliance	35
Cost factors	25
Unreliability of appliance	21
Have no need for appliance	18
Don't know	10
Total	*
Base	70

* Multi-response and therefore the column does not total 100

multi-response – some respondents gave a reason for not intending to buy which falls in two or more code categories. Tables showing this type of coded response to open-ended questions can of course also include cross-analyses.

The coding of open-ended questions in market research is quite a problematical activity. From a theoretical perspective it can introduce errors, and quite serious ones, in the data output. The coding frame itself may be inappropriate and produce a data analysis output that leads to misinterpretation and possibly wrong conclusions. Also, even if the code frame has been well designed, the actual coding process may be poorly done – every response must be related to the frame, the 'correct' grouping selected and the corresponding code assigned. This work is usually carried out by clerical staff with little or no understanding of the overall objectives of the research. Even with the right aptitude and effective training mistakes can be made. Even CATI and CAPI interviews need coding where open-ended questions are used; the principles are just the same as for paper questionnaires except that the work is done on screen. To a large extent errors of this sort can be minimized, if not totally eradicated, by good project management (see shortly). However, this leads on to another sort of problem with coding of open-ended questions: it is expensive. Coding introduces an additional labour-intensive stage that is not present at all with closed questions and the inclusion of open-ended questions significantly increases survey costs. Considerable thought and development work has been put into automating the coding of open-ended questions. This is generally based on word recognition packages including those that link words to context. However, as yet, none wholly replace human judgements – the basis of traditional coding. The best solution to either sort of problem may be not to include open-ended questions at all in the questionnaire or at least keep them to an absolute minimum. Often, open-ended questions are included because the questionnaire designer did not try hard enough to close questions with pre-coded responses. In large surveys it can be appropriate to change open-ended questions to closed after analysis of a pilot stage. For further discussion of coding and its problems see Owen (1991).

SIMPLE QUANTITATIVE DATA ANALYSIS – NUMERICAL RESPONSES

A final type of simple analysis to mention is of questions that produce responses in the form of numerical values, eg:

Q11 How much did you pay for this appliance?

Do not prompt, record actual value
£...

The individual responses can be listed, sorted into order (eg by ascending values) and then classified into intervals as illustrated in Table 12.7 – analysis software can take the hard work out of this. It will be seen that the intervals are not of equal range and this is deliberate since most responses fell into the narrow range of £340–£345.* The question responses could have been recorded by the interviewers under pre-coded intervals, but without knowing the likely responses it is very possible that the wrong intervals could have been used – eg £340–£350 would have accounted for two thirds of all responses and there would have been no indication of whether most would tend to the top or bottom end of this range.

As well as showing the distribution of numerical values by intervals (as in Table 12.7) various statistics also could be used to describe the responses, including: measures of location; mean, median and modal values or measures of dispersion; range, inter-quartile ranges and standard deviation. Such measures are often particularly useful in business-to-business market research and may be used in grossing up from the sample to the total population (eg having calculated the average consumption of a product among the sample, that of the whole population might be estimated by multiplying this average by the known total population).

---

* The internal of £340–£345 could be further broken down – it accounts for half of all responses. However, it may be that this range is considered narrow enough within the context of the particular project.

Table 12.7 *Amount paid for appliance (those who have bought the appliance in the last two years)*

Amount paid £	%
Up to 300	3
Over 300–340	19
Over 340–345	54
Over 345–350	13
Over 350	7
Don't know/can't remember	4
Total	**100**
Base	58

MULTIVARIATE ANALYSIS

Cross-analysis enables the relationship between two variables or 'dimensions' to be examined – eg likelihood of purchasing an appliance and home ownership as in Table 12.3. The relationship between three dimensions can (if with more difficulty) also be examined in a Table: we could for example take age as the third dimension in Table 12.3 and have both owners and non-owners in separate sub-columns of three age groupings (say under 25, 25–45 and over 45). The relationship between the three variables also can be represented in some sort of three-dimensional table with a vertical axis, although to do so and read it would be no easy task (and in practice not worth the bother). However, why stop at only three variables? The investigation of relationships between any number of variables may be worthwhile and produce a model (a representation of the reality restricted to selected but critical variables) which offers useful insights into how a market works and, therefore, provides guidance to effective marketing. The relationship between more than two or three variables is the outcome of *multivariate analysis* which is increasingly used in market research – particularly for handling product attribute and attitude data. In part the uptake of these techniques is because the mechanics of carrying out complex statistical operations has been made so much easier through widely available software run on desktop PCs.

The statistical concepts and techniques underlying multivariate analysis are beyond the scope of a general introduction such as this book and we limit ourselves merely to pointing to some applications of which, in broad terms, there are four main ones; segmentation, positioning, preference analysis and forecasting (see Jackling, 1990, for a succinct summary of these).

Marketing planning is now very much based on segmentation; the age of mass markets is waning and increasingly strategies are aimed at influencing specific market segments or niches. Segments can be defined in 'objective' variables such as demographics. This approach is widely used and has been for many years. Conventional cross-analysis of data is usually sufficient to segment the market in these terms. However, another approach is to focus on more subjective factors and especially attitudes consumers have to products; perceived attributes. Using appropriate scalar questions any number of such attitude variables can be obtained but the question then arises of how these can be used to group consumers into homogeneous segments, based on common attitudes, which can be addressed through appropriate (and different) marketing tactics. Two multivariate techniques used for such segmentation are *factor analysis* and *cluster analysis*.

Factor analysis focuses on the attitude attributes themselves and reduces them to a smaller number of *component factors*; groupings of attitudes which on the basis of responses appear to be empirically linked.

The focus of cluster analysis, on the other hand, is respondents themselves; as the term suggests they are clustered into relatively homogeneous groups on the basis of their attitudes to the product. In the drinks market, for example, one cluster may prefer drinks that are characterized by attributes that can be described as 'sophisticated' whereas another cluster may share attitudes more related to the intoxication effects of the products. Clusters are usually given fanciful names to help the nonspecialist (eg 'vintagers' and 'guzzlers'). Factor analysis and cluster analysis are often carried out together with clusters defined in terms of component factors from preliminary factor analysis.

Another application of multivariate analysis is for positioning brands; showing how brands are perceived by consumers to stand in relationship to each other in terms of responses given for each brand on a number of attitude scales. The output of such analysis is commonly a 'brand map' although it is important to understand that this is only a two-dimensional representation of a multidimensional relationship. Figure 12.2 illustrates such a map for four brands (A, B, C and D) in terms of six variables. From Figure 12.2 it appears that brand B, for example, is positioned as a value for money brand and quite reliable while other brands occupy different positions in consumers' perceptual maps. One of the specific techniques used in positioning analysis is *correspondence analysis*. For further discussion of positioning and segmentation see Blamires (1990).

Products and brands can be analyzed in terms of any number of attributes, limited only by what is included (or can be practically included) in the questionnaire. Not all attributes are, however, equally important; they almost certainly fall into some sort of hierarchy (price, followed by value for money, followed by

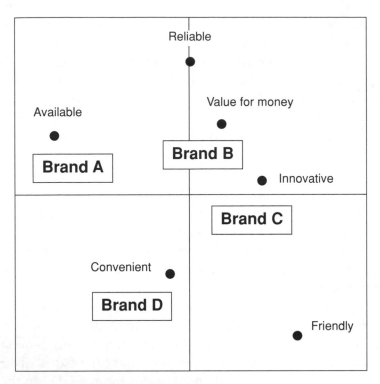

Figure 12.2   *Example of brand mapping*

durability, etc). This hierarchy can be established by direct questioning (eg please rank the following in terms of their importance...) but it is now recognized that this simple approach often fails to produce a realistic model of the consumer choice process; consumers just do not think in this way when making an actual purchase decision. An alternative is to link preferences for whole products (which can be purely artificial constructs of attribute bundles). The importance of the attributes is then derived from the two sets of data at the analysis stage.* A widely used multivariate technique to achieve this is *conjoint analysis* (see Morgan 1990) which calculates 'utility values' for attributes. *Trade-off analysis* is a variant of this based on respondents giving preferences between pairs of attributes. See Westwood *et al* (1974). A major benefit of conjoint analysis is that it allows the researcher to carry out simulations and forecast the likely effect of changing attributes and, therefore, components of a product mix. This can include the effect of pricing changes; conjoint analysis is often used in pricing studies. Other multivariate preference techniques include SIMALTO (see also Chapter 10).

---

* To facilitate the analysis the data commonly need collecting in a particular way and, therefore, multivariate analysis of this (and other) type must usually be planned at the questionnaire design stage.

Multivariate analysis is also used in statistical forecasting with the relationship between a dependent variable (what is to be forecast; eg market size, brand shares, etc) linked to a number of other variables and possibly with time-lags considered (the effect of changes taking some time to work through to the dependent variable). Often such forecasting is carried out with data other than that produced in primary research (eg using published macroeconomic variables) although it can be a useful technique in the analysis of continuous research programmes.

All multivariate analysis, and for that matter all market research analysis, seeks to represent key characteristics of a market and how they relate to each other. In other words, data analysis is a form of statistical model building (see Morgan, 1990; Davies, 1993; Freeman, 1994) which helps us to understand how markets work and can often be used to make predictions of the effects of taking certain marketing actions; asking 'what if' questions. Advances in computing make multivariate analysis, and models based on these statistical techniques, a practical possibility in many applications. However, a word of warning. Because computers 'do' the analysis the techniques can be applied without any detailed knowledge of the mathematics involved. But the output needs interpreting and particularly for the benefit of decision makers for whom the techniques always will be a mystery. In turn this requires a real understanding of what is being done to the data and what the output actually means. Multivariate analysis, therefore, requires more than just acquaintance with the terminology, and statistical experts cannot always be relied on to interpret the output of the analysis in a useful and practical way. Finally, it should be borne in mind that the most sophisticated analysis is not necessarily the best. Often simple cross-analysis produces adequate results and ones which decision makers can feel confident to use.

MANAGEMENT OF QUANTITATIVE DATA ANALYSIS

For a quantitative project of any size, the work required in data analysis is significant despite (or because of) the availability of cheap computer power. Figure 12.3 represents the process, and some of the issues involved in managing data processing will be discussed within this framework. Computer data processing is assumed. Even quite complex crosss-analysis can be produced by simple hand analysis – eg counting responses to each question, sorting questionnaires into piles or building a handwritten data logging sheet. However, with computers now so widely available and cheap, it is hard to imagine why anybody would want to take on this sort of drudgery. Very effective analysis can be carried out by using general purpose software such as spreadsheets and databases but anyone carrying out the work

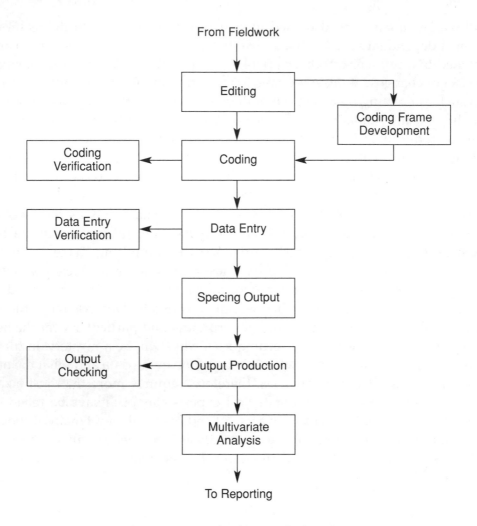

Figure 12.3 *The data analysis process*

regularly will eventually move to software specially developed for survey analysis; there are up to a dozen such packages on the market offering various levels of sophistication at different price levels.

The first step in the process is 'editing'. Each questionnaire is examined to establish whether it is fully complete, whether the routing is correct (ie question skipping has followed the right sequence) and whether responses (or key ones) are mutually compatible (eg if travel to work is on foot, is a journey distance of over 20 miles likely?). Such editing can be done by 'hand' checkers (who need some general training and briefing on the particular job). Alternatively, after the data entry stage, an edit check can be run by the computer although this is restricted to programmable logic checks. Where problems are identified in editing, ambiguities can be resolved either by inferring valid responses in place of dubious ones (on the basis of other responses or arbitrarily) or by re-checking with the respondents (often expensive and leading to considerable delay). Where computer editing is used the software can in some cases itself correct the data automatically within predefined rules ('forced' editing). However it is done, the result of editing is classified as 'clean' data – it was 'dirty' before. An additional part of the editing process is to allocate to (and mark on) each questionnaire a unique number.

Assuming the questionnaires being processed include open-ended questions, the next stage is coding. A coding frame is developed either by listing the responses to each open-ended question from all questionnaires or from a sample of them (the minimum recommended is 100). As already discussed, developing a code frame requires some skill and a knowledge of the objectives of the particular study – ideally the work should be done by the project manager/research designer. If this is judged impractical or too expensive (it usually is), staff preparing the coding frame should be at least adequately briefed and the frames they produce checked by the project leader. The frames are then used by the coding team (a number of coders is likely to be required in a survey of any size if the work is to be completed in a reasonable time). As already discussed, there is potential for mistakes in coding and the output (or at least a sample of coded questionnaires) should be verified independently by other staff.

The normal practice is to write the codes assigned to open-ended questions at the appropriate places on each questionnaire. These are invariably numeric codes in the range of 1 to 10 or 1 to 12 and the same convention is also used for closed questions (in this case it is the interviewer who records the appropriate code). The codes for both types of question are then entered, questionnaire by questionnaire (each forming a record), to form a database in the survey analysis package being used. In this database one field (sometimes more) is used to record the responses of each question and this may be arranged in various ways although it is common to use a 'punch card' format where the fields ('columns') are arranged into blocks of 80 (a 'card'), each of which is identified (by a 'card' number and the questionnaire number). Efficient data entry requires that the questionnaire is laid out in a format that matches the particular data entry method to be used (see also Chapter 8).

Data entry is normally treated as a routine task with any ambiguities in responses resolved beforehand (at the editing or coding stage) and with entries 'punched' as seen. Obviously mistakes are possible and some sort of verification is appropriate – commonly a sample of questionnaires is re-entered by another member of staff – with any inconsistencies that are found in the entries resolved or triggering a check of all the batch from which the verification sample was taken.

The required output from the analysis – the tables sought – are then 'speced'. This involves two distinct activities and often two sets of people. First, the project manager/research designer decides what tables (specified in terms of filters, cross-analysis and the inclusion of mean scores or other simple statistics) are required to meet the aims of the project. Often an initial table run of routine analysis may be requested, to be followed later by other tables which appear (on the basis of the initial output) to be additionally useful. The second aspect of specing is to write some sort of programme so that the software can produce the required output; with some user-friendly packages this may be carried out through menus rather than the more difficult (but efficient) approach of using a programming language. Various checks may be carried out to ensure the required output is correctly speced and this includes table titling and labelling; the finished product should be easy to read. As part of this work or to provide immediate top line results a 'hole* count' is often produced – this shows for each question the distribution of responses.

The cross-analysis tables are then produced – 'run' – and checked for conformity with the specification; appropriate filtering, the right cross-analysis, suitable labelling and titling. The tables are then the material for data interpretation and drawing conclusions at the reporting stage. Often, as this work is done, the need for additional analysis becomes apparent. This may include the application of multivariate analysis techniques although generally the use of these is planned from the start (eg as part of the questionnaire design).

QUALITATIVE DATA ANALYSIS

In qualitative research the samples are usually smaller than in quantitative surveys. However, the data may (or should) be more subtle and complex. It is likely, for example, that questions will be mainly open-ended and the interviewer will have prompted for full responses. Also the interview or discussion may be unstructured with the sequence and even range of topics covered varying between different respondents. Some of the types of data analysis already discussed for quantitative research may have a place in qualitative research as well. However, coding open-ended responses is seldom appropriate since too much detail is lost in this way and it is more usual to list and compare full responses. If the number of responses are few, then it may be enough just to read through the relevant parts of the questionnaires or other records. Often in the report produced of the research it will be

---

* The uninitiated often think this is a misprint for 'whole'. It is not. The term comes from the days when data was inputted through real punch cards with responses represented in each field – column – by punched holes.

appropriate to illustrate with verbatim quotations from individual respondents and sorting in this way will make this easier. Responses also can be transcribed on a word processing or database package and this will facilitate electronic rather than manual sorting but the benefits of this have to weighed against the work involved. See also Catterall and Maclaran (1998) for a wider discussion of using computer analysis for qualitative data. Full verbatim listing of open-ended responses is also sometimes used in quantitative work as well as (or instead of) coding.

Where interviews or group discussions have been tape recorded – a common practice in qualitative research – it is generally considered good practice to transcribe them into typed-up text and carry out analysis with this material. However, it may be enough simply to listen to the tapes and take notes and, arguably, even if full transcription is carried out the tapes should still be used as well to capture some nuances lost in text. It will be obvious that while tape recording interviews is efficient at the interview, it imposes much additional work afterwards and this is one reason why qualitative research is expensive either to do or to buy-in.

Table 12.8   _Sources of qualitative findings from fieldwork_

	Focus groups	Individual depth interviews
Output	4 focus groups generate over 100 pages of text and 30,000+ words	30 depth interviews generate 200 pages of text and 10,000+ words
Analysis tools	Videos, transcripts in Word, observers notes	Questionnaires, Excel, Word documents
Structure guidelines	Brief, proposal, discussion guides, social science frameworks	Brief, proposal, discussion guides, social science frameworks, marketing and business frameworks

The analysis of qualitative data is a neglected subject with only a limited literature (though see Wells, 1991; Robson, 1993). This may be because, like other aspects of qualitative research, much depends on the flair and particular interpretation put on the data by the practitioners involved. No two qualitative researchers are likely to produce identical outputs from their groups, nor would they analyse the data in the same way. However it is done, qualitative analysis requires the input of professional level staff and preferably those who carried out the data collection work.

NOTES ON STANDARD DEVIATION, STANDARD ERROR AND SAMPLING ERROR

The reader with no background in statistics may well have skipped over references to standard deviation and standard error. An adequate introduction to these measures of dispersion cannot be attempted here (there are many useful books on this subject – eg Hague and Harris, 1993). However, for completeness, the relevant formulae for standard deviation (dispersion of data within the sample) and standard error (standard deviation within the population from which the sample was drawn) are as follows:

Formula for standard deviation of a frequency distribution

$$s = \sqrt{\frac{\Sigma f(x - \bar{x})^2}{\Sigma f}}$$

where:
s = standard deviation   *x* = values
f = frequency of *x* $\bar{x}$ = arithmetic mean of the values

Formula for standard error

$$e = \frac{s}{\sqrt{n}}$$

where:
e = standard error   *s* = standard deviation   *n* = sample size

Working with a 95 per cent confidence level, the sampling error is +/– 1.96 times the standard error (see Chapter 7).

13

Report writing

To be more correct, this chapter should be called 'document writing'. Nowadays, market researchers write fewer and fewer reports, relying on PowerPoint presentations to capture their findings. However, there are a number of occasions when a traditional text report or document is required. Typically these are at the beginning of the study when a brief and proposal are prepared to show the scope and the cost of the project, and at the end when a full or an executive summary captures the findings.

For most of us, writing is a daunting task. It requires us to commit words and information to the page. A document is prepared that can be scrutinized, assessed and challenged. When we write we have to sort out muddles and heaps of information into clear and actionable words. Many a researcher can be seen polishing under his or her computer to put off the fateful time when writing must begin.

As with most research tasks, repetition is the mother of skill. The more we write, the better we get. We learn the tricks of writing and grow in confidence. The greater our confidence, the more we loosen up, the more adventurous we become and the faster the documents are written. Long gone is the era where writing was the tortuous process of scratching words on paper followed by the ping pong of editing and typing until a document emerged with a crust of correcting fluid. Of course, it goes without saying that the ability to type and use a computer is a prerequisite.

TARGETING THE REPORT

Reports are not written for just anybody, they have an audience in mind. This can present problems because the audience could be mixed in composition with very different needs. The higher up the organization, the greater will be the interest in the broader issues and conclusions and not the nitty gritty of the findings.

A survey carried out among users of market research reports showed that market research managers were more concerned with the detail of reports (eg typographical errors, poor grammar and inaccuracies) than were the other managers whose priority was that the report should be simple and easy to read. Also, several market research managers wanted detailed and thorough reports; this was not mentioned by those in other management positions.

Differing requirements of managers of a similar level are exemplified by the following contrasting quotes. The first person wants detail, the second wants clear, action-oriented recommendations.

> I like to see detailed methodology – the sample size, breakdown, etc. The data should be presented clearly with tabulations as well as graphs. I like to see an executive summary and the report must be 'meaty' enough. What I don't like are bar charts where you do not get the actual numbers. There is not enough background information or data so you can't do further analysis. I hate bland executive summaries.
>
> *Manager, Research and Planning*

> I like reports that are action oriented. A report should know its audience. It should be clear and display awareness of the initial objectives but be mature and flexible enough to highlight related issues. I dislike illogical reports and those with a poor summary – I don't like to see too much methodology. Also, I dislike reports which show an ignorance of the subject and objectives of the research.
>
> *Business Analyst*

The dislikes and gripes of people who are on the receiving end of reports are in the main the opposite of their likes. Thus, the main dislikes are reports that do not answer the brief, are too long/too full of padding or waffle, have an unclear structure/poor sign-posting, have a naive interpretation and do not come to firm conclusions. Many people have very specific hates, which might not be any great problem to others, such as poor grammar/punctuation/spelling, drawing spurious conclusions that cannot be supported by the data, too many verbatims, jargon, too many tables, reports which are structured around the questionnaire rather than the objectives, stating the obvious rather than providing commentary, and not understanding the client's business.

Table 13.1 *What makes a good market research report?*

	Total % mentioning	Market research managers % mentioning	Other management % mentioning
Answers the brief	33	45	27
Clarity/clear structure	29	18	35
Interpretation/conclusions	27	18	31
Recommendations/action points	21	33	15
Concise/to the point	21	21	21
Graphics/well-presented	19	24	17
Clear, concise executive summary	18	21	17
Total	*	*	*
Sample size	100	33	66

*People mentioned several factors, therefore the total does not add up to 100

A STRUCTURE FOR A RESEARCH BRIEF

A brief lays out the background to and requirements of the research project. It is important that the brief should be in writing as the very act of putting words on paper helps sort out the real issues. Sometimes, the preparation of the brief itself is sufficient to sort out the problem or at least to suggest to the writer an easier and faster solution.

A brief need not be a long document – a page or two is quite sufficient. The following provides an example.

Brief: a segmentation strategy for Joe Soap's Chemical Company

Background information

The Speciality Chemicals Group of Joe Soap's Chemical Company sells chemicals that are a speciality either because of their high purity or special composition. The key markets we serve are the analytical market and the pharmaceutical industry. In the analytical market, the chemicals are used to perform analyses for process control and quality assurance. In the pharmaceutical industry the chemicals are used as reagents in chemical reactions. The analytical customers can be found in the petro-chemical, pharmaceutical, other chemical industries, universities, private and public laboratories. We sell direct through our own sales engineers.

Joe Soap's Chemical Company has previously segmented the market by SIC code/usage. For example, we have done marketing focused on the laboratory market. We now believe it is necessary to have a deeper understanding of the needs and behaviour of buyers and specifiers of speciality chemicals in order for us to re-address our segmentation strategy.

Objectives

The research will have three objectives:

1   To segment customers based upon the key criteria on which they buy speciality chemicals. Previous work indicates the four main drivers are price, quality of product, service (sales, administration, training, technical support etc) and image. However it must not be assumed that these are the only factors. It is also essential to understand what 'quality' and 'service' mean to the customer.
2   To understand why a particular driver is the most important for certain customers and what factors (environmental, company specific, economic situation, personnel) would change the relative importance of the drivers.
3   To understand the role of buyer versus specifier, and whether they have different drivers.

Decisions to be made

To develop the optimum offering for each identified group of customers and to position it using the best mode of communication for each group of customers. We recognize that the research may identify a group of customers better suited to supply through distributors, in which case we would be prepared to reconsider our channels to that market.

Scope

Initially we wish to carry out the research in one country (possibly The Netherlands where we have a customer base of approximately 500). If the results provide a clear segmentation then we expect to carry out similar research in all major European countries.

Our previous experience is that customers often give a superficial and generalized view of what drives their selection of a speciality chemicals supplier. It is therefore possible that we may wish to put specific concepts or propositions to the customers to understand which are more valuable.

Confidentiality

It is imperative that the information either shared by Joe Soap's Chemicals or gathered on behalf of Joe Soap's Chemicals during this project remain in the strictest confidence of the research supplier.

Description and project design

We rely on you to make a suggestion as to the best methodology to fully understand and quantify the segments in this market. But very important to us is that the recommendations coming out of such a research project should be clear and manageable.

Deliverables

We are looking for a report containing the details of the responses per customer contacted as well as recommendations on how to segment the market as per objectives. The report will be acceptable as a presentation but it must be supported by all research material such as tabular analysis, the findings of any desk research, interview scripts, etc.

Qualifications of the consultant team

Please provide a short synopsis of the experience and qualifications of the consultants who will be leading this project. We would also like confirmation that the personnel who will carry out the interviews in the Netherlands are native Dutch speakers.

Budget

$20,000 including all expenses

Project timetable

Please provide a timetable for the research showing the key milestones for each major activity and the number and date of review meetings.

All proposals and inquiries should be addressed to:

Joe Soap's Chemicals N.V.
Mrs Whita van White
Belgium
Tel: 00.32.71.677.234
Fax: 00.32.71.677.235

We are happy to receive proposals by e-mail. E-mails should be sent to whita.vanwhite@joesoaps.com

Kind regards,

Whita van White
Market Research Manager
Joe Soap's Chemicals

A STRUCTURE FOR A RESEARCH PROPOSAL

A research proposal is the return of brief – the document that is returned to the client demonstrating an understanding of the problem, detailing the objectives that can be achieved, showing how they can be achieved, at what cost and over what timescale.

The following guidelines and structure would be applicable to most proposals.

Summary

A proposal is a complex document and merits its own summary. This should cover:

- Who the research is for and why it is being considered.
- The key objectives of the research.
- The important methods.
- The timetable.
- Any other key issues such as how it will be reported or who will manage the project.

The summary should be no more than a tenth of the length of the whole document.

Introduction

In the introduction section there should be a description of the client company – who they are, what they produce, where they operate. It would also be appropriate to clearly and simply state what need or problem will be addressed by the research. A short history of the problem or opportunity would provide a useful context.

A concluding paragraph in the introduction should refer to the names of the individuals in the client company who gave the brief, and the person in the research agency that has prepared the proposal.

Objectives

Project scope and aims

The first part of the objectives section is a short paragraph that defines the scope of the products, applications, and geographies that will be covered.

It may also be useful to say what will not be covered by the research.

Statement of problem or need

In this subsection there should be a clear statement of the need or problem that the research will cover. It can sometimes be helpful to use a diagram to illustrate a full understanding of the subject and to add clarity and interest.

Finally, in this section it is helpful to describe the action that the client will take with the information when they have got it.

Detailed list of objectives

In this subsection the many objectives of the project should be listed, grouping them under headings and sub-headings. For example:

Market size and structure
- To assess the market size for roofing tiles in Germany in numbers and value.
- To assess the size of the market for roofing tiles for new buildings and for re-roofing.
- To assess the size of the roofing tile market:
  - by major geographical region
  - by material type (clay, concrete, slate)
  - by colour.
- To describe the channels to market for roofing tiles and to assess the volume and value of that move direct and through distributors.

Trends
- To identify all the forces that are shaping the future of the roofing tile market in Germany.
- To quantify the trends in the roofing tile market over the last five years.
- To produce a forecast of demand for roofing tiles over the next three years.

and so on.

Methods

This is a crucial section. The method you choose will determine whether the objectives can be achieved successfully. This is the section that indicates the professionalism of the proposal, as it will show whether the researchers have thought through the practicalities of doing the work. As with most research projects, it is not the aims and objectives that are special – we can all dream up the most fanciful of these. It is a convincing demonstration that the method will deliver the objectives that demonstrates the quality of the good researcher.

The methods section could include:

- A general description of the approach that is being proposed for collecting and analysing the data.
- The factors that have influenced the choice of method.
- Desk research or secondary sources that will be consulted.
- A description of the primary research methods stating the reasons for choosing the interview method and, if relevant, the reasons for rejecting other methods.

It is necessary to state the number of interviews (and to separate this number into those that will be by telephone and those that will be face to face) and who they will be with. A table is a useful way of summarizing the number of interviews by demographic group, by country or industry sector. Table 13.2 is an example.

Table 13.2   *Telephone depth interviews by country and size of user*

Country	Large users	Medium users	Total interviews
US	3	3	6
UK	3	3	6
Germany	3	3	6
France	3	3	6
Benelux	3	3	6
Total	15	15	30

If possible it is helpful to give an indication of the accuracy of the data that will be collected.

In the methods section the devil is really and truly in the detail. If the project is international in scope, it may be appropriate to confirm how the translations of the questionnaires will take place, and by whom.

Analysis of the data

This section will state how the data (especially the primary data) will be analyzed and if any use will be made of statistical models.

Deliverables

Deliverables are the things that a research sponsor will receive during and on conclusion of the project. The proposal should clearly state what these are. For example, they could include:

- A commissioning meeting to fine-tune the method.
- The ability to comment on and sign off the questionnaire.
- Interim reporting sessions.
- A personal presentation of findings supported by soft and hard copies of the slides.
- Executive summary.
- Tables from the fieldwork.
- Open-ended responses written up and in a spreadsheet or Word document (sometimes referred to as 'verbatims' since these are, as near as possible, the answers that were given and recorded).

The research team

This will cover who will be in charge of the project day to day, who will control the fieldwork and who will carry out the data processing.

Timetable

The factors that are driving the timetable should be listed and these could include the size and nature of the interview programme, stages of the research, reporting sessions, holidays and so on.

A Gantt chart or a table should be given outlining the key elements of the project. Table 13.3 provides an example.

Table 13.3 *Timetable for project*

Research stage	Date
Commissioning meeting	End March
Agreement of questionnaire	Early April
Pilot interviews	Mid April
Mid-term review of fieldwork	End April
Completion of fieldwork	Early May
Analysis	Mid May
Draft presentation	End May
Final presentation	Early June

Costs

The research sponsor needs to know the cost of the project. Sometimes it is sufficient to give a single figure for the cost of the project. At other times it may be necessary to break the price down to show the cost of individual modules. For example, see Table 13.4.

Table 13.4 *Estimated cost of the project*

Module	Fieldwork	Management and design	Total
Module 1: first stage qualitative	$16,000	$5,200	$21,200
Module 2: quantitative	$39,000	$6,000	$45,000
Module 3: second stage qualitative	$12,000	$3,500	$15,500
Total	$67,000	$14,700	$81,700

It should also be made clear what the cost does not include. Costs are normally quoted exclusive of VAT and this should be stated.

Sometimes research fees exclude travel costs and out-of-pocket expenses for client meetings, in which case this should be stated.

Finally, within the costs section, any terms of payment should be stated. Many market research companies invoice a 50 per cent deposit on commission with the balance (plus any out of pocket expenses) on completion.

Credentials

In this section of the proposal the reader would hope to see examples of the experience and qualifications of the researchers. It is helpful to mention earlier projects that were similar and that will give confidence to the person deciding if the researchers can deliver against their proposals. Most research agencies work within the code of practice of the Market Research Society, in which case this should be stated. It may also be necessary to make assurances about the confidentiality of the research findings and any information that may be passed to the researchers by the client at the briefing or during the project.

A STRUCTURE FOR A REPORT ON RESEARCH FINDINGS

The key to writing a report of any kind is a good framework of headings and sub-headings that take the reader through the subject in a clear and orderly fashion. In a report on research findings, three major levels of heading are sufficient. For example:

Level 1: Chapter heading (eg 'Importance of Factors Influencing the Buying Decision').
Level 2: Topic heading within the chapter (eg 'The Importance of Price').
Level 3: Issue heading within the topic (eg 'The Role of Discounts').

The researcher should not begin writing until this structure of headings is in place at all three levels. The very act of preparing the structure provides a map for the report with balance and direction. As consideration is given to which and how many headings to use, the researcher will be encouraged to parcel up the report into manageable sections. Once the skeleton of the headings is in place, a major part of the planning of the report is finished. It is less intimidating now as it is no longer a task of writing a report. Rather it is a task of writing a maximum of around 300 words under the level 2 or level 3 subject headings, until finally all the headings have their following text.

DEVELOPING A STORY LINE

Finding appropriate headings is clearly important but there is usually a starting point. A report on the findings of a study will have the foundations for the framework laid out in the brief, the proposal and/or the questionnaire. The objectives of the research will almost certainly be a series of topic headings that could be used in the report. The questionnaire will have a logic and sequence to it that has produced findings which may help provide subject headings.

This is not to say that a market survey report should follow the sequence of the questionnaire or steps in the research process. The questionnaire may have been laid out to unfold an issue or to ease a respondent into his or her responses. It may not offer the best flow for the story line of a report. A report on findings may also bring together information from different sources. Interviews may have been carried out with end users as well as with respondents from further up the channel to market. Desk research may also need weaving into interview findings to fully explain a point.

The best reports, as with the best presentations, tell a story. Not a story as in a novel, but a story that builds a picture. Working out the theme for the story is crucial and it may not be as obvious as it seems at first glance. For example, the findings of a survey on customer satisfaction may suggest a structure as follows:

Chapter 1: Introduction
Chapter 2: Summary
Chapter 3: Factors Influencing Customer Satisfaction
● The importance of quality
● The importance of price
● The importance of availability
● The importance of service
Chapter 4: Customer Satisfaction Ratings for Key Suppliers
● The ratings of key suppliers on quality
● The ratings of key suppliers on price
● The ratings of key suppliers on availability
● The ratings of key suppliers on service
Chapter 5: Conclusions
● The most important issues influencing customer satisfaction
● Strengths and weaknesses of our company
Chapter 6: Recommendations
● Areas of the business where satisfaction should be improved
● Action required to improve customer satisfaction

There is nothing wrong with this structure and it may be adequate for some surveys. However, it may miss the point. The study may have been commissioned not just to measure customer satisfaction but to increase customer loyalty and build higher spending levels with greater profitability. If this is the case, then a more appropriate structure could be:

Chapter 1: Introduction
Chapter 2: Summary
Chapter 3: The Problem of Customer Churn
● The effect of customer churn in our company (ie turnover)
● Customer churn levels in different industries
● Trends in customer churn in the last five years
Chapter 4: Factors that Build Loyalty Amongst Customers
● Hygiene factors driving loyalty in the industry
● Differentiating factors that drive loyalty in the industry
● Summary of all factors driving loyalty in the industry
Chapter 5: Our performance in Building Loyal Customers
● Levels of satisfaction amongst our customers on loyalty building issues
● Ratings of loyalty drivers for key suppliers
Chapter 6: Conclusions
● Factors driving loyalty in our business
● Our strengths and weaknesses on these factors
Chapter 7: Recommendations
● Areas of the business where improvements would lead to greater loyalty
● Action required to improve customer loyalty

The suggestion that a report should have a story does not give the researcher the licence to reinvent the objectives of the study at the final reporting stage. So, without compromising the research objectives, a story line should be developed that clearly describes the findings and leads to action.

A story may have sub-plots, but it should have an overriding single message. The objective of the study may have constituted quite a few words such as:

> To establish the drivers that result in the selection of suppliers of polyethylene raw material, to determine their unmet needs and to recommend ways that Polyethylene International can increase its share of the market from 15 per cent to 25 per cent in the next three years.

What is the research really about? In the above example, the findings from the research may have determined different groups of customers with different needs and behaviours leading to a story line such as 'Segmentation – The route to becoming number one in polyethylene'.

Finding a succinct title helps in the search for the story. There is nothing wrong with the descriptive title 'The market for bitumen products in road building in Italy' except that a more engaging title such as 'Roads Beyond Rome' may draw the reader in and be just as effective in communicating the subject that will be covered.

WORKING OUT A REPORT STRUCTURE

It is quite normal nowadays for a presentation in PowerPoint to also double as the report. In the section that follows, guidelines are presented for a traditional narrative report written in Word.

There is no single, accepted structure for a report. For example, it is a matter of preference as to whether the summary is at the beginning or follows the introduction. There are no hard and fast rules and the researcher must develop a structure that feels comfortable. A suggested structure could be:

● title page;
● table of contents;
● summary;
● introduction;
● findings;
● conclusions and recommendations;
● appendices.

These are the main chapter headings and within them are subsections covering detailed issues. Each section or chapter and subsection is identified numerically and a standard practice is to use a 'legal' notation with two levels of numbers.

Below is a further explanation of the main structural headings that are used in a report.

The title page

The title page may also be the front cover of the report. It is the first thing people see and is, therefore, the shop window. It needs to create an image of professionalism and engage the interest of the reader, encouraging people to pick it up and read. The title must clearly state what the report is about and is best if short, to the point and slightly intriguing or tantalizing.

The date of the report should be clearly shown. If the report is confidential, this should be stated clearly somewhere on the title page. The report may have a filing notation or job number that could be tucked away in some corner of the page. It can be helpful to show on the title page the person and company who has carried out the work and the name of the research sponsor.

Table of contents

The table of contents is a map describing the report structure. It should list all main and sub-headings together with their page numbers. The table of contents should also mention any appendices.

Summary

Reports of ten pages or more should have a summary that contains all the salient points from the body of the document, including the introduction, findings and conclusions. As a rule, a summary should be a tenth the length of the body of the report.

Arguably, the summary is the most important section of the report, taking pride of place at the front to be read by everyone. Indeed, some people will only read this section. Although it is positioned at the front of the report, the summary is the last section to be written. Given its importance, care must be taken in the writing of the summary and it is most definitely not a section to be thrown together at the last minute when the researcher is tired of the project and ready to move on.

The style and layout of the summary requires careful attention. Summaries are generally in words but, depending on the objectives and findings, tables, charts or diagrams can be effective in adding impact. The summary can probably be broken down into 20 or so key points with as many paragraphs, each containing just a few sentences. Even though it is a summary, sentences should not be abbreviated.

Introduction

Following on from the summary is a chapter that introduces the report, telling the reader why the research was carried out, the aims of the study and how the results have been achieved. These topics can be covered under three sub-headings: background, objectives and methods.

Within the subsection entitled 'Background' the scene is set, describing the lead-up to the commissioning of the study. This may include a short account of the problem that was faced by the research sponsor, for example:

> Jones & Co. is considering entering the French market for domestic burglar alarms. An investment of $1 million is required in production and marketing resources. In order to evaluate the viability of the project, Jones & Co. requires a full understanding of the French market for burglar alarms. Ace Research was commissioned to study the market against objectives agreed in a proposal dated March 2002.

The 'Objectives' subsection provides a statement of the overall aims of the study and the areas of information that will be covered. It can be helpful for the reader to see a short statement of the aims expressed in just one or two sentences, such as:

> The broad objectives of the study were agreed in advance to be:
>
> To analyze the market for domestic burglar alarms in France; to show the opportunities for Jones & Co., and the barriers that could prevent these opportunities from being realized, and to make recommendations on whether the company could enter the market, and how.

There may then be a listing of some of the 'Sub-objectives' that will lead to the overall aim being fulfilled. For example:

- To assess market size and segmentation over the last three years.
- To assess market shares and provide a profile of the competing suppliers.
- To predict future trends over the next three years.
- To show the importance of installers, builders and householders in the decision-making process that results in the selection of a certain make of alarm.
- To show what motivates the specifiers of domestic burglar alarms in their choice of a certain make/supplier.
- To identify any barriers that could prevent a British company entering the market and to show if and how they could be overcome.
- To recommend a suitable product range for Jones & Co.
- To recommend sales targets for each of the next three years, and show the marketing strategies that will enable these to be achieved.

The third subsection of the introduction chapter would describe the 'Methods' by which the information was obtained, mentioning the secondary sources and the sampling procedures in the primary research. Depending on the subject or type of report, the length of the method section can vary enormously. In some industrial projects the method may merely involve desk research and a small number of informal interviews. In consumer studies it is customary to include details of the sample profile, how and when the data were collected, whether the data are weighted, and whether respondents were given any incentives.

Findings

The findings constitute the body of the report. They present all the relevant facts and opinions collected by the researcher but make no attempt to show the implications for the research sponsor's plans since this is the role of the conclusions.

The subjects that are discussed in the findings will, of course, vary from project to project. Sometimes they cover market size, market share and market trends; at other times they may be confined to image or attitudinal data. Whatever the content, the sequence should be logical. For example, buyers' awareness of companies should be discussed before any consideration of attitudes to the companies. The results of open-ended questioning should precede those from prompted questions. All the time the findings will take the reader from the general to the particular.

The findings attempt to bring to the fore any patterns in the industry or in the responses. This inevitably means that some generalizations will be made, although this does not preclude specific comments to exemplify and highlight points. Quotes (also known as 'verbatim comments' or simply 'verbatims') add authenticity to a report and make the results all the more credible. To make sense of the quotes it may be necessary to attribute them to a certain type of person or company, but this should only be with the respondent's permission, obtained at the time of the interview.

Quoted comments are especially useful for enlivening and adding personality to a report. They forcibly remind the reader that the views that are being expressed are those of the respondents and not the researcher. The onus is on the researcher to ensure that the quotes genuinely reflect the general view and have not been selected to support his or her own prejudice. It is also important to remember that a whole string of quotes should not be used without providing a meaningful commentary, leaving the poor reader to draw a pattern or some conclusions.

Conclusions and recommendations

Conclusions vie with the summary as the showcase of a research report. They provide an opportunity for the researcher to sparkle over and beyond some of the pedestrian information that very often forms the body of the findings.

Many market research projects focus on very specific issues. For example, the market research may set out to answer a question such as: Would the pack sell better if it was red rather than green? What is the optimum price for the product (or service)? What is the best way of segmenting the market? What aspects of our service could we improve? Of course, in each of these cases, there would be a host of detailed questions required to answer the principal objective.

We have seen in Table 13.1 that answering the brief is a crucial requirement of a good market research report. It is also important that the report has a good structure, has a clear interpretation and arrives at setting a clear way forward. Positioning the specific market research objective in a business framework can lift a market research analysis to a higher level and improve the presentation.

A framework is a model or system that locates the market research problem in a wider context and thereby helps in interpretation and arriving at the conclusions, especially leading to the longer term recommendations. The framework offers a theory for showing how things work and clarifies it by showing the component parts. There are many business and marketing frameworks available for the researcher. In drawing together the findings they could be classified into three types – those that describe a situation, those that help in establishing a way forward, and those that lead to action.

Table 13.5 *Three types of frameworks for drawing conclusions and making recommendations*

Section of the conclusions	Purpose of the section	Examples of frameworks
Situation analysis	To summarize the key issues and bring them together	Life cycle, Ansoff grids, SWOT
Marketing and business goals	To show what could be achieved	Porter's generic strategies, adoption models for new products, hierachical communication models (eg AIDA)
Recommendations	To show how the goals can be achieved	Four Ps, XY grids, process flows

Frameworks for situation analysis

It is helpful to begin the conclusions with a review of what has been determined in the research. This could be simply a summary bringing together main points from the findings. However, a framework may provide a better locator for the problem.

A common framework for positioning a product or service is the point on its life cycle. The life cycle concept in business follows the theory that products, just as people, have a birth, a youthful period, they enter maturity and, unless rejuvenated in some way, they enter old age and die. It may not be easy to recognize the position of the product on the life cycle but the attempt to do so with supporting arguments may raise an interesting debate and lead to thoughts for a medium to long-term strategy. At the youthful stage a product may be seeking to build market share by aggressive pricing and promotion. Later in its life it may be more concerned with brand building and customer loyalty.

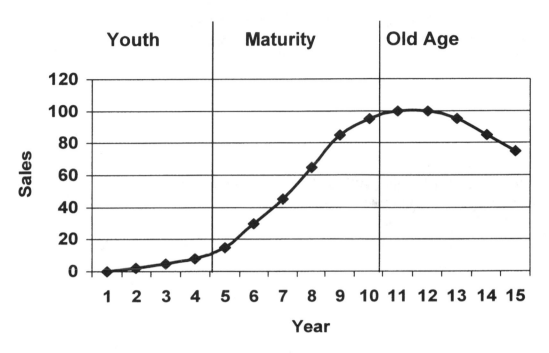

Figure 13.1 *The product life cycle for determining future strategy*

Professor Igor Ansoff suggested a framework (such as that shown in Figure 13.2) with four quadrants representing the position of a product according to whether the product itself is new or existing, and whether the market that is being targeted is new or existing. The grid may be a useful framework for illustrating the challenges that face the product. For example, a product in the south west quadrant can use many conventional qualitative and quantitative market research tools to measure its position in a market. However, market research is at its most necessary and is most challenged when helping to determine the potential for a new product in a new market – seen here in the north east quadrant.

Existing markets New products	New markets New products
Existing markets Existing products	New markets Existing products

Figure 13.2 *Ansoff's grid for locating products and markets by whether they are old or new*

One of the most valuable frameworks for analyzing a situation is to pull from the study the 'Strengths' and 'Weaknesses' of the product (or service), and the 'Opportunities' and 'Threats' that it faces in the market (SWOT), as shown in Table 13.6. The SWOT may only be from the point of view of the research, as there will be many more strengths, weaknesses, opportunities and threats that are not visible to the researcher unless he or she has complete access to 'whys' and 'wherefores' of the client company.

Table 13.6 *SWOT analysis for drawing together key findings that lead to recommendations*

Strengths	Where the product is seen to have an advantage, especially against the competition
Weaknesses	Where the product is considered inferior to the competition
Opportunities	Gaps in the market, trends in the market, unmet needs that could be satisfied by the product
Threats	Factors that could limit the market such as adverse trends, legislation, new competition or technology (very often the corollary of the opportunities)

A framework for the situation analysis does not have to be a universally known model or one that has been developed by an august academic. Some of the best frameworks are those that are constructed as a one off to pull together the strands of the specific survey. A researcher examining the house buying market on behalf of one of the national house builders created a framework to great effect by suggesting that people saw it as a game of chance – the framework became a snakes and ladders board. The die was loaded by the luck in getting a good (or bad) sales agent. Even before throwing the die, the game may be affected by the choice of buying a new or an older house. The graphic images in such a framework are so powerful they will be remembered long after the hard statistics have been forgotten.

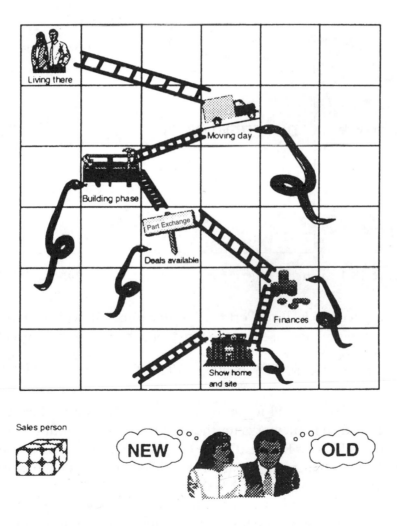

Figure 13.3 *A game of chance for house buyers*

Frameworks for setting marketing and business goals

Some frameworks lend themselves helpfully to deciding a way forward. Professor Michael Porter has successfully developed a number of models that are widely accepted as helpful frameworks for both situation analysis and goal setting.

Porter's 'generic forces' (Figure 13.4) is a useful model for determining where a company is positioned in its strategic intent, or where it could be positioned. The model is all the more powerful for its simplicity in that it implies that focus on differentiation, focus on lowest cost to serve or focus on a market niche are three worthy strategies.

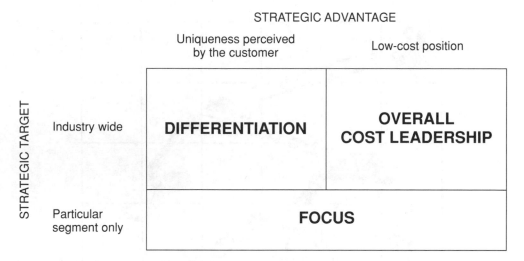

Figure 13.4 *Porter's 'generic forces' for determining strategic intent*

Another often quoted model from Porter is his 'five forces' in which he considers the rivalry between competitors based on the threat of substitutes, the degree of rivalry, buyer power, supplier power and barriers to entry. The researcher would be well advised to read Porter first hand for his frameworks, which have become standards for business strategy.

New product studies account for around 14 per cent of the total expenditure on market research, and so frameworks for the adoption of new products are useful. A well recognized model from Rogers (Figure 13.5) suggests that there is a sequence to the adoption of new products such that it is possible to recognize the proportions of certain groups that will buy a product over time.

Many market research studies are commissioned to examine the buying process and to establish what triggers people to buy. There are a number of models for

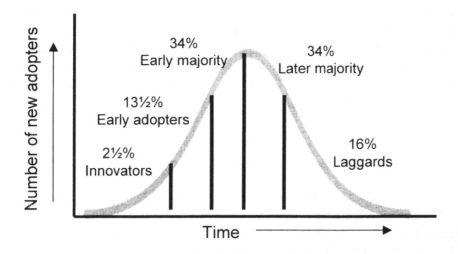

Figure 13.5 _Rogers diffusion of innovations for the adoption of new products_

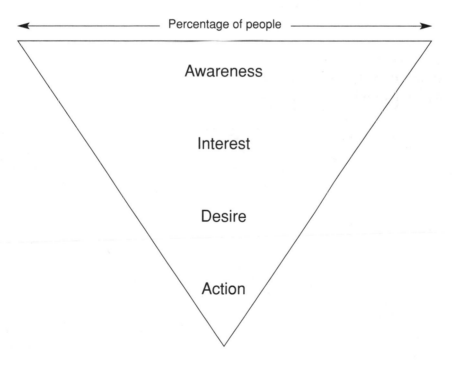

Figure 13.6 _The AIDA model of communication effectiveness_

determining the effect of communications on the intent to buy. The AIDA frame-work (awareness, interest, desire and action) is perhaps the best known (Figure 13.6). The model argues that communications work first at the cognitive level, when awareness is acquired. Communications, if they work effectively, begin to affect liking and preferences so that an interest is built up in the product with a desire to purchase it. Thereafter, a purchase is made for trial and hopefully for continued use. In this model people move through the hierarchy with smaller and smaller propor-tions showing interest, desire and action at each level.

Frameworks for making recommendations

Following on from the situation analysis and the setting of goals is the final part of the report – the recommendations for action. Almost always a market research project will offer some obvious points for action. Those that jump out from the study will be the things to fix straightaway – increase the activity of the sales force, improve the clarity of the invoices, make the pack red instead of blue, and so on. Most clients value a checklist of things to do as a result of the research. These are the 'low hanging fruit', the quick fixes. It is the medium and longer-term implications that are sometimes more difficult to determine. The frameworks used in the situa-tion analysis and the goal setting could be helpful here.

Plotting findings on an XY grid is a simple and yet powerful means of finding out where the goal lies. For example, if the attributes from a customer satisfaction survey are plotted against importance (Y axis) and satisfaction (X axis), there will be clear calls for action (see Figure 13.7).

Figure 13.7 *Importance against satisfaction leading to recommendations from a customer satisfaction survey*

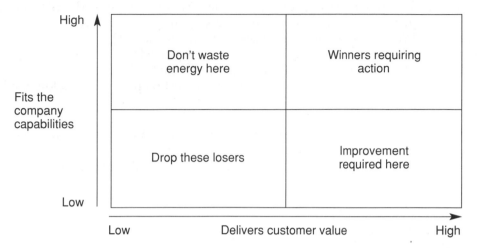

Figure 13.8 *XY analysis to determine where action should take place*

Many opportunities arise from a market survey by exploiting XY grids. Figure 13.8 is an example, plotting issues that deliver customer value against the capabilities of the company to competitively offer those issues.

The research may have focussed on one issue, such as price. This being the case, a process flow framework could help with a course for action (see Figure 13.9).

Perhaps one of the best known and most widely recognized frameworks for making recommendations is the four Ps – product, price, promotion and place (meaning distribution), as in Table 13.7. Sometimes extra Ps are added such as 'people' and 'processes'.

Table 13.7 *The 'four P' framework for arriving at recommendations*

Product	How could the design, quality and range of the products be changed to bring them more in line with the needs of the market? How could the packaging be improved? What services associated with the product (such as delivery, technical service, speed of answering enquiries) could be improved?
Price	How could the price of the product or services be changed to ensure an optimum return? What improvements could be made to the pricing structure, such as the discount policy, rebates, payment terms, etc?

Promotion   What could be done to improve the awareness of the products or services?
What would prompt people to 'pick up the phone' and take action?
What messages have most resonance in the market?
How could the value of the brand be improved?
What are the best media for communication?
What role does above-the-line communication play versus below-the-line and the sales force?

Place   How effective is the current segmentation of the market and how could it be improved by linking closer to customers needs?
What improvements could be made to the distributor network and route to market?

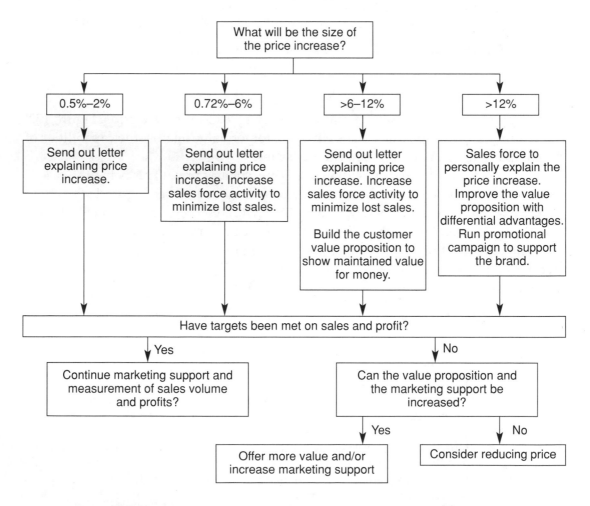

Figure 13.9 *Pricing framework for launching a price increase*

Appendices

Appendices are for data that, while of possible value or interest to the reader, are not essential to the presentation of the findings or conclusions. They could include questionnaires, sources of information, statistical methods, detailed tables, descriptions and definitions and any relevant support literature.

Appendices should not exist in isolation. They should be referred to in the text and only be included if they truly supplement the findings. There are no hard and fast rules for the length of appendices but they are not a dumping ground for vaguely related material, and a reasonable balance should be maintained between the length of the report and that of the appendix.

PREPARING THE REPORT

A good report is a planned report. The more detailed the planning, the better will be the finished document and the easier to write and read. A mistake that many researchers make in attacking the findings is to write up the results in the sequence that the research was carried out – desk research in one section, qualitative research in another, and quantitative in yet another. The quantitative research may similarly follow the format of the questionnaire, each question forming a small section as the researcher ploughs through it in sequential order. The result would be:

The easy (but not the best) way to structure findings:

A	B	C
Desk research	Qualitative findings	Quantitative findings

This type of structure may contain everything that was discovered in the study but would be repetitive for the reader. Some of the subjects covered in the desk research may well be mentioned later in the qualitative research. Likewise, the same issues raised within the qualitative research section would crop up yet again in the quantitative section, this time wrapped up in numbers. It is far better to bring together the findings from the different sources to build a picture within chapter headings, which have meaning to the reader. For example, desk research may be the principal source of data used in the chapter on market size and market structure. The chapter on buying behaviour may draw on findings from both the qualitative and quantitative parts of the study with no input from desk research. However, the chapter on trends could draw on all sources: desk research (A), qualitative (B) and quantitative (C).

The more difficult (but best) way to structure findings:

Chapter 1	**Chapter 2**	**Chapter 3**	**Chapter 4**
Market size	Market structure	Buying behaviour	Trends
A	A	B + C	A+B+C

The main chapter headings and sub-headings for a report will come out of the knowledge that has been built up on the subject, but reference should also be made to the initial proposal. Bearing all these things in mind, the researcher should begin to construct the report's main headings and the subheadings. At this early stage, when the map of the report is being formed, it is useful to write a word or two summarizing the subjects to be covered in each subsection. The structure as it stands, before any real words have been written, is only a starter. It is probable that changes will be made with new subsections added and others deleted, since the very act of writing throws up new and better ways of presenting the data.

Headings and sub-headings are vital signposts in reports, guiding the reader quickly through the pages. They should be short and snappy – wherever possible around half a dozen words or so – and limited to just one line. The headings could draw the reader forward with questions such as 'What are the chances of premium prices?' or be descriptive, for example 'Opportunities for premium prices'.

Once the bones of the structure are laid out with headings and sub-headings, notes can be compiled on the contents for each section. A reader should not have to face a page full of dense text, so at least one subheading should break each page with a headline. If the narrative in a subsection exceeds 300 words, the researcher should think of splitting it and creating a new one.

GETTING THE REPORT TO READ WELL

Reports contain text supported by tables and charts or diagrams. Careful attention to the presentation of the data will impress the reader and help the report to achieve greater conviction.

The correct balance between text, tables and graphics will depend on three factors:

1.   the type of research/subject matter;

2. the type of data;
3. the wishes and expectations of the client.

The type of research/subject matter

In a qualitative report it is customary to write a narrative report interspersed with verbatim quotes to illustrate the points made. The researcher still has the difficult decision to make of how many chapters or sections there should be and which topics should be dealt with under each. Qualitative reports can also be enhanced with imaginative diagrams, which communicate more readily and powerfully than lengthy text a complex issue such as the buying decision for a house (see Figure 13.3).

With a quantitative report a decision has to be made whether or not to use tables or diagrams or both and whether they will be integrated into the text, be positioned on facing pages or be relegated to the appendices. The most common practice is to combine tables and text.

The type of data

The purpose of diagrams is to give a quick visual impression as to a pattern or a trend in data. They can simplify and communicate figures more quickly than words or tables. However, they are not always the answer and there may be occasions when a table is more acceptable. For example, a balance sheet or profit and loss account of a company is better laid out as a table in a conventional format, since a diagram could not possibly show all the detail. As a rule, anything required for reference (where the reader needs precise figures rather than a broad idea) is better left as a table. So a list of prices or currency conversion rates are more suited to a conventional tabular format.

Client wishes

The importance of knowing what a client wants and expects in terms of his or her report cannot be stressed too much. The culture of the client organization may dictate the preferred type of report. For example, some clients prefer graphs with little text; some are keen on detailed tables and feel that graphics fudge the facts; others like a good narrative report with the minimum of tables or diagrams. As we have seen earlier in this chapter, there is likely to be wide variations in preferences, even within the same company.

A note on style

Documents prepared by market researchers are not novels. There is no place for flowery prose, long sentences, evocative passages or 'too-clever-by-half' words requiring the reader to reach for the Oxford Dictionary. They are business documents with the objective of quickly and clearly communicating a message. Brief sentences that introduce a subject followed by bullet points and lists are an excellent way of helping the reader speed-read the findings. Bullets have the advantages of:

- letting the reader see immediately how many points you are trying to make;
- relieving the boredom of long pages of dense text;
- making each point simple and easy to understand.

As with all devices used too much, bullets can make the report stilted. However, in the commercial world, most clients would rather read a snappy report than a literary work with long, convoluted sentences.

In the spirit of the bulleted list, here are some tips on style:

- Reports used to be written in the past tense. However, it is increasingly common to write in the present tense as it brings the report alive and makes the information seem more current.
- It is safer to write a report in the third person as an indication of neutrality.
- Sentences should be short. If a sentence contains more than 20 to 25 words, consider splitting it into two.
- Footnotes and bracketed text can be used to add more information on a point.
- Keep the use of capitals to a minimum. They should only be used for beginning sentences, for proper nouns such as names of people or places, for titles of an individual (for example the Prime Minister), and for headings.

There are no gold stars for using the longest, most obscure words in the dictionary. Where there is a short word it should be used. Jargon should not be used, unless it really cannot be avoided. Likewise, slang is usually inappropriate, except in verbatim comments. The good news is that you need not concern yourselves with the intricacies of the split infinitive, as such points of precision are much more relaxed nowadays – and how many people understand them anyway?

WORKING TO A DEADLINE

All market research projects have a timetable with a date for completion and this becomes the driver from the outset. The report and the presentation come at the very end of the project and so are squeezed if things fall behind schedule. Working at the last minute threatens the whole project with a 'deadline bias'. There is no chance to re-run the analysis and the final report is more likely to contain errors because there is no chance for an independent edit or for sections to be rewritten if they are not up to scratch. Work that would otherwise be rejected goes through if a deadline is screaming.

For all these reasons, care must be taken to plan the timetable for the report and the presentation and to secure sufficient time for them to be carried out properly. This may mean working backwards from the date of the presentation and report delivery to ensure that a number of critical things happen.

There is no simple answer to the question 'how long does it take to write a market research report?'. The skill and experience of the researcher are two more variables that affect the time required to write a report or prepare a presentation. Someone with experience and a strength in report writing will be able to prepare a report in half the time of someone who is new to the task. In general, quantitative reports are quicker to write than qualitative reports where the researcher has to sift through mountains of transcripts looking for insights.

When all the analysis has been carried out and it is just a question of putting the report together, it would be reasonable to expect a skilled researcher to be able to write between 1,500 and 3,000 words per day. Bearing these factors in mind the following table gives some approximations as to the time required to prepare three different types of market research reports.

Table 13.8 *Time required to write different types of market research reports*

Type of report	Days to write report
Quantitative study with 30 questions (20 pages – 4/5,000 words)	2–4
Qualitative study with four group discussions (20 pages – 6/8,000 words)	3–5
International business-to-business project with desk research, interviews with producers, distributors and end users (80 pages – 15/20,000 words)	6–9

Certain assumptions have been made in arriving at the estimations in the above table, namely:

1. that the report writer is experienced and types directly into a computer;
2. that the analysis has been completed prior to report writing;
3. that the report is written in a mixture of prose and bullet points;
4. that the reports will include a mixture of text, tables and charts as appropriate.

The time required to prepare the presentation depends very much on how much of the structure of the report has been completed. Where the findings are assembled, it should be possible to get a presentation of around 50 charts together in a couple of days. Of course, presentations can be put together much quicker than this simply by copying chunks of text straight out of a report, though this is not to be recommended.

PRESENTATIONS

The presentation, together with a bound copy of the slides, is fast replacing the narrative report. A presentation deck of slides offers a faster read, is harder hitting and is more interesting than a 15,000 word report. The presentation pack has become the reporting document and will require at least four or five days of a researcher's time to reflect on its composition and construction.

Whereas a sales presentation may aim to *hit hard* with graphics and a minimum of words, a market research presentation aims to *work hard* and therefore may contain a good deal of data on each slide. Not every slide in the print out will necessarily be shown in the personal presentation of the findings, but they will all form part of the handout and the reference document.

Bar charts are a particularly useful device for showing the percentage of people responding to a question but they can become over-used in the too easy to produce PowerPoint slide presentations. The audience requires some texture in the type of diagrams and charts being shown. The tedium of horizontal bar charts should be interspersed with flow diagrams, scatter diagrams and other imaginative means of presenting the data.

Researchers are lucky to have more than a few days to get this final but most important part of their act together. The presentation itself is merely a moment in time compared to the total time expended on the project, perhaps lasting only a couple of hours. During this time the researcher has to be selective in focusing on key findings, adding emphasis to points, answering questions and stamping personality on the project.

At the de-brief, or personal presentation, the researcher will explain and add to the bullets and charts on the screen. However, the slides should be designed to be self-explanatory so that anyone picking up the pack of slides some time later, and who did not attend the presentation, can work out what is going on. This means that a presentation requires the same format and structure as a report with a title slide, an agenda slide, a description of the aims and methods and then the findings, each divided into subsections as appropriate for the subject. The conclusions and recommendations are at the end. Unlike the written narrative report, a presentation document is unlikely to have a summary at the beginning, although there may be a couple of pages of summary in the conclusions section as the lead in to the recommendations.

Delivery of the presentation centres on the spoken word and it is a great opportunity to make an impression. At an early juncture reconnaissance is required to find out as much as possible about the venue, what projection facilities will be available, how long has been allocated and who will attend.

The time allocated for the presentation and the composition of the audience will influence the story line. If only an hour is available, the presentation will have to be pithy, concentrating on the overall picture, keeping it light on the detail, and maybe with questions held until the end. Equally, a two hour presentation requires pacing. In this case it will be necessary to unfold the data and build a picture to keep people interested.

Mixed audiences create potential difficulties. The chances are that in an audience of around 10 people there will be different interests and levels of seniority. The market researchers in the audience will want to hear about the technicalities and detail of the study; marketing managers will want to know what action to take; directors will be interested in the strategic implications of the study. The researcher must decide at what level to pitch the presentation and recognize that it may well not be at the most senior person present. If choices have to be made, it is the person who commissioned the study and those who will have to use the findings who are the most appropriate target since their acceptance will ensure that the greatest value is obtained from the results.

The presenter's verbal commentary needs to be tight and to the point. The audience is capable of reading the bullet points themselves and they do not need to be read out word for word. The presenter should emphasize the key findings on each slide and talk about their implications, adding interest with brief anecdotes.

With a structured presentation and clear and interesting charts, the researcher is well prepared. The skills of presentation are very personal and researchers must try to find their own style. Remember the dictum – it is not what you say that matters, it is how you say it. Even the most interesting data sounds boring if its delivery lacks enthusiasm. This is easier said than done for junior researchers struggling to keep nerves under control. There is an understandable concern that they will be questioned on what they do not know, and yet this is almost always a misplaced worry. It can be overcome by focusing on the depth of knowledge that is sure to exist, and ensuring that little is left to chance in the presentation by practice and rehearsals. Junior researchers will need to invest at least five or six hours on dummy runs and polishing their act for every hour of presentation.

14

The market research industry

In this book we have discussed market research as a subject in terms of its techniques and how these are used. In practice, however, market research is carried out within an institutional framework; a market research industry made up of organizations using and supplying market research services. Anyone new to market research will find it useful to have an overview of this industry and this is the purpose of our final chapter and with a focus on the UK industry.

THE DEMAND FOR MARKET RESEARCH

Market research is bought by companies and other organizations marketing goods and services and which require this sort of information to increase the chances of making effective decisions. To this we can add government and other organizations that buy information obtained through market research techniques to assist decisions and policy making in areas outside commercial marketing. In 2001 the total spend on market research by UK companies and organizations was in excess of £1 billion. This is the value of *ad hoc* and continuous market research bought-in from specialist market research suppliers. It excludes research carried out by non-specialists such as management consultancies, the value of work carried out 'in house' and the purchase of some information from databases, publications and from some other sources. These additional activities may add another £200 million to the total UK value of market research. Figure 14.1 shows the estimated breakdown of this expenditure by sector. Consumer markets of one kind or another account for by far the greatest market research spend, with only 10 per cent attributed to business/industry. The business/industrial spend is almost certainly understated, as many specialist companies, as well as the large management consultancies, serve this field and they do not report figures to the British Market Research Association (BMRA).

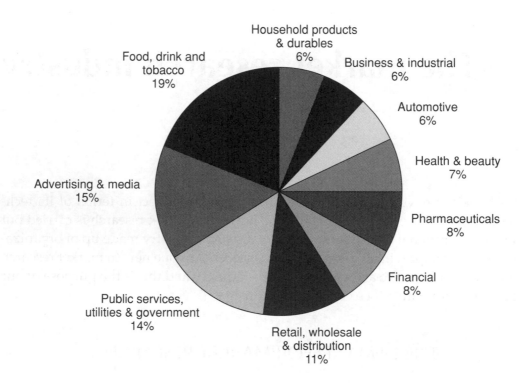

Figure 14.1 *Share of market research expenditure by sector*

The demand for market reserach services continues to grow and even in the recession of the early 1990s market research stood up better than many other businesses – the average growth rate in market research agencies' turnover since 1990 has been over 10 per cent pa with a slowdown only apparent in 1991 and 2001. Some of this buoyancy was due to high rates of growth in work for overseas clients, but even if this is stripped out, sales to UK customers increased. While market research budgets may sometimes be seen as 'luxuries' that can be slashed as part of cost cutting and while clearly, in recession, some sorts of research are postponed (eg that linked to capital investment), the counter argument is that, in a difficult economic climate, companies have to try even harder in their makreting and therefore have an increased need for market research.

As well as the variation in demand for market research by sector, there are enormous differences in the spend on market research between user organizations and in the way they organize the market research function internally. At the top, in terms of expenditure, are organizations each spending several million annually on market research. These include some of the very largest commercial companies and the Government (although spread through many departments and agencies). Research buyers of this scale often have central market research departments which act as service providers to the line management throughout their organizations. These departments not only act as professional buyers of market research but also carry out much work themselves including analyzing, interpreting and communicating data – they add value to the services of market research agencies. Even the largest departments, however, are seldom involved directly in data collection – this is very largely left to outside agencies – although they may be closely involved in sampling and other aspects of research design. Market research departments of this sort are staffed by research professionals and there is a considerable interchange with agency staff. There is a trade association representing the interests of these larger buyers of market research – the Association of Users of Research Agencies (AURA).*

In user organizations spending less but still major amounts on bought-in research (this includes some of the largest groups but where market research is carried out at the operating company level), research buying is also carried out by specialists who may work internally on a service basis for marketing departments and who are often in market research as a long-term career. As in the larger internal departments, the requirement for market research is continual, with projects commissioned regularly and continuous research taken on long-term contracts. Below these sorts of market research buyers, in expenditure terms, are the very many organizations commissioning research a few times a year or more spasmodically.

Apart from market research bought by individual organizations to meet their own needs, there is a significant expenditure by industry groups collectively. Trade associations may commission *ad hoc* or continuous research and in some areas there are special joint research programmes to meet industry-wide information needs – media research is the most notable example of this with much audience and readership data obtained in this way.

---

* A contact list of organizations is provided at the end of the chapter.

As well as users and suppliers of market research, there are some types of organizations which fall somewhere in between. The most significant of this group are advertising agencies who commission research on behalf of their own clients and may, for example, build in advertising testing and evaluation into the planning of major campaigns. The largest advertising agencies often have their own research departments staffed by professionals and involved in the development of sophisticated techniques for media and advertising-linked research (there is a monthly journal specializing in this area – see *Admap*). Other types of organizations buying research on their clients' behalf include management consultancies. A few of these have their own market research departments and many others will carry out research as part of wider assignments – with greater or lesser skill.

MARKET RESEARCHERS

Before moving on to describing the supply side of the market research industry in terms of the companies involved, it is useful to discuss the type of people who work in market research and particularly within the agencies, although, as already mentioned, there is a significant level of interchange in staff between research user and provider organizations. To simplify, there are three broad groups involved in market research work: professional level staff, support staff and interviewers or fieldworkers.

While, in the narrow sense, market research is not a full profession such as the law, medicine or accountancy since it lacks the restrictive practices and control over entry which are distinguishing features of these longer established callings, it is certainly a profession in a wider sense. Although anyone can call themselves a market researcher, being able to offer this service with any credibility requires education and training, together with a grasp of constantly evolving theory and its practical application. There is also a professional body to which most practitioners belong – Market Research Society (MRS) – and there are recognized codes of practice. The practitioners forming this layer within the industry are responsible for all aspects of research design – defining the coverage and selecting appropriate methods for a project – overall management of research activities and the interpretation of data and communication of findings to research users. In the case of qualitative research, professional level staff are also closely involved in data collection (moderating group discussions, depth interviewing). Desk research also can be part of their work. In other words, all the aspects of carrying out market research with a significant intellectual content. Because market research is not a fully regulated profession, it is difficult to estimate the numbers of professional level staff involved but it is less than 15,000 in the UK.

Support staff working in market research include some technical specialists and particularly those working in data analysis and statistics and who, like more general research practitioners, are nearly all graduates. There are also staff managing the work of other staff and especially interviewers (field management). Research agencies also, of course, employ a range of staff who have counterparts in most other businesses – administration, secretarial work and finance.

The largest group of workers in market research is, however, interviewers or fieldworkers. It is they who actually collect, through structured interviews, nearly all the data on which quantitative research is based and even in qualitative research, it is their efforts which ensure respondents attend groups or depth interviews. Most work is out in the 'field' carrying out face-to-face interviews, but in recent years there has been a growth in phone interviewing carried out from central locations – phone unit offices. There are about 35,000 market research interviewers, the large majority are women (professional level staff are also by no means male dominated), working nominally part time and often intermittently for several market research agencies. There are no formal qualifications needed to become an interviewer, beyond a reasonable level of secondary education. Training of interviewers from scratch typically involves two or three days in the 'classroom' with on-the-job support afterwards. The interviewer's task is largely a matter of administering a predesigned structured questionnaire and the training focuses on this and associated requirements. The real skill in interviewing is, however, successfully obtaining the co-operation of respondents – no mean task, taking up to an hour or even longer of respondents' time, and with no or at the most only a token reward. Some of this skill can be taught but a certain flair and temperament is also required. Research agencies recruit, train, organize and control their interviewing forces through local supervisors and any career progression of interviewers is limited to this avenue or occasionally office-based field management. Office-based phone interviewers may also progress to supervision. Market research agencies also employ part-time workers in data processing (including home workers) who have conditions of employment comparable to interviewers.

THE PROFESSIONAL BODIES

The main professional body in UK market research is the Market Research Society (MRS). This has a membership of around 8,000 and full-time staff based at offices in London. Most professional level staff belong to the MRS. The range of activities MRS undertakes is diverse and includes setting and enforcing a code of practice (see later), taking initiatives to develop and advance techniques of market research, providing a forum for members (with an annual conference as a main event), acting as a pressure group in relation to market research industry concerns and running an extensive education and training programme. The Society also produces publications including *Research* (monthly) and the *Market Research Journal* (quarterly).

There are a number of groups devoted to particular specialisms in market research, eg the Association of Qualitative Research Practitioners (AQRP) and the Social Research Association (SRA). Most members of these bodies also belong to the MRS. Finally, there are some international organizations based on individual membership, including the broadly-based European Society for Opinion and Marketing Research (ESOMAR).

MARKET RESEARCH AGENCIES

The total number of specialist UK market research agencies is uncertain but probably over 300. The BMRA (British Market Research Association) – the trade association of market research agencies – lists its members, turnover each year, with Taylor Nelson Sofres topping the bill with a turnover of over £100 million, one thousand times that of the smallest member, ranked out of the 101 in the table. In addition there are several significant companies in this field that are not members of the BMRA, plus many very small operations, with an imprecise boundary between small agencies and freelance workers (of whom there are many at the professional level). There are various listings of market research companies but the most authoritative is usually regarded to be the *Organization Book* (annual) published by the MRS.

Table 14.1 lists the 20 largest members of BMRA by turnover. Below these 20 there is a very long 'tail' of smaller companies and in fact the large majority of all agencies have turnovers of under £1 million. Despite the growth of larger agencies, both organically and by acquisition, market research remains an industry typified by small businesses.

Nearly all the medium and smaller companies (those with turnovers of under £1 million) are owner-managed. This is also true of some larger agencies and most of them started off this way. However, quite a few larger research agencies, although operated as separate companies, are members of larger groups with business interests outside market research. Three of the larger companies (Research International, Millward Brown and BMRB) are, for example, owned by WPP: the biggest advertising group in the world. Some companies, including most of the largest, have international connections including through offices or subsidiaries overseas, sister companies under the same ownership or other forms of link-up. Such connections make them well placed for carrying out international research projects.

Table 14.1 *Twenty largest BMRA members by turnover*

Company	2000 Turnover £ million
Taylor Nelson Sofres plc	110
NOP Research Group Ltd	68
Research International Ltd	65
Millward Brown International plc	65
NFO Worldgroup	43
BMRB International	40
Ipsos-RSL Ltd	39
Information Resources	31
MORI (Market & Opinion Research International)	27
Martiz TRBI	25
Martin Hamblin Group	17
GFK Marketing Services	16
ISIS Research plc	12
ORC International	11
Added Value Ltd	11
Hall & Partners Europe Ltd	9
Hauck Research Services Ltd	9
Davies Riley-Smith Maclay	7
Simon Godfrey Associates Ltd	7
Promar International Ltd	7

Source: BMRA published statistics

As already mentioned, the trade association representing market research agencies is the British Market Research Association (BMRA). This body was formed in early 1998 through the amalgamation of Association of Market Survey Organizations (AMSO) and Association of British Market Research Companies (ABMRC). The BMRA's primary purpose is to represent the interests of its member companies including by acting as a lobbying body. However, ethical and commercial issues are within its remit. The BMRA, for example, supports the work of MRQSA (see page 252) and requires its members to work to the standards of that body.

As well as the national trade association, there are several international equivalents to which agencies can belong, either by direct membership or indirectly through a UK body. These include the Association of European Market Research Institutes (AEMRI) and the European Federation of Associations of Market Research Organizations (EFAMRO). The activities of these bodies mirror the national associations but on a European and international level. One particular involvement is as a pressure group to the European Commission and monitoring the likely effects of EU legislation on market research work and businesses.

RESEARCH AGENCY SERVICES

Between them, UK market research agencies carry out all types of market research, in every market where there is a demand for this type of service. Few if any agencies, including the largest, however, claim to be able to carry out every type of project; they specialize either in markets or techniques. Some (many of the smaller companies) for example are only involved in qualitative research. The services offered can usefully be classified under four main headings: *ad hoc* research, continuous studies, publishing market research and data collection and processing services.

Ad hoc research

Ad hoc research is the mainstay of the large majority of agencies. Projects are carried out for individual clients and designed as one-offs to meet specific needs and objectives and with an appropriate research design developed (although to some extent the specialization of the agency is also a major determinant of the methods proposed). The normal commercial practice in *ad hoc* research is for the agency to discuss the requirement with a prospective client and then prepare a formal proposal. This includes a quotation and timetable for carrying out the work, but also details of the intended research design – market research is one of the few activities where client design work is carried out (as no charge) before any commitment is made. The output of *ad hoc* research normally includes full interpretation of the data produced plus conclusions relevant to the marketing problem to be solved or decisions to be made; for this reason the term 'full service' research is used. The delivery of this output is often in the form of a full narrative report although this may be backed or even replaced by a face-to-face presentation. Because *ad hoc* research agencies usually work closely with clients and involve themselves in the full background to the research requirement, their service shades into management consultancy. Some researchers, feeling mere research to be not sufficiently grand (or profitable), are anxious to move their service to a greater extent in this direction.

Anyone new to market research always want to know what *ad hoc* research costs. Unfortunately, with such wide variation in the scope of projects, generalization is impossible. However, as a very rough indication, the starting level for 'complete' projects is about the £5,000 mark and can go up to six figures but most *ad hoc* projects are in the £15,000–£50,000 range (2002 prices).

Continuous research

Some would say that it is hard to become seriously rich (agencies are profit seeking businesses) by offering *ad hoc* research alone and in fact the largest agencies earn most of their turnover from clients that subscribe long term to continuous research programmes. The boundaries between *ad hoc* and continuous research are not always clear-cut but typical types of continuous programmes involve the provision of data from respondent panels and retail audits; Taylor Nelson Sofres and Nielsen are two large companies heavily involved in these areas. There is also the output from large continuous interviewing programmes covering consumption and media exposure patterns – eg the TGI service from BMRB. Continuous research is mainly sold on a syndicated basis with a number of clients contributing towards what are very costly projects. The data may also be offered to anyone wishing to buy-in to them. For most continuous research charges are substantial even though costs are shared.

Published research

Published research is another form of syndicated research and may be based on continuous data. However, it is distinguished by being offered to a wide market and in a written report format (although other media such as CD ROM are starting to be used and some reports are also accessible from online databases). There are perhaps 30,000 titles available internationally covering virtually every market and subject and these can be located from a number of sources including *Market Search* (annual) and some online databases. Publishers of the reports include market reserach agencies whose main business is *ad hoc* or continuous research but there are also some specialists outside mainstream agencies, including Mintel, Euromonitor and Frost & Sullivan (specialists in industrial and technical markets). The scope of the reports is often international. Costs range from little more than the price of a hardback textbook up to several thousand pounds per report. However, much published research is modestly priced and can offer considerable savings over *ad hoc* research. Of course, a published report may well not exactly match specific requirements but buying it may reduce the contribution required from far more expensive tailored studies. Locating and selecting published research reports merges into desk research activities.

Data collection and processing service

The services discussed so far are all aimed in a sense at the final user of research – marketing decision makers who commission *ad hoc* research, subscribe to continuous programmes or buy published reports. The final types of service to be discussed, by contrast, are aimed at other market research professionals who buy them as cost-effective methods of data collection and processing. There are two common services of this type: field and tab and omnibus surveys.

In field and tab research, the client is responsible for the research design including questionnaire drafting and defining the sample method (field and tab is largely a quantitative research service) and at the other end of the process, interpreting the data and preparing a report. The agency carries out the labour-intensive legwork in between: interviewing (either by phone or face to face) and data analysis (where access to software and computer resources are also important) with the output delivered as 'tabs' – data tables. Field and tab services are also offered separately. The advantage of this type of service to clients is that they can carry out some parts of the work in-house and, therefore, save costs which would be incurred in full service *ad hoc* research. They can also have tighter control over some parts of the work. Such services are also bought by other research agencies to supplement their own resources. Providers of field and tab services include agencies that also offer full service research as as well as companies specializing in this type of business.

Omnibus surveys are interviewing programmes carried out regularly (weekly, monthly, etc) with specified and often large samples of respondents (including consumers, specialized subgroups and business and professional sectors). In this case, however, the agency concerned has no questionnaire content of its 'own' (apart from demographics) and instead offers space, on a question-by-question basis, to subscribers. This service is, therefore, ideal where only a limited range of data is sought either as a one-off or repeatedly as part of tracking research. The costs concerned are very much less than for a one-off survey (since no matter the length of an interview there is some fixed charge to cover) while the methodology including sample size is usually quite rigorous. Omnibus surveys also can be a cost effective way of locating minority samples – eg users of niche products; if necessary an adequate sample can be built up by buying into consecutive waves of the omnibus. The output of an omnibus is a tabulation of 'your' question cross-analyzed by the survey's standard demographics. Omnibuses, therefore, are very useful tools but they have some limitations including quality of response; each questionnaire covers a range of unrelated topics (the questions of different subscribers) and it has been argued that low respondent interest and possible confusion affects responses. Some, therefore, consider omnibuses only suitable for simple questions.

A final point to make about the service offered by market research agencies is that, with the internationalization of business, the scope of research is also increasingly international and this applies to *ad hoc* and continuous research. Published research is also often international in coverage. Around 30 per cent of UK market research companies' turnover is derived from international research.

CODES OF PRACTICE AND QUALITY SCHEMES

Market research in the United Kingdom is carried out to widely recognized codes of practice including those of the MRS and of the trade assocations. These cover the ethical aspects of market research, responsibilities to fellow members of the bodies setting the codes, as well as to clients, survey respondents and the public at large. The MRS code, in particular, is taken quite seriously by all professional rsearchers and even if they are not personally members of the Society, they are likely to subscribe to the principles embodied in this code. A copy of the code is obtainable from the MRS and research users should be familiar with its main provisions since it affects and to some extent restricts the user/supplier relationship. Some important aspects of the code in this respect include the following:

- Information can be collected from respondents only by fair means. Respondents must be told that the information is for research purposes and that their partici-pation is entirely voluntary. The only exception to this is observation, including mystery shopping, where the observed behaviour is public (eg shoppers, looking in a window).

- Information given by respondents is confidential and may not be passed, in an identifiable form, to anyone outside the agency carrying out the research. This includes the client. Confidentiality even extends to the identity of respondents. This requirement, therefore, largely excludes using formal market research (as understood by the MRS) to build up personal details of potential customers and produce lists of databases that can be used in subsequent marketing. The requirement for confidentiality, however, can be relaxed with the freely given and express permission of the respondent at the time of the interview.

- Equally a research sponsor – the client – has a right to confidentiality. Respondents or others should not be told, therefore, for whom the research is being carried out unless the client gives permission for this to be done.

- The results of research carried out for specific clients is confidential to that client and may not be disclosed to others or used to the benefit of other clients.

- The code also sets standards for reporting the results of research, including that any results must be supported by adequate data. Research agencies cannot, for example, be asked to lend their name to promotion claims (...the results of market research show that our brand was rated consistently better...) which are untrue or not backed by research data.

- Agencies are required to safeguard all data to meet the requirements for confi-dentiality and ensure that for a reasonable time (two years minimum) records are kept to allow queries arising from the research to be answered.

Market research is also subject to the statutory provisions of the Data Protection Act 1998 (at least when any of the data is computer processed and this covers nearly all quantitative research). The Act effectively gives legal force to some of the provisions of the MRS code (eg in relation to how information is collected).

Linked to ethical issues covered by the codes of practice is the question of quality standards. Clearly research, if it is to be of any use, must be carried out to at least a minimum standard. Most of the standards that are relevant to market research have been until now informal but, nonetheless, recognized within the profession. At the frontiers of techniques there may be some debate, but for most of the methods used day to day there is common agreement on what constitutes good practice. The specifics of this are learnt through participation in the profession and for agency clients quality is often a matter of choosing practitioners with a good track record and length of experience. However, in addition, there is a long established quality scheme relevant to one part of the research process and a wider scheme that has been in operation for a few years.

There can be little debate that the foundation of reliable market research is the quality of interviewing. Questionnaire design and other office-based activities certainly affect the output but so does how well and conscientiously individual interviewers carry out their work. Yet these workers are not of professional standing and often have only limited training before starting work. Moreover, face-to-face interviewers (phone interviewers are in a different position) work largely unsupervised and with limited contact with head office. Also they often work part-time and for several companies and this is bound to affect their loyalty to any one organization. A specific scheme called the Interviewer Quality Control Scheme (IQCS) has been in place for several years with the objective of developing and raising fieldwork standards. The detailed requirements of the scheme change year to year but include:

- Minimum training periods for new interviewers and a requirement that even experienced interviewers have some training on starting work for another company.
- Monitoring of interviewers' work through independent re-contacting of a sample of respondents (back-checking) – the purpose of this is especially to ensure that interviews are not just made up by a dishonest interviewer (rare but not completely unknown).
- Appraisal of interviewers' work including ongoing accompaniment by trained supervisors or head-office staff.
- Office based systems to ensure that all the above is carried out.

These requirements are as set out for face-to-face inteviewing; there are comparable IQCS requirements for phone interviewing. Agency membership of the scheme involves an annual visit by IQCS inspectors to ensure that the requirements are being met.

There are currently over 70 agencies in the IQCS plus a number who have no fieldwork activity of their own but are committed to buying the service from IQCS members only. A number of major research users give support to the scheme and prefer to buy research from IQCS agencies.

While vital, fieldwork is only part of the research process and it has been increasingly recognized that published standards (which can be independently assessed) also have a place in activities such as client contact and contracting, research design and planning, data processing and reporting. To meet this need the market research industry set up a new body in 1995 – Market Research Quality Standards Association (MRQSA). This association sets key minimum standards across the whole research process and arranges an assessment service for research agencies adopting the standards. MRQSA's standards are now formalized as a full British Standard – BS 7911.

Quality standards, whatever they are, have to be more than just good intentions and companies adopting them need to put in place methods to ensure the standards are met consistently and constantly. Above a certain size of operation, these methods need formalizing as a quality management system. Like businesses in all sorts of industries, some market research companies have chosen to develop such systems in conformity to the international standard of ISO 9000 and have been assessed and formally registered to this standard. MRQSA standards (BS 7911) also include a quality management element compatible with ISO 9000.

LIST OF CONTACTS

Association of European Market Research Institutes (AEMRI), 35 Perrymead Street, London (tel: 020 7736 4445; fax: 020 7371 9542).
www.aemri.org

Association for Qualitative Research Practitioners (AQRP), Davey House, 31 St Neots Road, Eaton Ford, St Neots, Cambs PE19 7BA (tel: 01480 407227; fax: 01480 211267).
www.aqrp.co.uk

Association of Users Of Research Agencies (AURA), c/o Institute of Chartered Accountants, PO Box 433, Moorgate Place, London EC2P 2BJ.
www.aura.org.uk

British Market Research Association (BMRA), Devonshire House, 60 Goswell Road, London EC1M 7AD (tel: 020 7566 3636; fax: 020 7689 6220).
www.bmra.org.uk

European Federation of Associations of Market Research Organisations (EFAMRO), 26 Chester Close, North Regent's Park, London NW1 4JE (tel: 020 7224 3873).
www.efamro.org

Interviewer Quality Control Scheme (IQCS), 6 Walkfield Drive, Epsom Downs, Surrey KT18 5UF (tel: 01737 379261; fax: 01737 351171).

Market Research Quality Standards Association (MRQSA), c/o Market Research Society, 15 Northburgh Street, London EC1V 0JR (tel: 020 7490 4911; fax: 020 7490 0608).
www.mrs.org.uk

Market Research Society (MRS), 15 Northburgh Street, London EC1V 0JR (tel: 020 7490 4911; fax: 020 7490 0608).
www.mrs.org.uk

Social Research Association (SRA), PO Box 33660, London N16 6WE (tel: 020 8880 5684; fax: 020 8880 5684).
www.the-sra.org.uk

References and further reading

1 WHAT IS MARKET RESEARCH?

Achenbaum, A A (1993) 'The future challenge to market research', *Marketing Research: A Magazine of Management & Applications*, 5(2), pp 12–18

Baker, M J (1993) 'Look before you leap', in *Research for Marketing*, Macmillan, London, chapter 1, pp 1–40

Chisnall, P (1992) 'Role and development of marketing research', in *Marketing Research*, 4th edn, McGraw-Hill, London, chapter 1, pp 3–22

Cowan, D (1993) 'Understanding in market research', *Marketing Intelligence & Planning*, 11(11), pp 9–15

Cowan, D (1994) 'Good information', *Journal of the Market Research Society*, 36(2), pp 105–14

Crimp, M and Wright, L T (1995) 'An introduction to the marketing research process', in *The Marketing Research Process*, 4th edn, Prentice-Hall, London, chapter 1, pp 1–19

Elliott, R and Jobber, D (1995) 'Expanding the market for market research', *The Journal of the Market Research Society*, 37(1), pp 143–58

Freeling, A (1994) 'Marketing is in crisis – can market research help?', *The Journal of the Market Research Society*, 36, pp 97–104

Goodyear, M (1996) 'Guest editorial', *The Journal of the Market Research Society*, 38(1), pp 1–6

Hooley, G J and West, C J (1984) 'The untapped markets for marketing research', *The Journal of the Market Research Society*, 26(4)

Kent, R (1993) 'Perspectives on marketing research', in Marketing Research in Action, Routledge, London, pp 1–21

Lazier, W (1974) 'Marketing research: past accomplishments and potential future developments', The *Journal of the Market Research Society*, 16(3)

Morello, G (1993) 'The hidden dimensions of marketing', *The Journal of the Market Research Society*, 35, pp 293–313

2 APPLICATIONS

Byrne, M and Langmaid, R (1990) 'The Marilyn project: avoiding the soldier blues', *The Journal of the Market Research Society*, 32, pp 435–56

Goodyear, M J (1990) 'Qualitative Research' in Birn, R, Hague, P and Vangelder, P (eds) *A Handbook of Market Research Techniques*, Kogan Page, London

Hague, P and Jackson, P (1992) *Marketing Research In Practice*, Kogan Page, London

Hansman, H and Schutjens, V (1993) 'Dynamics in market segmentation', *Marketing and Research Today*, 21(3), pp 139–48

Laitin, J A and Klaperman, B A (1994) 'The brave new world of marketing research', *Medical Marketing & Media*, 29(7), pp 44–51

Marks, A P (1990) 'The Sinclair C5 – why did it fail?', *Management Decision*, (28ª4), pp 9–14

Newton, S (1993) 'From hearses to horses: launching the Volvo 850', *The Journal of the Market Research Society*, 35, pp 145–59

Pickersgill, P (1991) 'How research helped to measure the effects of display and assess the contribution of salesmen and merchandisers', *The Journal of the Market Research Society*, 33, pp 153–62

Shingleton, J (1994) 'Black Rhino to leaping gazelle – how an integrated research programme helped rejuvenate Lex Vehicle Leasing Limited', *The Journal of the Market Research Society*, 36, pp 205–16

3 PLANNING MARKET RESEARCH

Brewer, T (1986) 'Don't make a move without doing research', *ABA Banking Journal*, 78(11), pp 76–85

Butler, P (1994) 'Marketing problems: from analysis to decision', *Marketing Intelligence & Planning*, 12(2), pp 4–13

Chapman, R G (1989) 'Problem–definition in marketing research studies', *Journal of Services Marketing*, 3(3), pp 51–59

Czinkota, M R and Pronkinen, I A (1994) 'Market research for your export operations: Part I – using secondary sources of research', *International Trade Forum*, 3, pp 22–33

McDonald, M (1992) *Marketing Plans: How to Prepare Them, How To Use Them*, Butterworth Heinemann, Oxford

Smith, D and Dexter, A (1994) 'Quality in market research: hard frameworks for soft problems', *The Journal of the Market Research Society*, 36, pp 115–33

Stephen, E H and Soldo, B J (1990) 'How to judge the quality of a survey', *American Demographics*, 12(4), pp 42–43

Weinman, C (1991) 'It's not "art", but marketing research can be creative', *Marketing News*, 25(8), pp 9–24

Yuspeh, S (1989) 'Dracula and Frankenstein revisited: two research ogres in need of restraint', *Journal of Advertising Research*, 29(1), pp 53–59

4 HOW TO GET INFORMATION FOR NEXT TO NOTHING

Baker, K (1989) 'Using geodemographics in market research', *The Journal of the Market Research Society*, 31, pp 37–44

Brown, P J B (1991) 'Exploring geodemographics', in Masser, I and Blakemore, M (eds) *Handling Geographical Information*, Longman Scientific & Technical, London, pp 221–59

Cornish, P (1989) 'Geodemographic sampling in Readership Surveys', *The Journal of the Market Research Society*, 31, pp 45–51

Crimp, M and Wright, L T (1995) *The Marketing Research Process*, 4th edn, Prentice-Hall, London, pp 246–54

Evans, M (1994) 'Domesday marketing', *Journal of Marketing Management*, 10(5), pp 409–32

Evans, N and Webber, R (1995) 'Geodemographic profiling: MOSAIC and EuroMOSAIC', in Crimp, M and Wright, L T, *The Market Research Process*, 4th end, Prentice-Hall, London

Jackson, P (1994) *Desk Research*, Kogan Page, London

Leventhal, B (1990) 'Geodemographics', in Birn, R, Hague, P and Vangelder, P (eds) *A Handbook of Market Research Techniques*, Kogan Page, London

Market Research Society (1993) *Introductory Guide to the 1991 Census*, NTC Publications, Henley-on-Thames

Mitchell, V W (1992) 'The future of geodemographic information handling', *Logistics Information Management*, 5(3), pp 23–29

Newson–Smith, N (1986) 'Desk research', in Worcester, R and Downham, J, *Consumer Market Research Handbook*, 3rd edn, ESOMAR, McGraw-Hill Book Company, London, chapter 1, pp 7–27

Powell, T (1991) 'Despite myths, secondary research is valuable tool', *Marketing News*, 25(18), pp 28–33

Sleight, P (1993) *Targeting Customers, How To Use Geodemographics and Lifestyle Data in Your Business*, NTC Publications, Henley-on-Thames

Sleight, P and Leventhal, B (1989) 'Applications of geodemographics to research and marketing', *The Journal of the Market Research Society*, 31, pp 75–101

5 QUALITATIVE RESEARCH

Bhaduri, M, de Souza, M and Sweeney, T (1993) 'International qualitative research: A critical review of different approaches', *Marketing & Research Today*, 2(3) pp 171–78

Byers, P Y and Wilcox, J R (1991) 'Focus groups: a qualitative opportunity for researchers', *Journal of Business Communication*, 28(1), pp 63–78

Collins, L (1991) 'Everything is true, but in a different sense: a new perspective on qualitative research', *The Journal of the Market Research Society*, 33, pp 31–38

Colwell, J (1990) 'Qualitative market research: a conceptual analysis and review of practitioner criteria', *The Journal of the Market Research Society*, 32

Cooper, P (1989) 'Comparison between the UK and US: the qualitative dimension', *The Journal of the Market Research Society*, 31(4), pp 509–20

de Groot, G (1986) 'Qualitative research: deep, dangerous, or just plain dotty?', *European Research*, 14(3), pp 136–41

Esser, W (1995) 'From the "triad" to a "quadriga": a systematic qualitative marketing research programme for the Far East', *Marketing & Research Today*, 23(1), pp 20–24

Gabriel, C (1990) 'The validity of qualitative market research', *The Journal of the Market Research Society*, 32, pp 507–20

Glen, R (1998) 'New skills now', *Research*, 384, pp 46–48

Goodyear, M (1990) 'Qualitative Research' in Birn, R, Hague, P and Vangelder, P, *A Handbook of Market Research Techniques*, Kogan Page, London, p 229

Griggs, S (1987) 'Analysing qualitative data, *The Journal of the Market Research Society*, 29(1), pp 15–34

Hayward, W and Rose, J (1990) 'We'll meet again … repeat attendance at group discussions – does it matter?', *The Journal of the Market Research Society*, 32, pp 377–408

Henderson, N R (1990) 'Focus groups for the last decade of the twentieth century', _Applied Marketing Research_, 30(2), pp 20–22

Johnson, B C (1990) 'Focus group positioning and analysis: a commentary on adjuncts for enhancing the design of health care research', _Health Marketing Quarterly_, 7(1), pp 153–68

Kaushik, M and Sen, A (1990) 'Semiotics and qualitative research', _The Journal of the Market Research Society_, 32, pp 227–43

Marks, L (1998) 'New horizons of qualitative research', _Research_, 384, pp 44–45

Robson, S and Hedges, A (1993) 'Analysis and interpretation of qualitative findings. Report of the MRS Qualitative Interest Group', _The Journal of the Market Research Society_, 35, pp 23–35

Rowan, M M (1991) 'Bankers beware! Focus groups can steer you wrong', _Bottomline_ 8(4), pp 37–41

Rust, R T and Cooil, B (1994) 'Reliability measures for qualitative data: theory and implications', _Journal of Marketing Research_, 31(1), pp 1–14

Sampson, P M J (1967) 'Commonsense in qualitative research', _The Journal of the Market Research Society_, 9(1)

Spiggle, S (1994) 'Analysis and interpretation of qualitative data in consumer research', _Journal of Consumer Research_, 21(3), pp 491–503

Sweeney, J C _et al_ (1997) 'Collecting information from groups, a comparison of methods', _The Journal of the Market Research Society_, 39(2), pp 397–411

Sykes, W (1990) 'Validity and reliability in qualitative market research: a review of the literature', _The Journal of the Market Research Society_, 32, pp 289–328

Sykes, W (1991) 'Taking stock: issues from the literature on validity and reliability in qualitative research', _The Journal of the Market Research Society_, 33, pp 3–12

Warren, M and Craig, A (1991) 'Qualitative research product and policy', _Marketing & Research Today_, 19(1), pp 43–49

Warren, M (1991) 'Another day, another debrief: the use and assessment of qualitative research', _The Journal of the Market Research Society_, 33, pp 13–18

Wells, S (1991) 'Wet towels and whetted appetites or a wet blanket? The role of analysis in qualitative research', _The Journal of the Market Research Society_, 33, pp 39–44

Yelland, F and Varty, C (1997) 'DIY: consumer driven research', _The Journal of the Market Research Society_, 39(2), pp 297–315

6 QUANTITATIVE RESEARCH

Albaum, G (1987) 'Do source and anonymity affect mail survey results?', _Journal of the Academy of Marketing Science_, 15(3), pp 74–81

Appel, V and Baim, J (1992) 'Predicting and correcting response rate problems using geodemography', *Marketing Research: A Magazine of Management & Applications*, 4(1), pp 22–28

Blyth, W (1990) 'Panels and diaries', Birn, R, Hague, P and Vangelder, P (eds) *A Handbook of Market Research Techniques*, Kogan Page, London

Brehm, J (1994) 'Stubbing our toes for a foot in the door? Incentives and survey response', *International Journal of Public Opinion Research*, 6(1), pp 45–64

Brennan, M, Hoek, J and Astridge (1991) 'The effects of monetary incentives on the response rate and cost–effectiveness of a mail survey', *The Journal of the Market Research Society*, 33, pp 229–42

Brown, M (1994) 'What price response?', *The Journal of the Market Research Society*, 36, pp 227–44

Buck, S (1990) 'Peoplematters', in Birn, R, Hague, P and Vangelder, P (eds) *A Handbook of Market Research Techniques*, Kogan Page, London

Faria, A J, Dickinson, J R and Filipic, T V (1990) 'The effect of telephone versus letter prenotification on mail survey response rate, speed, quality and cost', *The Journal of the Market Research Society*, 32, pp 551–69

Farrel, B and Elken, T (1994) 'Adjust five variables for better mail surveys', *Marketing News*, 28(18), p 20

Gajari, A M, Faria, A J and Dickinson, J R (1990) 'A comparison of the effect of promised and provided lotteries, monetary and gift incentives on mail survey response rate, speed and cost', *The Journal of the Market Research Society*, 32, pp 141–63

Gaynor, J (1994) 'An experiment with cash incentives on a personal interview survey', *The Journal of the Market Research Society*, 36, pp 360–65

Helgeson, J G (1994) 'Receiving and responding to a mail survey – a phenomenological examination', *The Journal of the Market Research Society*, 36, pp 339–47

Kamins, M A (1989) 'The enhancement of response rates to a mail survey through a labelled probe foot-in-the-door approach', *The Journal of the Market Research Society*, 31(2), pp 273–83

Martin, C L (1994) 'The impact of topic interest on mail survey response behaviour', *The Journal of the Market Research Society*, 36, pp 327–38

Martin, W S, Duncan, W J, Powers, T L and Sawyer, J C (1989) 'Costs and benefits of selected response inducement techniques in mail survey research', *Journal of Business Research*, 19(1), pp 67–79

Mason, N (1990) 'EPOS', in Birn, R, Hague, P and Vangelder, P (eds) *A Handbook of Market Research Techniques*, Kogan Page, London

McCarthy, T (1990) 'Retail audits', in Birn, R, Hague, P and Vangelder, P (eds) *A Handbook of Market Research Techniques*, Kogan Page, London

McKee, D O (1992) 'The effect of using a questionnaire identification code and message about non-response follow-up plans on mail survey response character-istics', *The Journal of the Market Research Society*, 34, pp 179–91

Meier, E (1991) 'Response Rate Trends in Britain', *Admap*, 26(11), pp 41–44

Nebenzahl, I D and Jaffe, E D (1995) 'Fascimile transmission versus mail delivery of self-administered questionnaires in industrial surveys', *Industrial Marketing Management*, 24(3), pp 167–75

Ratneshwar, S and Stewart, D W (1989) 'Nonresponse in mail surveys: an integrative review', *Applied Marketing Research*, 29(3), pp 37–46

Schlegelmilch, B and Diamontopoulos, A (1991) 'Prenotification and mail survey response rates: a quantitative integration of the literature', *The Journal of the Market Research Society*, 33, pp 243–56

Schuldt, B A and Totten, J W (1994) 'Electronic mail v. mail survey response rates', *Marketing Research*, 6(1), pp 36–40

Semon, T T (1994) 'Projecting survey results is always a problem', *Marketing News*, 28(15), pp 17–18

Steele, T J, Schwendig, W L and Kilpatrick, J A (1992) 'Duplicate responses to multiple survey mailings: a problem?', *Journal of Advertising Research*, 32(2), pp 26–33

Swires-Hennessy, E and Drake, M (1992) 'The optimum time at which to conduct survey interviews', *The Journal of the Market Research Society*, 34(1), pp 61–78

Tse, A, Ching, R, Ding, Y, Fong, R, Yeung, É and Au, A (1994) 'A comparison of the effectiveness of mail and facsimile as a survey media on response rate, speed and quality', *The Journal of the Market Research Society*, 36, pp 349–55

7 SAMPLES

Baker, M J (1991) 'Sampling', in *Research for Marketing*, Macmillan, London, chapter 6, pp 100–31

Bolton, R N (1994) 'Covering the market', *Marketing Research: A Magazine of Management & Applications*, 6(3), pp 30–35

Cowan, C D (1991) 'Using multiple sample frames to improve survey coverage, quality, and costs', *Marketing Research: A Magazine of Management & Applications*, 3(4), pp 66–69

Crimp, M and Wright L T (1995) 'Sampling in survey research', in *The Marketing Research Process*, 4th edn, Prentice-Hall, London, chapter 6, pp 107–31

Dent, T (1992) 'How to design for a more reliable customer sample', *Business Marketing*, 17(2), pp 73–77

Fish, K E, Barnes, J H and Banahan, B F (1994) 'Convenience or calamity? Pharmaceutical study explores the effects of sample frame error on research results', *Journal of Health Care Marketing*, 14(1), pp 45–49

Frankel, M R (1989) 'Current research practices: general population sampling including geodemographics', *The Journal of the Market Research Society*, 31(4), pp 447–55

Geurts, M, Whitlark, D, Christensen, H and Lawrence, K (1994) 'Calculating sample sizes for population with multinominal proportions', *Marketing & Research Today*, 22(3), pp 214–19

Hague, P and Harris, P (1993) *Sampling and Statistics*, Kogan Page, London

Hahlo, G (1992) 'Examining the validity of re-interviewing respondents for quantitative surveys', *The Journal of the Market Research Society*, 34, pp 99–118

Harris, P (1977), 'The effect of clustering on cost and sampling errors of random samples', *The Journal of the Market Research Society* 19(3)

Marsh, C and Scarborough, E (1990) 'Testing nine hypothesis about quota sampling', *The Journal of the Market Research Society*, 32, pp 485–506

Noble, I *et al* (1998) 'Bringing it all back home', *The Journal of the Market Research Society* 49(2), pp 43–120

Semon, T T (1994a) 'A good sample of accounts may not always be a good sample of your customers', *Marketing News*, 28(9), pp 8–11

Semon, T T (1994b) 'Save a few bucks on sample size, risk millions in opportunity loss', *Marketing News*, 28(1), p 19

Shiffler, R E and Adams, A J (1987) 'A correction for biasing effects of pilot sample size on sample size determination', *Journal of Marketing Research*, 24(3), pp 319–21

Swan, J E, O'Connor, S J and Seung, D L (1991) 'A framework for testing sampling bias and methods of bias reduction in a telephone survey', *Marketing Research: A Magazine of Management & Applications*, 3(4), pp 23–34

Watson, M A (1992) 'Researching minorities', *The Journal of the Market Research Society*, 34(4), pp 337–44

Whitlark, D, Geurts, M D, Christensen, H B, Kays, M A and Lawrence, K D (1993) 'Selecting sample sizes for marketing research surveys: advantages of using the coefficient of variation', *Marketing & Research Today*, 21(1), pp 50–54

8 QUESTIONNAIRE DESIGN

Bolton, R (1993) 'Pretesting questionnaires: content analyses of respondents' concurrent verbal protocols', *Marketing Science*, 12(3), pp 280–303

Carroll, S (1994) 'Questionnaire design affects response rate', _Marketing News_, 28(1), pp 14–23

Crimp, M and Wright, L T (1995) 'Questionnaire design', in _The Marketing Research Process_, 4th edn, Prentice-Hall, London, chapter 7, pp 132–62

Diamontopoulos, A, Reynolds, N, Schlegelmilch, B (1994) 'Pretesting in question-naire design: the impact of respondent characteristics on error detection', _The Journal of the Market Research Society_, 36, pp 295–313

Douglas, V (1995) 'Questionnaire too long? Try variable', _Marketing News_, 29(5), p 38

Hague, P (1987) 'Good and bad in questionnaire design', _Industrial Marketing Digest_, 12(3), pp 161–170

Hague, P (1993) _Questionnaire Design_, Kogan Page, London

Martin-Williams, J (1986) 'Questionnaire design', in Worcester, R and Downham, J, _Consumer Market Research Handbook_, 3rd edn, ESOMAR, McGraw-Hill Book Company, London, p 111–45

Oppenheim, A (1970), _Questionnaire Design and Attitude Measurement_, Heinemann Educational Books, London

Payne, S (1951) _The Art of Asking Questions_, Princeton University Press, Princeton, NJ

Prunk, T (1994) 'The value of questionnaires', _Target Marketing_, 17(10), pp 37–40

Reynolds, N, Diamontopoulos, A and Schlegemilch, B (1993) 'Pretesting in question-naire design: a review of the literature and suggestions for further research', _The Journal of the Market Research Society_, 35, pp 171–82

Sawyer, C (1990) 'The art of the question: it can make or break your research effort', _Sales & Marketing in Canada_, 31(10), pp 16–17

Sudman, S and Bradburn, N M (1982) _Asking Questions – A Practical Guide to Questionnaire Design_, Jossey-Bass Publishers, 1982

Vittles, P (1994) 'Question time', _The Health Service Journal_, May 94, pp 34–34

9 DATA COLLECTION METHODS

Blyth, B and Piper, H (1994) 'Speech recognition – a new dimension in survey research', _The Journal of the Market Research Society_, 36, pp 183–203

Curry, J (1990) 'Interviewing by PC: what we could not do before', _Applied Marketing Research_, 30(1), pp 30–37

DePaulo, P and Weitzer, R (1994) 'Interactive phone technology delivers survey data quickly', _Marketing News_, 28(1), p 15

Dickson, J R, Faria, A J and Frieson, D (1994) 'Live v automated telephone inter-viewing', _Marketing Research_, 6(1), pp 28–35

Dodd, J (1998) 'Market research on the Internet – threat or opportunity?', *Marketing and Research Today*, February, pp 60–66

Gates, R H and Jarboe, G R (1987) 'Changing trends in data acquisition for marketing research', *Journal of Data Collection*, 27(1), pp 25–29

Gershowitz (1990) 'Entering the 1990s – the state of data collection – telephone data collection', *Applied Marketing Research*, 30(2), pp 16–19

Havice, M J and Banks, M J (1991) 'Live and automated telephone surveys: a comparison of human interviews and an automated technique', *The Journal of the Market Research Society*, 33, pp 91–102

Jones, P and Polak, J (1993) 'Computer-based personal interviewing: state-of-the-art and future prospects', *The Journal of the Market Research Society*, 35, pp 221–33

Keller, W J (1993) 'Trends in survey data processing', *The Journal of the Market Research Society*, 35, pp 211–19

Merton, R K (1987) 'The focused interview and focus groups: continuities and discontinuities', *Public Opinion Quarterly*, 51(4), pp 550–66

Morrison, L J et al (1997) 'Mystery customer research: cognitive processes affecting accuracy', *The Journal of the Market Research Society* 39(2), pp 349–61

Morton-Williams, J and Young, P (1987) 'Obtaining the survey interview – an analysis of tape recorded doorstep introductions', *The Journal of the Market Research Society*, 29(1), pp 35–54

Neffendorf, H (1993) 'Survey computing in the 1990s: a technology update', *The Journal of the Market Research Society*, 35, pp 205–10

Perkins, W S and Roundy, J (1993) 'Discrete choice surveys by telephone', *Journal of the Academy of Marketing Science*, 21(1), pp 33–38

Perrot, N (1998), 'Will you be an ostrich or campaigner?', *Research*, 385, pp 50–55

Schafer, M (1990) 'Data collection in the UK and how it differs from the US', *Applied Marketing Research*, 30(2), pp 30–35

Sweeney, J C et al (1997) 'Collecting information from groups, a comparison of methods', *The Journal of the Market Research Society*, 39(2), pp 397–411

Yovovich, B G (1991) 'Focusing on customers' needs and motivations', *Business Marketing*, 76(3), pp 41–43

10 PRODUCT TESTING

Chay, R (1989) 'Discovering unrecognized needs with consumer research', *Research-Technology Management*, 32(2), pp 36–39

Cramp, B (1994) 'Research propels innovation', *Marketing*, 27 January, pp 33–36

Davis, R E (1993) 'From experience: the role of market research in the development of new consumer products', _Journal of Product Innovation Management_, 10(4), pp 309–17

Davis, R E (1994) 'From experience: role of market research in the development of new consumer products', _IFEE Engineering Management Review_, 22(2), pp 30–35

Deschampes, J P (1989) 'Creating the products the market wants', _Marketing and Research Today_, pp 4–16

Eassie, R W F (1979) 'Buy-response analysis: a practical tool of market research', _European Journal of Marketing_, 13(4)

Ehrenberg, A S C (1991) 'New brands and the existing market', _The Journal of the Market Research Society_, 33, pp 285–300

Eisenhart, T (1989) 'Advanced research finds a new market', _Business Marketing_, 74(3), pp 50–61

Juster (1966) _Consumer Buying Intentions and Purchase Probability_, occasional paper 99, National Bureau of Economic Research, Columbia University Press

Mitchell, V W and Davies, R (1996) 'Does marketing research encourage the development of frivolous products?', _Marketing Intelligence & Planning_, 13(1), pp 28–34

Morgan, R P (1995) 'Modelling techniques for product prediction and planning', in Crimp, M and Wright, L T, _The Marketing Research Process_, 4th edn, Prentice-Hall, London, chapter 10, pp 209–27

Opatow, L (1986) 'Making the best out of product development', _Bankers Magazine_, 169(4), pp 23–28

Ortt, R J, and Shorrmans, J P L (1993) 'Consumer research in the development process of a major innovation', _The Journal of the Market Research Society_, 35, pp 275–88

Palshaw, J L (1991) 'Using marketing research effectively for launching new products', _Medical Marketing & Media_, 26(9), pp 60–64

Power, C (1993) 'Flops', _Business Week_, 16 August, pp 76–82

Sanchez, R and Sudharshan, D (1993) 'Real-time market research', _Marketing Intelligence & Planning_, 11(7), pp 29–39

Wagner, C and Hayashi, A (1994) 'A new way to create winning product ideas', _The Journal of Product Innovation Management_, 11(2), pp 146–56

Workman, J P (1993) 'Marketing's limited role in new product development in one computer systems firm', _Journal of Marketing Research_, 30(4), pp 405–21

Wyner, G A (1994) 'Evaluating innovative products', _Marketing Research: A Magazine of Management & Applications_, 6(3), pp 44–46

11 CUSTOMER SATISFACTION SURVEYS

Heskett, J, Sasser, W E and Schlesinger, L A (1997) *The Service Profit Chain*, Free Press, New York

Kaplan, RS and Norton, DP (1996) *The Balanced Score Card*, Harvard Business School Press, Boston

McCarthy, D (1997) *The Loyalty Link – How Loyal Employees Create Loyal Customers*, John Wiley, New York

12 DATA ANALYSIS

Alt, M (1990) *Exploring Hyperspace: A Non-Mathematical Explanation of Multivariate Analysis*, McGraw-Hill, London

Baker, K (1991) *Research for Marketing*, Macmillan, London, chapter 9

Blamires, C (1990) 'Segmentation' in Birn, R, Hague, P and Vangelder, P (eds) *A Handbook of Market Research Techniques*, Kogan Page, London

Catterall, M and Maclaren, P (1998) 'Using computer software for the analysis of qualitative market research data', *The Journal of the Market Research Society*, 40(3), pp 207–22

Davies, R (1993) 'Statistical modelling for survey analysis', *The Journal of the Market Research Society*, 35(3), pp 235–47

Freeman, P (1991) 'Using computers to extend analysis and reduce data', *The Journal of the Market Research Society*, 33(2), pp 127–36

Freeman, P and Rennolls, K (1994) 'Modelling methodology. Basics to neural nets – a return to ignorance?', *The Journal of the Market Research Society*, 36, pp 69–77

Funkhouser, G R, Chatterjee, A and Parker, R (1994) 'Segmenting samples', *Marketing Research: A Magazine of Management & Applications*, 6(1), pp 40–6

Gatty, R (1966) 'Multivariate analysis for marketing research: an evaluation', *Applied Statistics*, Series C, 15(3)

Hague, P and Harris P (1993) *Sampling and Statistics*, Kogan Page, London

Holmes, C (1986) 'Multivariate analysis of market research data', in Worcester, R and Downham, J (eds) *Consumer Market Research Handbook*, McGraw-Hill, London, pp 351–75

Hooley, G (1980) 'A guide to the use of quantitative techniques in marketing', *European Journal of Marketing*, 14(7)

Jackling, P (1990) 'Analysing data-tabulations', in Birn, R, Hague, P and Vangelder, P (eds) *A Handbook of Market Research Techniques*, Kogan Page, London

Kent, R (1993) *Marketing Research in Action*, Routledge, London, chapter 6

Michell, V W (1994) 'How to identify psychographic segments: Part 1 & 2', _Marketing Intelligence & Planning_, 12(7), pp 4–16

Moore, K, Burbach, R and Heeler, R (1995) 'Using neural nets to analyze qualitative data', _Marketing Research: A Magazine of Management & Applications_, 7(1), pp 34–39

Morgan, R (1990) 'Modelling: conjoint analysis', in Birn, R, Hague, P and Vangelder, P (eds) _A Handbook of Market Research Techniques_, Kogan Page, London

Nichisato, S and Gaul, W (1988) 'Marketing data analysis by dual scaling', _International Journal of Research in Marketing_, 5(3), pp 151–70

Owen, D (1991) 'Every decoding is another encoding', _The Journal of the Market Research Society_, 33(4), pp 321–33

Punj, G and Stewart, D W (1983) 'Cluster analysis in market research: review and suggestions for application', _Journal of Marketing Research_, 20

Robson, S (1993) 'Analysis and interpretation of qualitative findings', _The Journal of the Market Research Society_, 35(1), pp 23–35

Schwoerer, J and Frappa, J P (1986) 'Artificial intelligence and expert systems: any applications for marketing and marketing research?', _European Research_, 14(4), pp 10–24

Venugopal, V and Bates, W (1994) 'Neural networks and statistical techniques in marketing research: a conceptual comparison', _Marketing Intelligence & Planning_, 12(7), pp 30–38

Wells, S (1991) 'Wet towels and whetted appetites or a wet blanket', _The Journal of the Market Research Society_, 33(1), pp 39–44

Westwood, D et al (1974), 'The trade-off model and its extensions', _The Journal of the Market Research Society_, 18(3)

13 REPORT WRITING

Britt, S H (1971) 'The writing of readable research reports', _Journal of Marketing_, May

Hague, P and Roberts, C (1994) _Presentations and Report Writing_, Kogan Page, London

Mohn, N C (1989) 'How to present marketing research results effectively', _Marketing & Research Today_, 17(2), pp 115–18

Sussmans, J (1991) _How to Write Effective Reports_, Gower, Hampshire

Van Embden, J (1987) _Report Writing_, McGraw-Hill, London

14 THE MARKET RESEARCH INDUSTRY

Bowles, T (1991) 'Issues facing the UK research industry', *The Journal of the Market Research Society*, 33, pp 71–81

Demby, E H (1987) 'The future holds everything from better sampling to brain research', *Marketing News*, 12(18), pp 19–20

Goodyear, J (1989) 'The structure of the British market research industry', *The Journal of the Market Research Society*, 31, pp 427–37

Jackson, P (1994) *Buying Market Research*, Kogan Page, London

Jackson, P (1997), *Quality in Market Research*, Kogan Page, London

Laborie, J L (1990) 'Marketing research in the decade ahead', *Marketing & Research Today*, 18(4), pp 221–6

Oostveen, J and Wouters, J (1991) 'The ESOMAR annual market study: the state of the art of marketing research', *Marketing & Research Today*, 19(4), pp 214–18

Index

WARWICKSHIRE
COLLEGE
LIBRARY